THE DAY BRITAIN DIED

Andrew Marr has been a political commentator for the *Observer*, the *Express*, the *Independent*, *The Economist* and the *Scotsman*, as well as making and presenting television and radio programmes for the BBC and independent broadcasters. He was editor of the *Independent* for two years. He has written two previous books, *The Battle for Scotland* (Penguin, 1992) and *Ruling Britannia* (Penguin, 1995), which was described by Anthony King as 'the best book on the British political system since Bagehot' and by Matthew Parris as 'a work of brilliance'. He has received two awards as columnist of the year and recently made *If John Smith had Lived* for Channel Four. Andrew Marr is 40, Scottish-born and lives in West London with his journalist wife and their three wicked children.

For Citizens Harry, Isabel and Emily

Andrew Marr

THE DAY
BRITAIN
DIED

PROFILE BOOKS

First published in 2000 by
Profile Books Ltd
58A Hatton Garden
London ECIN 8LX
www.profilebooks.co.uk

Copyright © Andrew Marr, 1999

Typeset in Bembo by
macguru@pavilion.co.uk

Printed and bound in Great Britain by
St Edmundsbury Press, Bury St Edmunds

A CIP catalogue record for this book is available from the British
Library.

ISBN 1 86197 223 7

Contents

Preface

This is a book which has been written, in passion and at speed, after several months touring Britain. I have been asking a single, simple question. Is Britain dead?

What does 'dead' mean? Lost in spirit and bereft of soul; about to decay physically; unable to imagine, lacking self-consciousness, no longer able to affect the living future. Passive. Finished. These phrases are clear enough applied to an animal, but are subjective when applied to a social construction. Nations have no heartbeat and do not breathe. The corpse of a nationalism, with its clothing of parliaments and flags, its solid mass of territory and varied human communities, can be sprawled out for decades before it starts to stink; or it may only be sleeping. But the death-signs exist, and can be investigated. I have had a picture of myself in my mind as an amateur pathologist carrying my little leather case, slinking onto buses and trains, driving to the possible site of the crime, sniffing the air for putrefaction, taking the pulse of friends and strangers. And looking for what?

Physical decay is the easiest part: will Scotland fall away, a lost limb? Wales? Is the body of England, its skin of town and countryside, still smooth and whole, or is it mouldering, crusted with neglect? In terms of loss of consciousness, I have been looking for a country that no longer knows what it wants to be, or do, in the world. This means a country that is not able to affect the future of anywhere else, just lying there glassy-eyed, while other nations and peoples around about are still brimming with energy and ideas. That is one way of looking at things, something out of Swift, the state as a single human. 'Britain', however, is all of us who live here. It is an idea inside our minds – billions of synapses in millions of brains that have been altered to recall dates, famous people, fragments of geography or writing. Like all nationalisms, it is an agreed, consensual, act of collective imagination. If, in some science-fiction attack from outer space, the men, women and children who move about on the islands of Britain, had their memories erased, then Britain would immediately cease to exist – as one with Nineveh and Tyre. Britain *is* to the extent that we choose it, by act of will. And *is not*, similarly, by other choices – a lack of conscious remembering and multiple assertion.

This suggests that the travelling pathologist, poking about in anonymous clothes, must ask about individuals' sense of themselves, how strong their will to be British really is. When I went to my own past, to Scotland, through my education and the landscapes that matter most to me, I found matter-of-fact, friendly but distant voices, a land of kind strangers, noting in passing that Britain meant nothing at all to them. South of that border, talking to a host of busy people, campaigners and writers, singers and business executives, lorry-drivers and farmers, I noticed a fuzziness, a confusion, where identity should be.

There was a rising sense of bemused hurt about the Scots and a more serious concern about the buzz of activity on the continent of Europe, where the political elites are building a new political space. Is this European Union a great, pride-driven Tower of Babel, an impious heathen monument doomed to fall? Or is the EU the genuine, post-Holocaust union of peoples which will be Europe's destiny for hundreds of years to come? No one knows, but the question hangs unanswered wherever people who think about the future gather and talk. Stay with it or leave, the EU is too massive a structure to be ignored. Whichever way we turn, however we raise our voices and try to think of other things, its shadow crowds out other choices.

Meanwhile, as they spoke about the Scots, the Irish, the Welsh, 'Europe' did the English have a pride in Britishness, the self-consciousness and essential unity that pumps through healthy nations? Many of them did not. They were beginning to use the word English once more to describe themselves.

This is a difficult case. To ask about identity is not only to ask about political identity. There must be questions about culture, about the spirit, or lack of it, in television programmes and about assumptions hidden in computer software, in music and fictions. A pathologist of nationalism must tap the bones, the armature of the state, test the knuckles of power and knock against the brainpan of faith. And always, we must have a sense of the medical history of the subject, how this creature grew strong, and what it looked like in its prime, striding about, and where it was born and how many relatives it may have.

So that is what I have been doing. Even asking the question infuriates a lot of people. Of course Britain is not dead, they say. It is a thousand years of history, it is the Mother of Parliaments, it is the people of empire and of the rule of law. You are on a wild goose chase, a corpseless whodunnit. 'You cannot be serious'. I am. And not only me – there are plenty of serious people on the right and left of politics who think Britain either is likely to die, or – more disturbingly – passed away some time ago, with nobody watching, no final friendly voice, no rite, no sentimental goodbye. Many of their voices will be heard in what follows.

In the final stages of this project, *The Economist* asked the polling company MORI to find out from people the two or three levels of authority 'you most identify with' from a list shown to them. Among the Scots, a derisory 18 per cent identified with Britain (72 per cent identified with Scotland). Among the Welsh, Britain managed 27 per cent (Wales got 81 per cent). Most surprising of all, perhaps, was that among the English themselves only 43 per cent identified with Britain against 41 per cent with England – and 49 per cent with their region. Asked to look 20 years ahead, 8 per cent of Scots thought Westminster would be the most influential body overseeing them, and in Britain as a whole just 22 per cent gave Westminster their vote of confidence, half the figure for the EU. These are striking figures, which give some statistical backing to the journalistic verdict I had reached in the previous few months: the *Daily Telegraph* splashed them across the front page with a headline proclaiming that the British were losing their 'sense of nationhood'. That is my feeling too.

Before continuing, it seems right to explain who I am – because everyone is coming from somewhere. First, I am a Scot, born in 1959. But, second, I am a British male. I was brought up to think of myself as both British and Scottish. I had visited England just once before I went there to university. Even so, educated in private schools, I had the kind of traditional British-history education that is rare now; we learned kings and queens, of England as well as Scotland; studied Nelson's victories; and were taught in detail about missionaries, the Empire and the public landmarks of 'our island story'. It was a similar historical grounding that most people in their fifties and sixties once had; I was probably the last generation to get it and then only because Scottish private schools were a bit behind the times. We read books by children's authors like Rosemary Sutcliffe and Henry Treece, about Romans and Vikings and crusaders, which filled in imaginative details. Like many families, British pride was an intimate thing: my father had been in the Navy for his national service, and his family had worked for a Scottish tea company in India. One grandfather had fought with the Eighth Army in Italy. One uncle was killed in his ship at Dunkirk; a great-uncle was a Spitfire pilot, killed over Norway. The family did not bang on about any of this but it was there in the background.

Third, all this is very male: my boyish imagination was fed on Second World War comics and storybooks, notably the War Picture Library series and Commandos, produced by D.C. Thomson in my home town of Dundee. Beyond that, films like *Waterloo* and *The Battle of Britain* stand out in my memory. In a more homely sense, Britain was the country of self-deprecation and silliness, of Eric Morecambe and Ernie Wise, the stream of television sitcoms, comic-strips in the *Sunday Post*, cartoons from *Punch*, long lists of football results on the weekend television, and occasional state events, glimpsed dimly from afar. I felt that I was privileged; to be born British was to be a member of one of the most success-ful, brave, fair and rich nations on the planet, a small nation which had ruled half the world and then handed it back to grateful, now-educated people after we had taught them how to run things; a nation whose democracy was ancient but which was also facing an exciting future. Hornblower was past, but Dan Dare was still to come.

From very early on, I was aware that there was a distinc-tively Scottish way of squinting out at the world. The stories of Bannockburn (played at home, won) and Culloden (home, lost) were well known; I had picture books about Robert the Bruce as well as English heroes like Warwick the Kingmaker and Nelson. We Scots lost, but we were nobler and braver and more tragic than the English, who were a bit dull and smug. We were rough, they were smooth. We were gritty, they were suburban. I read a lot of Scottish history and poetry. Once, when we driving back in the family car from our annual holiday in the West Highlands, my youngest sister, then about five, was listening to the conversation. 'The English?' she asked with genuine puzzlement, 'are they the black ones?' My parents are Conservatives, of a moderate, pro-European and distinctly non-Thatcher stamp. My earliest political memories are of going canvassing with my mother, and attending a public meeting about British membership of the Common Market, at which a Scottish Nationalist warned that it would all lead to starvation, much to my father's amused contempt.

Later, I became a journalist and considered myself challengingly left-wing. In Edinburgh, as a trainee on the *Scotsman*, I became enthused about the idea of Scottish self-government and supported the Campaign for a Scottish Assembly. I became and remain an enthusiast for political reform and have written two books and many political columns on the subject. Now, I live in London with an English wife and three children who are more English than Scottish. The very modest Scottish intonation in my voice has disappeared except when I go home, when it rises from zero to barely perceptible. So, of course, the thought of full Scottish independence and the disappearance of Britain after 300 years is a little uncomfortable for me. Also, as a lifelong pro-European, there are aspects of the current EU which make me uneasy. Have my chickens come home to roost? Perhaps. I am genuinely proud and pleased that there is a Scottish Parliament and I do not believe for a moment that the breakup of the UK would lead to disaster, or to English people feeling unwelcome in Scotland, or any of the various grim scenarios trotted out.

But there is a lot about Britain that I like – not just the history of battles and conquest, though some of them were fought against terrible tyranny and for human freedom. In personal terms, I like having a larger space to mooch about in. Friends from Scotland sometimes ask what it feels like, living for so long in England, and I say I do not live in England. I live in London. The pathology of Britain is curious and complicated and London feels more like a world city than an English one. It is a kind of mixed, urban-provincial buzzing city-state embedded in the southern counties of a different country, the 'green England' referred to by Jeremy Paxman in his book, *The English* (1998).

Once, clearly, cities were essential to nationalism and the very idea of countries. They were where people gathered, listened, had free time to think, read or watch. Without cities, no coffee houses, newspapers, bourgeoisie, film audiences, finance ministries or state funerals. But, recently, some cities seem to have changed their meaning, becoming anti-nationalist rather than nationalist in effect. The contemporary city is a zone of speed, distorting time and distorting space. It distorts time by its frantic devotion to change, so that history and tradition mean little, torn down and replaced endlessly. I walk in London past landscapes that have changed shape and meaning every few years. The contemporary city has a short attention-span, challenging national memory. And it distorts space too, because increasingly city-dwellers are more like one another than they are like the dimly seen people of their various hinterlands. What is happening in Tokyo is happening in Los Angeles, London, Bangkok. Styles slip at the speed of light among them. Their news stories, about congestion, mayoral corruption, the heavy-handedness of police, increasingly sound the same. As a city-dweller, though I know my familiar routes and the British history of piled stones and monuments I pass, I am more at home in Paris or Vancouver – same coffee-bars, films, bookshops, fashions – than I am in the remoter parts of 'my' country. As with the distortion of time, the playing-around with space caused by the growth of mega-cities is hostile to nations and nationalism.

But I like it, the jostling of communities, the cram and rush, the awareness of being next door to New York, Delhi and Paris. A Scottish Londoner, I am British in most ways I can imagine being British, always excepting enthusiasm for the monarchy. In the middle of my city, I cling on to inherited ideas of Britishness – the notions of fairness, liberalism, civic stroppiness, post-war welfare decency, all that; and the idea that Britain is a made-up identity, neither ethnic nor based on religion, under which I have the freedom to be myself, outside class, race or origin. This Britain is less imperial than reassuring – comfortable. So when some critics say, as they will, that in questioning the life left in Britain, I am a wrecker, more psychic murderer than careful pathologist, all I can do is deny it. Journalism, done with any decency, means you have to try to tell it straight and that has been the intention. Forced to choose one day, I would carry a Scottish passport not an English one. But I have no enthusiasm for that choice. Pathologist or hack, I am, in the end, a British man. If it is dead, then a lot of me is dying too.

Acknowledgements

As usual, there are people to thank. First, always, Jackie
Ashley, my wife, who was forced to juggle her journalism
while I got on with yet another book, not having cleared it
with her first, and my children, Harry, Isabel and Emily, who
saw less of me during the autumn of 1999 than they
deserved, and found me occasionally distracted, or worse,
when I should have been friendly. Next, Alan Clements of
Wark-Clements, whose idea the programmes and therefore
the book was but who disagrees with my conclusions and
should not be held accountable for them. Then, because this
was very much a joint exercise with them, the team with
whom I worked for the BBC films – Ian Lilley, the remarkably even-tempered and shrewd director/producer, who is
probably some kind of artist; Andy Jackson, the cameraman,
who is certainly some kind of artist, despite everything;
Dominique Middleton and Bavesh Hindocha, whose
research was brilliant and heavily influenced the final outcome; the BBC executive in charge of us, Katie Lander; and
the sound and lighting team, Nic Jones, Dave Kirkwood,
Douglas Kerr, Tom Wright and Dick Philips. Filming is a
very odd, cumbersome and time-consuming business if you
are used to doing words alone; they made it very nearly good
fun. Then, the man who kindly agreed to publish a book
which was originally meant to be half this size at very short
notice and very quickly, Andrew Franklin and Nicky White

who worked on it at horrifying speed; and my agent Cat Ledger, who fixed it. Finally, at the risk of sounding like a wet-cheeked thespian hysteric, I would like to thank all the people who generously agreed to talk to me, often going out of their way to do so and sometimes being ruthlessly expunged from history in the final editing; and my various indulgent employers, Clive Hollick at United News & Media, Roger Alton at the *Observer* and Rosie Boycott at the *Express*. Thanks, all.

1

Roll-back

Satellite photographs are a beautiful lie. If they are of the British Isles, they are heavily doctored to show us without the usual swirls of hiding cloud. They are gorgeously coloured, in bright living greens, soft browns and sharp blues, in a way our daily lives are not. Looking at Britain you see the familiar and very odd shape: Scotland a hump-backed old lady throwing the javelin of the Outer Hebrides; Ireland a straggle-chinned old man with a bulbous nose. Then the great spread of England and Wales, the Bristol Channel between them like a dirty grin. Beside the warts and callouses, the fissures and splatter of isles that mark the Celtic countries, England looks quiet and smooth, not much bigger than Scotland or Ireland. If you were an ignorant space-traveller staring down on that miraculous day when these islands were not hidden by cloud, you would say – yes, one place, clearly, two big islands very close together, all much of a muchness.

Yet the vast majority of the British live in England. The human populations of Scotland, Ireland and Wales are small and sparsely spread. It is in the quiet-looking, flat-looking reversed L shape of England that eight out of ten people live, work and die. In money and people, it is more dominant than it was 100 years ago; 200 years ago; 300 years ago. Though a satellite map, with its sharp colours and edges, seems real enough, it leaves out what matters to the political economy. It does not tell us that the smudge of brown in the bottom south-east corner is sucking in people and energy from everywhere else. It doesn't tell us which bits, the southern shoreline and parts of the middle, are particularly lived in by old people, or where the last smoking industries can be found. It cannot say which bits have different languages or which bits pay a net tax transfer to which other bits. And above all, there is no information about those lines on the political map, dividing the UK from the Irish Republic, Scotland and Wales from England. These lines do not exist, of course, except as ideas. From space, you cannot see them. Crouch a few inches above the wiry grass and clay where they are said to be. Nothing. They are only in our heads – which nevertheless makes them as real as the shape of the islands from space.

The people of the larger island are, at least legally and formally, British. Some of the people on the other island call themselves British and belong to the UK. That is, they are the citizens of a state which has existed in more or less its current form for 300 years though the south of the smaller island left it nearly 80 years ago. In those three centuries, it grew by trade and conquest until it ruled huge swathes of the world, an empire vaster by far than that of the Romans. Then it began to shrink. We live in a time of roll-back. First the Empire, dissolving into Commonwealth. Two world wars so emptied the home island of wealth and energy that it could not seriously oppose the politicians and people of India, Africa and Asia who wanted to rule themselves. Nor, by that stage, did the British want to stop them. For the story of Britain had been a strange one. At the same time as the

British were creating their empire, they were also building a democracy at home, in which more and more of the people were given a say in the nation's decision-making. And democracy is a catastrophic domestic system if you want to rule an empire; the talk of equality and rights at home does not square with rule by force abroad, unless you believe that some races of human are inherently better than others. Once upon a time, many British people did think that – perhaps most – but the idea was made completely unrespectable by the disaster of Hitler. So the empire went, leaving the island alone again, though tied to other English-speaking nations.

But the roll-back carries on. South of the island, the great, jagged land mass of Europe, source of wars, English kings, religions, alliances and enemies, is engaged in a grand project of federal union. It may be a good idea. It may be a bad idea. But it is undoubtedly a big idea, and for two generations now, fear and fascination with the EU has transfixed and paralysed those British leaders whose predecessors' roars – their very throat-clearings – were heard with concern and respect around the world. Is it a plot, wonders London. Are the Germans behind it? In one mood we ask, is it our best hope for the future, giving us a new beginning? In another we fear that it is, in the resonantly inaccurate words of the Labour leader, Hugh Gaitskell, in 1962, 'the end of a thousand years of history'. So far, we have been unable to decide. A great adventure or the vet's final needle?

'Roll-back' is most acute inside the big island, since the smaller island has long ago set out on its own constitutional path. Ireland still contains, of course, an outpost of the UK which has been under sustained siege from Catholic nationalists for a generation, people who were once intent on accomplishing by demography and murder what they had previously had stolen from them by political trickery and oppression. In Scotland, whose aristocratic leaders had abolished the country's independence at a particularly grim moment, when the northern nation was virtually broke, a Parliament sits again for the first time in nearly 300 years. In Wales, taken over far earlier by Norman knights, there is an Assembly which, like the Edinburgh Parliament, is busy causing new problems for London. So is it to be first the British Empire going; then the UK; then Britain itself? The so-called 'inner Empire' that the English created in the two islands is now in serious jeopardy too. Where does this roll-back stop? In Newcastle and Durham, Labour campaigners want an assembly for the north, while the Archbishop of York presided over a Campaign for Yorkshire, using arguments and tactics pioneered in Scotland 15 years earlier. Will the long story of English expansion end where many believe it began, with Alfred the Great's kingdom, no longer called Wessex but the Home Counties? Would this extraordinary power reduce itself to a series of European provinces? And if it did, would the people really care?

That is the most painful question of all. The cultural changes in Britain have been just as striking as the political retreat. Much of what once set the white British apart, in their own minds at least, has gone. Their carefully graded class system and the accents that established its topography; the sports teams of white Anglo-Saxon men; the insular food and drink; the great British corporations and industries: 'roll-back' is about more than borders. In the City, the British-owned merchant banks (set up, albeit, by families of Baltic immigrants or the great German-Jewish mercantile dynasties) have passed to American, Japanese or continental ownership. Hundreds of the great country houses have gone. Culturally the biggest influence has been the world's only superpower in the year 2000, the United States, whose technology, film and TV industry, food corporations, car and plane-makers, music and clothing, have coloured and shaped every life in these islands. Britons today dress, amuse themselves, eat and often speak in ways that are essentially American. In time, of course, this may change. The rise of China and other Asian countries may bring a new kind of world culture, with different languages, styles and ways of doing business. But the American era has had a huge effect on the way the British see themselves.

I grew up reading British-produced comics and history stories, and watching British films; I had a firmly British idea of the war against Nazism and our place in the world. Today, if my children see a war film, it is likely to be American and to contain no mention of the British – or at the most, a slighting one. If Enoch Powell was right when he said, 'It's really collective memory that makes a nation, its memory of what its past was, what it has done, what it has suffered and what it has endured,' then the British nation is in very fast retreat. Or, to quote the novelist Ben Okri, 'To poison a nation, poison its stories. A demoralised nation tells demoralised stories to itself.' Demoralising or not, American stories are edging out British ones. American technology, above all in computing, is even helping to erode the forms, spellings and pronunciations of British forms of English. As a distinctive people, we are becoming less ourselves all the time.

Partly, this is about the composition of Britain, which is further and further removed from the white simplicities of old. Never mind that this apparently homogenous white British group in fact contained great diversities, of Celtic peoples and Norsemen, English and Jew, Huguenot and Irish, living in very different circumstances and with very different attitudes. The whiteness of the British had become, as they spread around the world, one of their most obvious markers, both to themselves and the people they colonised. But that clearly describes a Britishness that has gone forever. One of the consequences of empire was mass immigration

into Britain during the twentieth century, particularly after
the 1950s. People who had been brought up with a strong
idea of Britain as a land of wealth and hope came from India,
Pakistan and Bangladesh, from the colonies of the
Caribbean, and from parts of Africa – first encouraged by
Powell, at a time when the country was desperate for labour,
then baited by him. At the same time, many white British,
lured by the thought of sun and a fresh start, emigrated to
Australia, New Zealand or Canada.

By the time racist British politicians and officials had pan-
icked and tried to construct a legal system for keeping Asian
and black immigrants out while allowing in white ones, it
was too late, and the country had changed, bringing problems at home but also huge opportunities for Britain as a
new global market developed. So the look and smell of the
country changed. New foods arrived. Mosques were built.
Today the most popular restaurant dish in Britain is not roast
beef but chicken tikka masala, a hybrid Indian meal invented
in East London by Bangladeshi chefs. Of the 3 million extra
people who demographers expect to be living in the UK by
2023, when they expect the population to peak, a high dis-
proportion (because of the birth-rate) will be Asian. Given
the large numbers of Asian families in London, and London's
marked cultural influence on the rest of Britain, that impact
will be even stronger than the raw numbers suggest, striking
though they are.

The shifting shape of the economy has had equally dramatic effects on the look and feel of Britain. Old trade union
and class allegiances which defined the mood of parts of the
British nation have been destroyed by the decline in mass
manufacturing, coalmining and shipbuilding. Towns which
used to be rich and confident, but dirty, are now poor and
silent. People have moved from parts of the north to the
increasingly crowded south-east corner. The mood of

anxiety was well caught by an article in London's newspaper, the *Evening Standard*, which pointed out that a new planning proposal would

> launch a city upon the South-east of England larger than the one Romulus started when he dug a ditch on an Italian hillside. This will not be a city that can be seen in any one place but it will consist of one million new homes built over the next 20 years in an area spreading from Bedford to Brighton, and Basingstoke to Dover, but not including greater London which will itself have to accommodate even more homes.

The writer went to on to admit that even the south's local authorities thought 800,000 new homes would be needed because 'at some point, the housing needs of teachers and nurses have to account for something against those of badgers and birds.'[1] In fact, London had already grown by 300,000 from 1989 to 1999, and included all five of the UK's most densely populated boroughs. London house prices were wildly inflating, rising at 20 per cent a year in 1999, while it was almost impossible to give away housing in some parts of the north – a Salford estate agent, for instance, was offering a 'two houses for the price of one' deal in some streets. A demographic map of Britain, altering its shape to show where people lived, would turn it almost into a teardrop, with the fattest bit covering London, Kent and Essex, though with significant concentrations in the West Midlands and Greater Manchester.

The emptying of parts of the north has been mirrored by the flight of the middle classes to suburbs and small towns. Despite official disapproval, not mirrored by the readiness of political parties to take money from the superstore shopping

giants, there has been a huge shift to out of town shopping
centres, with giant carparks and a centralised discounting
system which has in turn changed the shape of high streets
up and down the country. If you relied on the old high
streets, you would conclude that Britain was a nation of
charity shops and pizza delivery stores. Outside the towns,
new farming techniques have changed the countryside, ripping away thousands of miles of ancient hedgerow and
woodland. Although the main subject of this book is the
constitutional change that confronts British identity, it is perhaps these shifts in landscape and habit that shake people
more, even to their sense of national belonging – something
John Betjeman was already noting in the mid-war period,
when the first big ribbon development was wriggling out
from the cities.

The assault on traditional national self-image comes in
smaller-looking things too. Attitudes to gaining money and
flaunting it have changed, so that old 'typically British' values
like self-deprecation and a certain sober drabness have vanished. Homosexuality and smoking have swapped places as
things to be approved or disapproved of. The explosion of
scientific technique and understanding has damaged the
island's once dominant Protestant-Christian religion, leading
to a revival of alternative religions, cults and beliefs. Membership of the European Union has meant altering habits and
forms in politics, business and daily life. The old system of
coinage, with shillings, pennies, florins, sixpences and half-
crowns, was abolished in 1971, to bring in a decimal system
more like that of continental currencies. The government is
committed (ish) to abolishing the pound and replacing it
with the new EU currency, the euro. It may be, however, as
more of us use banks joined by the Internet to our homes,
credit cards and charge cards, that money as we have known
it simply becomes less and less used. From the end of 1999,

pounds and ounces, the old system of weighing foodstuffs, were made illegal and replaced by metric measurements.

This life of change is at the back of most of our minds, even if rarely examined or pondered on. It is like the shape of the skyline on the way to work, a surrounding context. The acceleration of change, the way it cuts into the corners and odd moments of everyday life, need have no effect on the legal survival of this or any other nation-state, but it makes us uneasy and, perhaps, more prone to extreme reactions. Rehearse some of the changes to the island people in the past few decades: our place in the world; laws and constitution; coinage and perhaps currency; racial mix; food and religion; sexual mores; the agreed territory of the nation; culture and (at the edges) language; the shape of industries and the look of the countryside; condition of towns; the system of weights and measures. And through all of this there have been phenomenal wider changes which are not directly related to us, but which shape our lives nevertheless. The revolution in genetics opens up possibilities of new kinds of crops, designer babies and even new species of living creatures. Last, but not least, climate change is changing the year, giving us less snow, and longer, drier summers, bringing new insects and birds further north, unexpected fish to our seas, and crops, such as wine, that we have not seen for centuries. We are spinning with change, drunk on change, maddened by it and yet mad for it too.

For despite this long litany, the people who actually live in the large island are mostly doing pretty well. A fifth or so of them are excluded from the good life enjoyed by the rest, tucked away on foul housing estates. But the majority have a comparatively high level of material prosperity. We are more secure from overseas invasion or the threat of being called up to fight than ever before in our history. Perhaps the greatest, and certainly the most influential modern essay on identity is

George Orwell's 'England your England' written in 1941. It is a wry, funny, highly critical but utterly passionate celebration of English national differences and national culture generally. But it opens with the sentence: 'As I write, highly civilised human beings are flying overhead, trying to kill me.' The oddness of that sentence now is a glaring reminder of my generation's extraordinary luck. No one is trying to kill me. I have not the slightest fear that my son and daughters will be asked to put on a uniform and be killed to defend their parents' freedom. This is, historically, unusual.

The luck does not stop there. We enjoy entertainments and learning that earlier generations would be entranced by. Those of us with money have a wider range of choice than any previous group of people on the planet; the choice to loot almost any interesting database in the world through the Internet; to go for a few weeks to Budapest or Vancouver or Madras; to consume what may be the central achievement of Western millennial civilisation, the ice-cream Mars Bar. We dress more comfortably, eat better and generally do less physically grinding jobs – as a result of which we live longer, and look better than our grandparents did at our age. A comparison between Prince Charles at 50, when he looked relatively young, and his father and grandfather, who seemed old men at the same age, makes the point for millions of other families. In all those ways, we are very lucky indeed.

To the extent that the British are unhappy, it seems to be because of stress and uncertainty, caused by the feeling of acceleration in daily life and insecurity about economic status and sex – none of which they are likely to connect directly to the future of the nation-state. The writer Oliver James coined the phrase 'the low-serotonin society' for the depression felt by many people. He pointed out that rates of depression have been increasing throughout the developed world in the past half-century. Suicides have increased, and among young British men, according to a report by R.F.W. Diekstra, they have tripled between 1970 and 1995. Violence against the person has increased in England and Wales by 10 per cent a year on average since 1950. James writes:

> Let us be absolutely clear about the scale of the
> problem. The proportion of adult Britons
> suffering from psychiatric morbidity at any one
> time is now almost one third ... If the definitions
> were widened to include all low-serotonin
> problems, such as violence and impulsive
> aggression, it would be around one-half – perhaps
> 20 million people. The majority of them receive
> no formal treatment (pills or therapy).[2]

This seems an extreme proportion. Even so, there are parts of James's picture which make sense. We are lucky-sad people.

This impinges remarkably little on our attitudes to politics or anything else in the public sphere. In earlier phases of British history, personal unhappiness was thought to be something to be dealt with either through religious consolation or political action and the hope of a better world ahead. Today, the unhappiness industry has been privatised, and is dealt with through self-help books, a constant flow of treatments, theories and cults that make us seem like the Imperial Rome satirised by Juvenal; and by the voyeur's confessional of the daytime television sofa. It is Prozac not Parliament, St John's Wort not St Stephen's Green. There is a lot of political ignorance bound up in these attitudes, since much unhappiness is caused by problems which public, political action can help – employment fears, bad housing, crime. But the membership of political parties continues to fall away. Thinking about public policy seems too difficult, too boring, for most people to bother with, compared to the glossy personal simplicities of the self-help dream. Perhaps because states do not kill you or send you to fight, it is too easy to forget that they exist and are still very powerful. The growth of a huge middle class and of middle-class politics, hostile to tax rises and redistribution of wealth through the state, has meant that public action is simply weaker. Oliver James has become a strong advocate of pills as well as therapy, but deplores how the number of people on low income, suffering from low status and great unhappiness, has grown in Britain, the USA, Canada and Australia.

> Liberals (amongst whom I count myself) will feel a sharp pain in their guts at the thought of trying to use drugs to address problems with blatantly socio-economic causes. The only reason I can advance for doing so is that I do not know a better way of immediately countering the ill-effects of modern inequalities and empowering those whose serotonin levels have been diminished by being made to feel like losers … Given the triumph of Market Economics which forbids increased welfare spending, the challenge to liberals is to come up with a better alternative.[3]

It is a challenge millions would echo. Rarely have the role of the state, national prestige and daily living seemed so disconnected as they are today.

But we are not going to have the option of simply turning away from public life, popping down the pills and pursuing our interests in a privatised world. The political crisis facing the British state is too near for that and touches us despite our lethargy. If Scotland leaves the United Kingdom, or if Britain withdraws from the EU, or if any one of a number of other combinations of things happen, the consequences for ordinary life will be real and, for a while, raw. The politics of Westminster will change, altering the balance of the political parties, with consequent effects on people's bank accounts, pensions and job prospects. For many, a residual sense of British identity, which affects their security and therefore their happiness, will also be touched – though a reviving Englishness and Scottishness might, of course, make many others feel happier too. Within weeks of the new Parliament and the new Assembly getting going, arguments about university student fees, help for farmers and whether it is safe to eat beef on the bone had divided the Scots, Welsh and English. The argument about whether the pound is to be replaced by the euro cannot forever be ducked. When it comes, probably in a referendum within a few years, it will be the decisive debate about our future in Europe and therefore the place of Britain, and England, in the world. That too affects most of us directly: where will our children work, what money will we use, will we be able to stop politicians doing things to us we dislike?

So for a writer on politics, this is an interesting time to be alive. This book follows others about the possible death, breakup or abolition of Britain. The right-wing journalists Peter Hitchens (*The Abolition of Britain*) and Simon Heffer (*Nor Shall My Sword*) have entered the fray with passionate and interesting books in 1999. Heffer bases his on criticising Scottish nationalism and concludes that 'the reinvention of England as an independent and proud nation' would be the best response. Hitchens accuses New Labour of a 'slow-motion coup d'etat' and says that this 'is a last unrepeatable moment at which we can halt our extinction as a culture and a nation.' The Conservative politician John Redwood has written *The Death of Britain*. All these follow the first, ground-breaking work from the left-wing Scottish writer, Tom Nairn, and the anti-devolutionist Labour MP, Tam Dalyell, who were predicting the *Breakup of Britain* in the 1970s. The late Raphael Samuel, whose writing on Britishness was particularly shrewd, said in 1995 that 'if the United Kingdom continues to unravel, the word "Britain" may be as obsolete as "Soviet" is in post-1989 Russia ... No less striking that the collapse of British power, and this country's relegation to a second- or even third-class industrial nation, is the unravelling of any unitary idea of national character.'[4]

The historian Norman Davies has published a monumental *The Isles: A History*, tracing British and Irish history from the Ice Age, which takes a distinctly Europeanist perspective, emphasising our links with the story of the continent. In the final chapter of that book, Professor Davies writes:

> I happen to belong to that group of opinion
> which holds the breakup of the United Kingdom
> to be imminent. I may be wrong. But the feeling
> has grown steadily over the last decades as I sat at
> my desk thinking and writing about history over
> the long term ... One receives the overwhelming
> impression that all states and empires are
> ephemeral; that all of them pass away; and that
> something is always found to replace them. The
> death of a state has overtones of sadness; but it is
> not necessarily a tragedy.

Six years earlier, Davies had expressed a doubt about whether the UK would live to see its three hundredth birthday in 2007:

> I have not changed my mind, though now I think
> that the belated introduction of devolution may
> prolong the UK's life for a season or two. At
> bottom, I belong to the group of historical

colleagues who hold that the United Kingdom
was established to serve the interests of Empire,
and that the loss of Empire has destroyed its *raison
d'etre*.[5]

What do the politicians think? Do they have other reasons
for the continuance of Britain that these writers omit?
Strangely, perhaps, Labour has become the prime unionist
force in the islands. Scottish and Welsh devolution was advocated and legislated by Labour and its allies for the simple
reason that, at least in the former case, it had become an irre-
sistable and popular demand which, if denied, would simply
accelerate the push for independence and the end of the UK.
The idea that Labour politicians have cooked up devolution
to benefit themselves is politically illiterate: the Scots in cabinet are the people today most threatened by Home Rule.
Gordon Brown's hopes of succeeding Tony Blair as Prime
Minister, for instance, depend upon a British settlement in
which the English are happy to continue with the top jobs in
the country held by Scottish MPs. More generally, Labour is
a party which has mostly relied for its occasional periods in
power on Scottish and Welsh votes – though that was not
true after the 1997 anti-Tory landslide.

So Labour's simultaneous support for devolution, trying
to put more elasticity into the centralised British state, and its
support for the Union, is no mystery. It may be a gamble, but
then Labour did not inherit a secure UK to start with – far
from it. The most stirring, thoughtful unionism on offer is
the left-of-centre variety which seeks to bind the peoples
back together with a revitalised and fairer state dispensation
– what Gordon Brown calls 'the Great British Society' in
which fairness and common interests balance the growing
sense of separate nationhood on the island. To expect a frank
discussion of the underlying fragility of the Union from

Labour is naive. Late at night and sotto voce, however, many Labour figures will readily admit that, in the words of one, 'none of us really knows where this is heading.'

The Conservatives under William Hague have been making the most of the contradictions in the devolved system, calling for 'English votes for English laws' and beginning to relearn the language of English nationhood. Hague is following a delicate line, since he says he is standing up for the (British) nation-state as well, particularly against the European federal threat. To scratch away at the current relationship between England and Scotland and yet to defend the Union when turning outside to confront continental Europe is a tricky double-act to pull off. But in the short term, English patriotism may well be a profitable tactic for a struggling opposition party to pursue, since the sense of grievance in middle England is real enough. In the longer term it is a great irony, of course, for a party which still formally calls itself the Conservative and Unionist Party to be following a course of logic which will loosen the current Union. But there are plenty of intelligent Tories who think it is over anyway, and note that they are likelier to return to power in England once the Celts have left than they are in the current British system. The Liberal Democrats, meanwhile, have the modest but real advantage of being federalists throughout the century; they, at least, have an answer ready.

Politicians will not feature much in what follows, however. The demands of party debate and the extreme sensitivity of this question, the survival of the state to which professional politicians owe allegiance and their hopes of advancement, mean that we are on firmer, ground talking to others. If there is a real crisis of Britishness, or if Scotland is to break from England, then that is more likely to be articulated by working people, business executives, farmers and the writers, than at Westminster. This is an issue where 'the people' lead politicians in seeing it plain.

In going round the country, I have found an assumption, spread far more widely than expected, that old Britain, the post-imperial, broadly united and homogenous country, is dead. Caution is in order. We have been here before, notably in the years before the First World War, when dissent was rampant and many observers thought a British civil war could not be avoided for long – and, in a lesser way, during the near breakdown of the 1970s. But Britain was immeasurably stronger in the first case and there are hard reasons for the debate this time to be a more serious one. The number of intelligent people who think that Britain cannot last more than a decade or so more is too great to be ignored or laughed at. We are at a genuine turning-point in the story of the British and this book, the product of a series of three television films made for the BBC during the summer and autumn in the run-up to 2000, is intended to help people find their bearings in the argument. Its title follows that of the TV programmes. When we first discussed *The Day Britain Died* I thought it had a certain ring but was a bit over the top. Now, I am really not so sure. You could even say that Britain is dead already, that the imperial project and core values, the class system and rules and religion that held the peoples of these islands together have fallen away, leaving only a husk and a flag and a shape on the map. It is not impossible that the flag will go too, and the name, so that my son and daughters, when they are middle aged, will live in the Kingdom of England, or the Scottish Republic, or South Anglia, Europe.

Unlikely. Not impossible.

2

Are There any British Left?

Imperial people

The British are a comparatively small group of people. Imagine the world's entire population represented by a thousand people, milling about. In the year 1900, 23 or 24 of them would be British citizens. Many more would be ruled by the British Empire. By 1920, about a quarter of the world's population were born, lived and died in that empire. It had more of the world's people in than China, almost four times as many as Russia, more than four times as many as the USA. Beside it, the other European nations were tiny. Today, the empire has gone and there have been vast increases in the populations of Asia and Africa, both proportionately and absolutely. Political shrinkage and the shifts in demography have worked together, so that today, out of that thousand people, only nine would be British citizens. On current trends, because our population is rising only slowly, and the world's is rising fast, that proportion will fall dramatically, so that by 2050, we would be down to five or six out of the thousand. Not even one in a hundred.

This may seem a strange way to start. What counts, after

all, is the power and influence of a people, not their raw or proportional numbers. The British story is partly about how a small island came to dominate a third of the inhabited planet, and then fell back; it is an essay in leverage and national energy. Yet there is no getting away from it. In an advanced global economy, the size of the population still matters. Companies frame their thinking for the largest and richest functioning markets. As the poorer parts of the world grow economically, trade agreements, military treaties and macro-economic policies will follow. This does not mean 'small' cannot prosper. Hong Kong prospers. Switzerland prospers. But as other peoples advance, they press in on our old power, our room for manoeuvre, even our imaginations. So before talking about Britishness, or the Scots and the English, or the tension between urban liberals and rural conservatives, it is as well to keep a sense of proportion. These are discussions or arguments among northern tribes which, in world terms, are now very small fry indeed.

Trying to define the character of the people of any nation is a slippery and dangerous game. Britain, or its constituent countries, holds such a variety of characters, so many views, styles, attitudes and different educations, that to say the English or Scots are all 'like this' is patent nonsense. Mostly when people assert something about the national character they are trying to bully the rest of us into a certain idea of what it should be like. Old nationalistic right-wingers may tell us that the British are uniquely brave fighters, a statement which cannot be justified. (Braver than the Russians and Germans at Stalingrad? Braver than the Americans fighting in the Pacific in 1944? Braver than the Polish Jews facing the SS in Warsaw?) Liberals, including myself, have been prone to say that the British are more tolerant and 'decent' than other people, more committed to fairness. How this matches the raw racism of some, or the increasingly exhibitionist attitude to sex, or our enthusiasm for politicians who promise a less fair taxation system, is hard to say. Really, what I mean is that I *want* us to be more tolerant and pro-fairness – and hope that if I keep saying it often enough, it will become so.

Even so, wise writers have in the past believed that they can describe, very generally, some aspects of national identity. In the essay by Orwell mentioned earlier, he speaks of many things that people would recognise today and know are worth preserving; the 'gentleness' of English civilisation, the relative lack of corruption in the law and politics. He writes that England will never be Germanised or Russianised:

> The gentleness, the hypocrisy, the thoughtlessness,
> the reverence for law and the hatred of uniforms
> will remain, along with the suet puddings and the
> misty skies … England will still be England, an
> everlasting animal stretching into the future and
> the past, and like all living things, having the
> power to change and yet remain the same.

It is generally at times of immediate threat or crisis that people cast around and ask: who are we? What is it about us that makes it right to hold together? And though the character of people of a nation is so various and unpredictable that it does not really exist, what does exist is the web of habits, laws, ideas and collective memories that holds the people together – their public, semi-formal identity. In short, there is no such thing as a national character, except as a commonly agreed myth, important in itself; but there is a national identity.

The trouble with the Orwell quotation is that it is about England, not Britain. It was common through most of British history for people to say England when they meant Britain; and perhaps it was inevitable, given the huge preponderance of English people in the Union. 'Britain' was the official word, the description of the state, and its Empire. But it was not the word that tugged most hearts; English poets, politicians, historians and later broadcasters used 'England' by preference. Even some Scots did. The main hotel in Edinburgh used to be called The North British Hotel. It has now been renamed, as the 'Balmoral'. But there was never a South British Hotel; nor did the English ever think of themselves as south Britons. There is not a passage as eloquent and authentic as Orwell's one, about Britishness, rather than Englishness. And it was not until relatively recently that rising Scottish and Welsh self-assertion produced a new mood of political correctness in organisations such as the BBC and national newspapers, so that the use of England rather than Britain dropped away.

So what would an average or typical British person look like? How would they sound? In broadcasting, a gentle Irish or Scottish accent has become popular precisely because it does not say to the English listener or viewer anything strong or potentially off-putting about the speaker's class. In a small but telling episode in October 1999, James Boyle, the (Scottish) controller of BBC Radio Four, sacked (English) Boris Johnson from presenting the programme *The Week in Westminster* allegedly because his voice, which is a plummy upper-class one, was thought to be inappropriate for a Saturday morning. It was, in Johnson's words, 'too posh, stuck-up, toffee-nosed, just too damn pukka for its own good.' Suddenly, he went on,

> here we are, deep in the fathomless morass of
> British class prejudice ... a British system more
> elaborate and stratified than in any other country
> on earth ... It's brilliant to be Brummie, super to
> be Scottish or anything else. But just you try

reading out a script in the received pronunciation
of the Queen's English on Radio Four at 11am
on Saturday and pow – you're sacked by Jimmy
Boyle. Frighten the horses, eh? What is it with the
horses that they should be frightened by a simple
braying noise?[1]

Johnson, it turned out later, had been overdoing it – tone
was also at issue – and he apologised to Boyle. But this was,
at the least, a telling glimpse of the Britishness problem. With
the fall of empire, the old elite has been forced into retreat
for decades and the pyramid of class and power that main-
tained the British system has crumbled. Voice is indeed a
good indicator of what has happened, because it is honest
and familiar. I was brought up to 'talk properly' and not in a
Dundee accent but now suspect that a Dundee accent, or at
least a modified central Scottish one, would have been an
advantage in life. Lacking a Scottish voice is certainly a disadvantage, and sometimes an embarrassment, in Scotland. In
England, the spread of what has been called 'estuarial English', a flattish southern accent with swallowed vowels, is the
latest attempt to overcome the old divisions. It follows the
fashion for Manchester, Liverpool and Newcastle accents
from the 1960s and 1970s onwards. (Boris Johnson is wrong
about only one thing: it has never been 'brilliant to be Brum-
mie', however helpfully alliterative.) Once, Johnson had the
voice which held the British nations together. It was the
voice of Reith's BBC, the voice of the empire, the voice of
monarchy and order. Today, it has become embarrassing.
There is no British voice. Britishness is becoming steadily
harder to hear.

So, what are the habits, laws, customs and memories that
hold all the people of the big island, and some of the people
of the smaller island, together? Is it possible that 'Britain' and

'British' are historically specific words, describing certain communities who came together during a certain part of their story, but not forever – and that we are close to the end of that period?

We know when it began. It makes no sense to talk of Britain before the Act of Union between the English and Scottish states in 1707. There had been a single monarchy for a century before that, when the Union flag, later nicknamed the Union Jack, was invented as a naval ensign by the Scottish and now English king, James VI and I. That royal order of union, which the English Parliament refused to extend to a political one, had been interrupted only by Oliver Cromwell's short, military British Commonwealth of 1649–60. But neither the regal union nor the republican one touched the identity of Scots and English very deeply, so far as we can tell from the way they recorded their daily lives. After 1707, however, Britain became a strong, self-certain nation, rising to extraordinary power and prominence in a very short time. It is only by looking at what happened to the peoples of the island after that date that any sense of Britishness can be found. There are some historians who would collapse that 300-year history quite substantially, taking the story of Britain proper from the failure of the Jacobite rebellion in Scotland in 1746 to the Irish treaty, establishing the Free State, in 1921. Still, that birthday of 1707 is the simplest and most generally agreed one.

The main things that reinforced British identity in the following three centuries were war and the militarisation of public life; the industrial revolution, and the internal divisions and mobilities it produced; and the empire. All of them touched every corner of the islands, except the agricultural fringes of the west of Ireland and Scotland, which saw little of the effects of industrial and scientific power until recently – though plenty of the manpower-draining effects of war.

After half a century of relative peace, and because we have never been invaded successfully, it is already hard to remember just what a bloody history the British one has been. There is a common view of the British story which sees the era of serious war as starting with the fight against Napoleon, and then allows our forefathers a long period of peace until the traumas of Flanders. This is a desperately unhistorical view. Britain was born in war: the war of the Spanish Succession; the war of the Austrian Succession; the war of Jenkin's Ear. Then came the American war of independence, the wars against revolutionary France and against Napoleon, then the war of 1812 against the United States. Imperial history involved a long chain of wars, against the Indian states, Bengal and against Mysore; the two opium wars against China; the Crimean war against Russia; and endless minor imperial wars we have mostly forgotten – small wars in Abyssinia, the Gold Coast, Burma, Persia, Canada, New Zealand, Afghanistan and the Punjab. (On the North-West Frontier there were nearly 20 wars between 1863 and 1901.) There were nasty little wars to put down rebellions, from Scotland and Ireland to India and South Africa. There was the forgotten war against Lenin's Russia. And then, of course, the huge wars, the ones that shook us to the marrow and destroyed the empire and changed everything – the First World War and the Second World War. After that, under the nuclear threat of the Cold War, there were only smaller ones, the wars in Malaya and Korea, Cyprus and Egypt, the Falklands and the Gulf.

But however you cut it, the history of the British has involved a huge amount of fighting. Much of it was at sea and the greatest wars were against real tyrannies: there have been limits to British bellicosity. Yet war has marked the British experience deeply. Even when the wars were small ones, generations of men from all classes served in the Navy or Army. The public schools' Officers Training Corps, the Boy Scouts and the Boys' Brigade, the military trappings of Empire Day, a now-forgotten annual ceremony, the popular songs of the music halls and the huge reviews of the forces, on land and sea, ensured that Britain was a remarkably militarised society – certainly more so than the self-image of an anti-soldier 'unPrussian' country suggested. Streets were named after victories and newspapers were crammed with military information. The Army gave a particular tone to the class system and to Victorian entertainment. The great wars emptied villages and towns of many of the men and produced two generations of widows and spinsters.

Similarly, it is impossible to imagine Britain without the imperial experience. We would have been a totally different people, and perhaps never united politically at all. Before the Union of the Scottish and English crowns, there was hardly any empire. England had colonised Wales, was in Ireland and had taken small corners of the American seaboard and few islands. The pre-British 'English Empire' was based on sugar, tobacco, slaves and piracy, all lucrative enough but hardly the achievement of a world-changing power. Outside their shores, the English were mostly known as heretics and pirates. The East India Company had been formed as early as 1600, following earlier trading ventures such as the Muscovy Company, the Venice Company and the Turkey Company, but was then engaged in a small, speculative business in spices and linens.

What really built the empire was already established during the seventeenth century – the seafaring tradition and the Navy, effectively re-founded by Cromwell to take on the Dutch. It is worth remembering that Britain itself was formed by empire in the negative sense that the Scots were forced into a form of Union which effectively submerged them politically, because of the failure of their own attempts at an empire. The 'Darien scheme' of 1698–1700 was intended to establish a Scottish colony at Panama but a mixture of malaria and Spanish and English hostility destroyed it. Some estimates suggest that a quarter of Scotland's entire liquid wealth had been sunk – almost literally – in the project and its failure had a devastating effect on the morale and wealth of urban Scotland. After the Union, however, Scotland provided a disproportionate share of the manpower of empire-building, as these islands became a global power, based on the military might of the Royal Navy and the ideological conviction of the Protestant religion.

The English led, in terms of firepower, money and political direction. But the Scots, and to a lesser extent the Welsh and Irish, were full and enthusiastic players almost all the way, providing large numbers of colonists, soldiers, missionaries, explorers, traders and, later, engineers. It really was a British Empire, not just an English one; Britain was born as a baby empire. Meanwhile, at home the surplus wealth, liberal political climate and strong commercial laws, which made it comparatively easy to raise money, had helped spark the industrial revolution. That was the third shaping force for Britain and cannot be disentangled from the other two, war and empire. And they all, in turn, derived from and shaped the constitution of the country.

The cost of building and maintaining a huge navy meant that the Crown was utterly dependent on Parliament in a way other European monarchies were not, so entrenching the 'Glorious Revolution'. Later, the industrial revolution created a new politics which made successive extensions of the franchise an urgent necessity. And the experience of war, particularly in the past century, was the main motor for the growth of a strong, centralised state machine. It all hung together: the Royal Navy and the Army carved out and protected the huge overseas territories that provided the raw materials and the markets for the world's first industrial power.

At home, the age of Britishness was also the age of the huge new cities. The staggering ugliness of stretches of the English and Scottish midlands, the gouging-out of the Welsh coal seams and the creation of a nation of factory-dwellers living in small brick houses, rather than peasants and farmers, is all a British thing, not a Scottish or English thing.

This is a crude summary, not a history; but what is not in doubt is that the new nation called Britain was, within a hundred years of its foundation, a staggering success. One historian of the empire says, without hyperbole:

> For the first three-quarters of the nineteenth
> century Britain appeared as a colossus astride the
> world. Britain dominated every field of human
> activity and its people seemed to possess an almost
> demonic energy.

Not surprisingly, he added, there was a developing national conviction that 'Britain had been chosen by Providence as an instrument of universal progress.'[2]

By the beginning of the First World War, the British Crown ruled a quarter of the planet and had a hugely disproportionate share of its people, wealth and firepower. Our cities would not be our cities without the empire. Our mix of races, our foods, come from the empire. The fact that the games we play, rugby and football and cricket, have become international games comes from the empire. The United States of America, our child, enemy, nemesis and ally, would never have happened in the way it did without British imperialism. Perhaps it would have been a German and French-speaking confederation with a Mohawk president ruling from its capital, New Paris, on the Hudson. The British

Empire, one way and another, for good and evil, made a lot of the modern world possible. We cannot begin to deal with our current national illness without talking about that. To deny the empire is to deny Britishness.

Yet we have done our best to do just that. In the end, it slipped away pretty easily. Two world wars reduced us and raised America. Our agonising about that was confined, by and large, to the ruling elite. The rest of Britain suffered the privations and losses and then enjoyed the material benefits of the twentieth century.

Another way of looking at it is that of all the imperial countries, which had grown great by denying democracy and self-determination to other peoples, Britain got out quickly and relatively cleanly. Britain had moments of imperial agony, most notably Suez. But we never had the civil disruption and war that plagued France in the 1960s – a British equivalent to the Algerian crisis would have involved, perhaps, the overthrow of the monarchy, the mutiny of a couple of famous regiments and IRA-style terrorism by former Rhodesian colonists living in Reigate and Dorking. It never happened. We ended up with a cosy Commonwealth, liked and respected as decent and well-meaning around the world. That, at least, is what we tell ourselves. Imperialism brought railways and industry, constitutions and cities to India, Africa, Australia, New Zealand, Canada and smaller territories. But if the British Empire had been so uniquely successful at evolving into an informal union of sovereign democratic states, then Africa might today not be a political disaster zone; half a million Indian and Pakistanis would not have died in that civil war; there would not be a nuclear confrontation on the sub-continent; and the modern history of the Middle East would have been far less bloody and dangerous than it has been, and still is. While countless millions of people around the world are still struggling to emerge from the consequences of British imperial power the British themselves appear to have almost forgotten it.

It may not be so easy. The empire made Britain. But its disappearance may mean the end of Britain. There is an almost uncanny balance between what we did to the world and what the world is now doing to us. We took our religions and peoples deep into Asia. Now Islam is in England and the British are black and brown as well as white. We built missions in India and churches in Africa. Now we have one of the greatest new Hindu temples in Neasden, the nearest thing, in terms of skill and detail, to one of the old stone English churches, but carved by a thousand stonemasons in Gujerat from marble and limestone; and of course, mosques in every sizeable town. We imposed our will by military power; now we are a junior partner in a world alliance. We fought wars to make the Chinese import and use opium; now the drug routes run from Afghanistan to every British village and school. We kept the continental Europeans divided and down. Now continental Europe suggests that, if we want to remain significant, we should next give up our currency, dividing us entirely. Why should this process not end in the disappearance of Britain, the political entity that gave rise to the empire? Almost every imperial collapse has ended with the collapse of the original empire-building centre, from the Romans to the Japanese, the Austro-Hungarians to the Incas. Why should Britain be different?

All this history – the empire, all those wars, the industrial revolution – is lightly worn today. More important is the last act, the greatest achievement of the empire – its role in defeating Hitler, a struggle which exhausted and finished it. For Britons of my generation, the wars against German militarism and the democratic welfare state that followed it were and are the defining acts of Britishness, the things that made it worthwhile. British war stories and films, then the democratic acts of the post-war era, were the imaginative glue which is now dissolving.

The war against Hitler may have lost the country its vast empire, but it also gave the idea of Britishness a great shot in the arm. It turned the monarchy from being a scandal-ridden and moth-eaten looking thing to a genuinely popular symbol of the nation. It made the still young BBC a force around the world. The wartime state made government respected and trusted again, and enabled the huge wave of nationalisations and state welfarism that followed, so that there was, for a while, no doubt at all what Britain was for. British Coal. British Rail. The National Health Service. British Steel. Britain morphed from being essentially about empire into being essentially about the state, the role of government in our lives. But this too has been undermined and eroded.

As the state retreats from the economy and from close oversight of daily life, other forces move in − few of them British. Industrial enterprises and former public utilities are sold to German and French companies. Of the 42 notable privatisations carried out by the Thatcher and Major administrations, 14 were of leading groups with the word 'British' in their title, four had 'National' and others, such as Rolls-Royce, Jaguar, Rover Group and the nuclear power industry, had mattered to the country's sense of itself. Privatisation may have been a great and liberating economic act, and some (though by no means all) of those groups retained their British self-identification in the free market. But because 'British' was so associated after 1945 with the power and achievements of the state − a public word, not a private or cultural one − the retreat of the state has also meant a retreat of Britishness. Indeed, there is a case for saying that Margaret Thatcher, by privatising, deregulating and demolishing much of the old state apparatus, helped to undermine key aspects of

British identity – unwittingly and ironically, since she was and is a passionate British patriot. Sir Bernard Ingham, her former press secretary and a living embodiment of the bull-dog breed who will disagree with much of my general thesis, says

> there is a case to say that during the 1980s, during the Thatcher years, the remorseless erosion of things British occurred. I have to say that having been with Mrs Thatcher throughout that period, it was not what she intended or hoped – but there again, there are a lot of things which politicians do not intend, but find happening.

Atlanticans

In culture, the pass was sold much earlier than that. Few forms of mass entertainment have been as important to modern nationalism as film. British commentators often mock France for its complex web of subsidies, tariffs, quotas and rules designed to maintain a native French film industry in opposition to Hollywood. French cinema is not left to the market but is championed and protected by the Ministry of Culture. In the words of Nicolas Seydoux, of the film pro-duction company Gaumont, 'It is essential that Europe pre-serves its cultural diversity. When you realise that children spend more time in front of the television than with their teachers, you have to encourage audio-visual creation. The Americans already have half the market'.[3] The French system, vigorously pursued since the 1950s by governments it is widely supported.

And, entirely forgotten by modern Britons, we tried to do exactly the same thing ourselves, much earlier. Part of the original task of the British Board of Film Censors, founded in 1912, was to protect the image of the nation and its empire; in 1925 it refused a licence to the great Griffith film *Birth of a Nation* because, in the words of one historian, 'it showed British soldiers behaving badly during the American war of independence'. Since film culture, both in the cinema and later on television, is so important to our sense of ourselves, it is worth retelling a forgotten story. The year after the Griffith film was rejected, the British government produced a secret paper for the 1926 Imperial Conference, headed 'Exhibition within the Empire of Empire films' and which began: 'His Majesty's Government have recently had under serious consideration the problem presented by the fact that the Moving Pictures exhibited at Cinema Houses throughout the Empire are almost wholly the product of foreign countries, particularly the United States of America.' This was seen as a social threat:

> A position in which so powerful an influence as that of the Cinema, reaching as it does all classes and all ages of the community, is exercised throughout the Empire almost wholly by non-British producers, is obviously a dangerous one. It is not suggested that foreign films are the medium of intentional anti-British propaganda ... the influence exercised is indirect and for that reason more difficult to deal with. It is clearly undesirable that so very large a proportion of the films shown throughout the Empire should present modes of life and forms of conduct which are not typically British, and, so far as setting is concerned, tend to leave on the minds of untutored spectators the impression that there are no British settings, whether scenic or social,

which are worth presentation. However good the
foreign films may be in themselves, there is still a
need for the shewing of more home-produced
films; however good foreign education may be, we
should still feel that if we sent our children to be
educated exclusively in foreign countries they
would miss something important in their
education.[4]

This is not so different from Seydoux, and still has reso-
nance today, when so many British stories and characters,
from Dickens's *Great Expectations* to Kipling's *Jungle Book* by
way of Pooh Bear, have been engorged by Hollywood and
presented back to British audiences in other accents and
with subtly, or unsubtly, altered messages.

The British analysis from the 1920s to the 1940s was very
similar to how the French elite sees things today: that film
matters hugely for national identity and America because of
the huge size of its home market, has a head start which will
destroy other film industries unless they are protected. But
the British experience was different because of language and
our indebtedness to the dollar during and after the war,
which meant that British quotas, levies and a short cinema
trade war, including a brief Hollywood boycott, ended with
US victory and a fast-shrinking British film industry. (In
1997 there were 158 French films produced, even if some of
them had miserable audience figures.) It was also, frankly,
because Hollywood was so much better at making films: as a
film historian puts it,

As if Hollywood's financial might were not
enough, by the 1920s Hollywood was a world
centre for talent ... It scouted vaudeville, the
legitimate stage, radio and other countries' films.

It scouted talent everywhere … Possible stars in
Germany, France, Italy, Britain and Scandinavia
were lured to Hollywood, then internationalised.
When we think of Garbo, Dietrich, Sonja Henie,
Shirley Temple, Anna May Wong, Dolores Del
Rio, Errol Flynn, Peter Lorre, Sir C. Aubrey Smith
and Basil Rathbone, we get an idea of the vast
reach of its talent search. Even Maurice Chevalier
and Gracie Fields worked in Hollywood.[5]

Britain, even in her imperial heyday, had no chance of
competing with that. Perhaps it was never possible for a
country with the domestic market of Britain's, sharing the
English language, to resist global American culture, and it has
become impossible to imagine what a dominant British film
culture would feel like today. In 1930, the splendidly named
General Sir Granville de Laune Ryrie, a Boer war veteran
and Australian high commissioner in London, suggested that
children across the empire should be 'marched to the cinema
in the morning to see wholesome British films depicting
what is going on in the Empire' rather than the violent and
sensational Hollywood fare. Some imperial British films
were made. But by then, nine films out of every ten shown
in the UK came from America.[6]

Since then, each decade has brought a crop of British films
which have done their bit to support a national sense of self,
from the short golden era of the wartime films, notably
Powell and Pressburger's *Colonel Blimp* and the Olivier *Henry
V*; the Ealing comedies such as *Passport to Pimlico*, *The Laven-
der Hill Mob* and *Kind Hearts and Coronets*; then the Michael
Caine films – *Alfie*, *The Italian Job*, *Get Carter*; the new realism of *Saturday Night, Sunday Morning*, *The Loneliness of the
Long-Distance Runner*; the endless James Bond and *Carry On*
films; Ken Russell's bloodshot, scampering surrealism; the

odd patriotic epic, *The Battle of Britain*, *Waterloo*; the flouncy Merchant-Ivory numbers, like *Passage to India* and *Howards End*; the contemporary comedies, *Four Weddings and a Funeral*, *Sliding Doors*, *Shakespeare in Love*, *East is East*; the Ken Loach films, and so on. How many of these Sir Granville would have considered wholesome fare is anyone's guess (not, presumably, *Trainspotting* or *The Full Monty*) but one could construct an entire history of twentieth-century British consciousness out of a minor film industry which, for all its weaknesses, we have enjoyed. It may not have been as important a mass medium in recent times as television, but because we tend to share films, talk about them more afterwards and find their catch-phrases, stars and issues recurring in our papers and broadcast material afterwards, it could be argued that film still matters as much. Films ripple, as television doesn't.

Yet clearly, despite that list, there have been scores of blockbuster American films for every home-made hit. The US produces some 750 films, both for screen and TV each year, compared to a tiny British output. Mergers and integration among the big US entertainment companies also mean that the regular blockbusters are not self-standing events, but come wrapped in layers of commerce which have a further cultural impact. Rupert Murdoch's Fox films are hyped in his British newspapers and on his Sky television channels. Each new Disney film comes with its merchandising, its tie-ins to American-owned fast food outlets, McDonald's or Pizza Hut; there are the videos and the books, the CDs of the soundtracks, the toys and the computer games, the tickets to theme parks, all creating something much more than simply a film, a kind of glowing mental capsule, a vivid blur of images and sounds which passes quickly but leaves its mark before the next film or 'culture-event' arrives.

An appeal of film in its first great era was precisely that it took British audiences out of their grey, cold island to a melodramatic land of cowboys, gangsters, impossibly beautiful women and hugely wealthy homes. It was an escape from the here-and-now: through sci-fi and other genres, it remains that. Nor have the British done so badly from Hollywood. Since the Oscars started in 1927, nearly a fifth of the best actor or actress awards have gone to British stars, and British-directed films have performed disproportionately well too. Admittedly, this is partly because British performers have been cheaper and readier to play niche roles; in the words of one recent analysis:

> Whilst many American actors prefer to play
> sympathetic characters or charming villains, the
> Brits believe that the outright bad guys are often
> the best roles. The Brits take happily to playing
> serial killers, Nazis, corrupt politicians, sexual
> perverts, child molesters and upper class idiots.
> The Brits also relish eccentricity and cameo
> parts.[7]

British made-for-television series and sitcoms have not exported as well, but it would be too gloomy to present all this as a one-way trade.

The same is true of television. The BBC has been a powerful reinforcer of British identity from the 1920s onwards, and not simply in broadcasting the accents, voices, stories and news that the middle classes imbibed as mother's milk. It quickly became the most important commissioner and distributor of culture in the broadest sense, from the Proms, which the BBC took over in 1927, to the time-pips of the Royal Observatory, Greenwich (1924), to spreading the great sporting events, the cricket series, the race-meetings and Wimbledon, to the promotion of British composers

(Walton, Vaughan Williams), to a pop music policy which launched new acts and by giving a huge early push to British rock performers, from the Beatles to Oasis, helped ensure that this least musical of European nations – historically – has been the only real rival to the US in the era of pop.

Generations of the modern British grew to understand their place in the world through the BBC. In fact, it is hard to imagine twentieth-century Britain without the BBC. Our sense of our politics has been shaped by programmes like *The Week in Westminster*, the world's oldest continuous current affairs show, *Newsnight* and the voices of emblematic reporters, from the numerous Dimblebys to John Cole and James Naughtie. Our idea of being an island has been delicately reinforced by decades of shipping forecasts, with its spare, practical poetry about Dogger, German Bight, Faroes, Rockall, Lundy, Malin, Forties. Millions of childhoods obtained their cultural grammar from *Blue Peter* presenters and the scalp-prickling music of *Dr Who*. Our understanding of class, intelligence and luck have been heavily influenced by successive sitcoms, quiz shows, game shows and chat shows. More of us have been educated by factual programming, wildlife shows, programmes about race, the human body, America, civilisation, art and science, than learned memorably about these things in schools or universities.

Despite its diversity and the sheer size of its output, it is even possible to talk about a particular and rather heartening BBC idea of Britishness, summed up by Raphael Samuel. The BBC, he argued, had done a lot to create

> that particular conceit, so potent as a mobilising
> force in the dire circumstances of 1940, according
> to which this island was peopled by a race of
> loveable eccentrics, averse to power worship,
> addicted to gardening and never happier than

> when laughing at themselves. Where British
> cinema depicted a nation of warriors ... the
> BBC, wedded by the circumstances of its being a
> more domestic view of the British people and
> discovering or rediscovering its comic muse,
> created an imaginary England of clodhoppers.[8]

England, not Britain: the BBC was, from the first, highly self-conscious about its role as prime propagandist for Britishness but only later, in response to growing national self-awareness in Scotland and Wales, did this mean deconstructing the notion of Britain as Greater England. This 'England of clod-hoppers', an island of eccentrics and strange ones, has been a constant and quietly powerful image, promoted from the Goons to *The League of Gentlemen*. It has been the homely, domestic Britishness, the warmer, weirder and more private sense of self that was largely concealed from outsiders and which shrugged at or mocked the official, martial, imperial Britain: *Dad's Army* not *The Longest Day*. It is closely related to a defiant British lack of stylishness, the beslippered, self-mocking, world of *Wallace and Gromit*.

True British heroes, in this reading, are not prime minis-ters but the late Lord Sutch; not Kenneth Branagh, but Eric Idle; not the supermodels but Cynthia Payne, the ruddy faced Streatham madam. It is the nation of bawdy not sex. Its bards were the Bonzo Dog Doodah Band and the self-mock-ing punks, rather than the pomp rock bands which were so successful around the world. In terms of high fashion, it is the jokes of Vivienne Westwood, not the formality of classic tai-loring; in the visual arts, it is the impish, playful anarchism of Damien Hirst rather than the grandness of the sub-French oil painters of the Royal Academy. Childish, anti-authoritarian and harmless, even when it tries to shock, this is one of the most attractive modes of British self-understanding and we would probably have all gone mad without it. The BBC has been hugely influential in promoting it but after the end of its broadcasting monopoly in 1955, the new commercial channels often out-thought and out-performed the state broadcasters; Channel Four quickly became a serious rival to BBC 2 just as the late-lamented *News at Ten* quickly rivalled the BBC offerings. The real question now, of course, is to what extent British broadcasting can retain its identity and its binding-together function in a digital market of hundreds of channels.

Again, we have to retain a sense of proportion. Even in the old days of the BBC-ITV duopoly American programming, which could be sold outside the US very cheaply, thanks to the economics of the industry there, was used in huge quantities to fill air-time. Endless Westerns and sitcoms such as *I Love Lucy* were staple fare long before the age of *South Park* and *The Simpsons* and, as with film, there is no evidence that British audiences were other than delighted by such fare. Radio, however, is a different matter. It is far cheaper to make and depends, much more than television or film, on the accents and stories of local performers; so, while we have imported US television culture and US radio formats, such as the phone-in, we have not imported any significant American radio programming; and the prospect of us doing so seems remote. Radio remains a more national, and more local, medium than the industries tied to the costs of film and TV broadcast.

In television format too, we bought into ideas pioneered in the US, the gameshows and the celebrity interview shows, the high-value-prize quiz shows, the sit-coms and the current affairs programmes, with 'character' presenters, and then Britified them, without losing any sense of ourselves as a result. As things stand today, the licence fee which underpins the BBC seems safe and there is no reason to suppose that

British television will not retain an important influence in the world of digital, cable and multi-casting. But the old world of a state-monopoly or semi-monopoly broadcasting system is more likely to sustain national difference and identity than a world of very many channels, each watched by a smaller proportion of the total market. Nationality is about common experience.

London has been at the centre of an American–dominated entertainment and communication system since the days of the first undersea cables near the beginning of the century. In publishing, books and music as well as in broadcasting, we have been woven into American business and thinking so deeply that it is hard to see a distinct 'join' or break when British culture suddenly became a minority culture even in Britain – we have for so long inhabited a mental Anglo-American country that might be called Atlantica. Writers as diverse as Kipling and T.S. Eliot, Henry James and Oscar Wilde lived there at the beginning of modern times and so too do their successors today – Martin Amis, Bill Bryson, Tina Brown, are all Atlanticans, neither quite British nor quite American. The spiritual children of the early Hollywood stars who left these shores, the Charlie Chaplins and Basil Rathbones, are the TV comedy-migrants of today, Billy Connolly, Tracey Ullmann and the sun-warmed wicker-basketful of expat Pythons. The big US publishing houses, HarperCollins, Warner and Simon & Schuster, are part of those US media companies, the 'culture-event' producers described above, such as NewsCorp and Viacom. US publishing is a rare area which has partly fallen to outsiders, such as Germany's giant Bertelsmann, which owns Random House, and to Britain's Pearson. But everything converges and they too are doing deals with US new-media companies. These publishers sell their books through US-owned (Borders, Amazon.com) or US-influenced (Waterstones,

Bol.com) bookshops. Often the authors are Atlanticans – Thomas Harris, Stephen King, John Grisham or, at a more elevated level, Simon Schama, and the large British academic community at Harvard or Yale, and journalists such as Christopher Hitchens. Atlanticans sit about in Atlantican coffee-bars, with names like 'Seattle', reading our Atlantican books from Atlantican retailers. British? Not very.

Does it matter? Does it have any bearing at all on the life, or death, of Britain? If you take the popular view that nations are 'imagined communities' created by print journalism and a political culture, then it must. And though I have defined culture in a fairly narrow sense, as films, music, books and broadcasting, the Atlantican culture also spills into newspapers, since it has given us owners who are instinctively North American in allegiance and hostile to European integration; and politics too. Both our main political parties now intuitively look to America for their latest thinking, slogans, strategies and techniques. Philip Gould, the pollster and focus group expert, learned many of his special skills working with the first Clinton campaign in Arkansas. Gordon Brown, the current Chancellor, spent holidays absorbing Democrat thinking from Washington friends and inhaling rows of books in the Library of Congress. The whole spin-doctor culture, with the emphasis on getting your retaliation in first, staying with a limited number of messages and using computerised databanks to hit the opposition with their U-turns, old embarrassing quotes and inconsistencies – all that is Atlantican politics. The Tories of the Thatcher years learned powerful lessons, particularly in advertising, from the Reagan Republicans; American conservatives like Newt Gingrich arrive in London to brief groups of leading Tories; William Hague borrows his 'Commonsense Revolution' agenda, name and all, direct from a Canadian conservative. Take a British politics which is saturated with American thinking,

fed by papers owned by North American proprietors, enter-
tained by US political and other films (*Primary Colors* and
Bulworth), lobbied by Atlantic companies and observed by an
educated elite which consumes American authors and
American films more avidly than anything at home. How do
you describe that nation? You may have a British Parliament
and British political language. But do you have a British
political culture?

Again I ask – does it matter? Numerous countries are
soaked by American attitudes, products and values while
staying politically independent – Canada, Australia, the
Caribbean, and, in a lesser way, much of Asia and continental
Europe. It is perfectly possible, as many small nations would
point out, to keep a sense of patriotism and difference based
on a modest fringe of activities – the Canadian enthusiasm
for ice-hockey and canoes or Dutch social liberalism. It may
be that the intensity of national difference is inevitably
diluted by global culture, and that we notice it more living in
Atlantica; but also that national identity can remain stable,
just more watery, less rich and noticeable. We can be British,
but less so, and that may be our fate. Yet sharing our culture
with a much larger and more energetic people is not the
whole story. Britain's loss of world power has been described
already. How about the internal, original sinews of identity,
the structures of the state?

Subjects, worshippers, voters?

Again, immediately, we hit the British/English distinction.
There is no British system of law. There is a currency, which
may or may not be abolished. There is a flag. And there are,
obviously, the institutions which ran things in the old days
and run on themselves today – the Crown, the Established

Church and the Westminster Parliament. Of these, the monarchy is still the best known thing about Britain around the world, our biggest point of difference inside Atlantica, and the most obvious surviving emblem of national identity. This is so because of, not in spite of, its foreign origins. Since 1066, the English Crown has been held by a succession of families whose only common quality was that none of them were English. Normans, French, Welsh, Scots, Dutch, Germans. As Norman Davies has put it, Diana, Princess of Wales, was 'the first person of English descent ever to approach the British throne.' And she, of course, died in a Paris traffic tunnel with her new love, Dodi al-Fayed.

Throughout the history of Britain, as distinct from England, the foreignness of the Royal Family has been important because it emphasised that it was a bought-in emblem of statehood, not an organic native power-source. The arrival of William and Mary was a revolutionary act by the Whig political establishment: it established that, instead of the Crown being the Heaven-ordained fount of authority (as the Scottish Stewarts had claimed) it was a convenient political servant of the parliamentary establishment. It was a hireling monarchy, dependent on its paymasters. It has been so ever since, despite the understandable blindness to this basic fact among some of the hireling monarchs themselves. It was a stroke of eighteenth-century genius to find, as the candidate Royal Family for the age of empire, one of the dullest and least imposing of the lot, the German House of Hanover.

The secret of the British monarchy's success was that it was rarely politically powerful. It never mattered enough to be the focus of a great wave of republican hostility. This was so despite its huge wealth and, as the British Empire expanded, its imperial pomp. The core of that wealth was in effect handed over to Parliament by George III, so that the great properties grabbed by successive monarchs over the centuries became a kind of hidden internal empire of the British state. Today, these 'Crown Estates' include land: the rollcall has great names like Ascot racecourse, Stapleford Abbots, including Hainault, in Essex and Savernake in Wiltshire and lesser known properties, such as Sunk Island and Swine in Humberside. It owns great chunks of central London, including Trafalgar Square, Regent Street, Kensington Palace Gardens and the Strand Palace Hotel. It owns business parks in Hemel Hempstead, superstores in Hereford and a golf course on the Isle of Wight. It has nearly 1,700 miles of foreshore, of mud, sand, rock and seabed, stretching out 12 nautical miles, and all the mooring, fish-farming and pipe-laying rents of that, and Windsor Great Park and a Welsh goldmine. Prince Charles once suggested a new funding deal for the Royal Family, including taking back control of the assets of the Crown Estates. Mysteriously, this was not warmly received by the politicians.[9] The Crown remains hugely wealthy today, in great buildings, paintings, land and investments, though the Queen's personal wealth is much less, and centred on the Balmoral and Sandringham estates, is worth some £110 million, plus up to £50 million in jewellery.

While Australia agonised about becoming a republic, and then narrowly rejected the form of republic offered, the British themselves have seemed relatively content with their genteel, imported monarchy. Organised, anti-monarchism is so marginal that in Britain 'republican' has become the recognised shorthand term for Irish nationalist, as if the word had no other discernible use. There have, admittedly, been moments when the monarchy has suddenly looked weak. In 1870–1, there was a surge of republicanism, with Charles Dilke leading the charge against Queen Victoria's alleged greed in a way that no senior politician would have dared in modern times. There was a huge anti-monarchy demonstration in Hyde Park; and a more general feeling that 'the Widow of Windsor' was not properly representing a self-confident imperial nation. The behaviour of King Edward VIII and the Abdication crisis was another thorough shock to the system and led to questioning of the whole institution, of a kind the older generation of the Royal Family, notably the Queen Mother, has never forgotten.

And, once more, in recent decades, there have been signs of dissatisfaction. The 1970s had seen a growth in satirical anti-monarchism, with the rise of the 'hard left' in the Labour Party, the Queen's head abused by punk bands, and then a new generation of cartoonists, including the *Guardian*'s Steve Bell and the *Spitting Image* team, laying in. As Rupert Murdoch rose to become Britain's leading media baron during the 1980s his chippy anti-establishment republicanism echoed, however intermittently, in the papers he owned. You could never be sure if the *Sun* was being ultra-loyal in its prurient and censorious coverage of the Windsors, enjoying the falling standards and rising sales, or if it wanted the whole edifice to fall.

By the early 1990s, after the toe-curling (and then toe-sucking) revelations about the sexual habits and infidelities of the younger Royals, above all the breakdown of the 'fairytale' marriage of Charles and Diana, there was something uneasy about the nation's laughter. The Queen was beginning to be compared to Queen Victoria in her fustiness and the long frustration of her heir. The great Victorian constitutional writer, Walter Bagehot, had described them as 'a retired widow and an unemployed youth' and Gladstone had complained that 'the Queen is invisible and the Prince of Wales is not respected.' Small wonder, perhaps, that courtiers in Queen Elizabeth's London were starting to talk about QVS, or 'Queen Victoria Syndrome'. Above all, the surrounding media atmosphere had changed utterly since the early years of her reign. There were overtly hostile and intrusive books, and no deference in the press.

Anthony Sampson, one of the veteran commentators on the British state, pointed out that

> The apparatus of royal events and rituals, from
> weddings and coronations to funerals, was built
> up in the Victorian era to strengthen the image of
> empire; and a century later, in the fifties and
> sixties, the ceremonials provided an ideal subject
> for television whose hushed commentators gave
> them a religious reverence at a time when other
> religious ceremonies were in retreat. But while
> the pomp was magnified, the imperial purpose
> was disappearing, and television and journalism
> could quickly turn from adoration to destruction.
> The extended family added to the danger.[10]

These factors crystallised around an argument in 1991–2 about whether the Queen ought to start paying income tax, as some of her predecessors had, and about the size of the tax-payer-funded Royal Household. On 20 November 1992, a devastating fire consumed the state dining room and three drawing rooms at Windsor Castle, horrifying and depressing the Queen. When the Conservative government announced that it would foot the repair bill for the uninsured castle, estimated at up to £40 million, there was uproar; polls showed the offer was very unpopular. According to the Queen's biographer, Ben Pimlott, 'the Windsor fire – which might have revived awareness of the historic role of the Monarchy, and brought a rallying of support for it – led to a huge revolt of public opinion on the topic of royal wealth and privilege in general.'[11] A few days later, she made her famous 'annus horribilis' speech, an unprecedented admission of vulnerability and unease about the future which was described by the *Guardian*'s Hugo Young as an act of penitence: 'appealing for decency, it relinquished command.' Soon after, the Queen agreed a new deal on the voluntary payment of income tax which she had in fact been preparing well before the fire. That did not placate the public mood, with the *Daily Mirror* publishing a savage cartoon attack on 'HM the Tax Dodger'.[12]

The next part of the story came five years later, when Diana and Dodi al-Fayed's Mercedes crumpled in a Paris tunnel. Her death did not spark a political revolution – Britain, in electing its first Labour government for 18 years had, in many people's eyes, had just had one – but the reaction amounted to something different, an emotional revolution. It was a moment when the British looked at themselves and did not quite recognise the people staring back from the mirror. The divisions were complicated. Many older people, and others, simply regarded Diana as an airhead with little sense of public duty. A few commentators hailed her as a republican heroine. Most people mourned a glamorous and troubled woman, who seemed more human than the Windsors.

As the family hesitated in its response, they felt the full blast of Diana-worshipping and media anger. But there were problems here. For a start, just how British was Diana in the first place? She might have been, as the placards said and Elton John sang, 'England's Rose', but she was a new kind of English, an aristocrat certainly, but far away from the formal, buttoned-up and dutifully dowdy Englishwoman of old. She was flawed, struggling with self-doubt, and uneasy in her roles. She was instinctive and confessional. She stripped herself bare, metaphorically speaking, on national television. She had the modern disorders – bulimia, self-hatred, celebrity. She did not have the Windsors' strange mix of stoic duty and

private self-pity. As an Englishwoman, she was too restless
and curious to be a fit representative of Britishness – which
was why she was so loved.

The historian Simon Schama, in a brilliant essay for the
New Yorker, put his finger on it. Diana understood, he argued,
that she was 'inventing herself' in a role which had no prece-
dent in British public life. But there was a fatal contradiction
in her sense of her plans for herself:

> For she badly wanted to be both Diana National
> and Diana International. The fallout from this was
> apparent in the notorious interview in *Le Monde*
> in which she said that if it were not for the boys
> any sane person would already have fled the
> sceptred isle. And her choice of lover was
> destined, in the long run, to make her adoring
> British public become disenchanted. For the
> ghosts of Suez have not all gone away. Though the
> treatment of the senior Al Fayed at the hands of
> the British naturalization authorities was
> evidently not cricket, Diana's alliance with the
> family that bought Harrods, the retailing world's
> equivalent of St Paul's Cathedral, and then leased
> the Paris mansion of the despised, exiled Duke of
> Windsor would finally have been seen as an act of
> wilful de-patriation.[13]

There, in one bravura flourish, is the Abdication crisis,
Suez, race, religion, the state, shopping and sex all tending to
the same conclusion: Diana was not quite British. She had
chosen her own path. But I was there in the crowd when
genteel-looking old ladies almost spat at the mention of
Charles or the Queen, and I am not sure that they would
have disliked Diana al-Fayed, the Harrods Princess. Her

charity work, her campaigning for Aids victims and against landmines (which angered the Ministry of Defence), her openness and vulnerability would not have changed; and the crowd itself was not British, or not in the old way. It was, as the *Independent* reflected in an editorial column at the time, as if

> Britain is becoming less British. The displays of grief and anger about the death of Diana have been not only mass, but impassioned, florid as well as floral, public not private. There has been crying, shouting – open displays of emotion, not private reflection. This is not how the nation popularly supposed itself to behave; we are meant to be a people of gritted teeth, suppressed feelings and stiff upper lips. The great mounds of flowers ... the clipped-out photographs from magazines, the piled teddy bears, the poems and pen messages ... all this seems somehow foreign to the received images of the British in public sorrow. Traditionally, we think of the grave, silent faces at the Cenotaph, of military processions and of the dignified but repressed and duty-lined expressions at establishment funerals or memorial services. Compared with that buttoned-up nation, the current torrents of grief over the dead Princess seem American, or even somehow Neapolitan.

There was a new nation here as well. In the queue for Diana's funeral service, snaking round Westminster Abbey, I found myself standing in front of a couple of Chelsea Pensioners, with their ancient scarlet tunics, military moustaches and medals. Old Britain at its oldest and finest. But in front of me stood two gay men, wearing mourning suits of matching black leather, with slashes and zips, belts and studs; also moustached and, in their way, uniformed, and certainly as solemn and aghast as the Pensioners. Inside the Abbey, the discordant echoes were even stronger. I sat watching men with a lifetime of state service and cavalry officers in flagstone-sparking spurs try to find a fit facial expression with which to greet Elton John's song for Diana, or her brother's bitter attack on the Windsors. I watched as the amazed realisation spread after him that there was a wave of clapping from outside, breaking into the Abbey.

Clapping in the Abbey? Just like the Mediterranean clusters of candles under trees, and the crying, and the tiny shrines, and the fury that the Queen had not broken protocol and flown the flag at Buckingham Palace at half-mast, or hurried south from Balmoral to share the people's grief ('Every hour the Palace remains empty adds to the public anger at what they perceive to be a snub to the People's Princess,' fulminated the *Sun*) the clapping was the applause of a nation burying its old self.

Yet here we are, a couple of years later, with the Royals back in business, not strikingly popular but as secure-looking as anything else on the islands. The British monarchy has reinvented itself yet again. It always does. The Royal Family has been good for business for the most powerful media voices in the land, battening on the family even as they chew it up; tabloid newspapers still crank out 'part-works' on the lives of minor members of the Royal Family and, more than two years after her death, a front-page story about Diana is considered certain to boost sales. The Royals are the apex of the tourism and heritage industry, which is a crucial earner for the UK. They are also at the apex of the residual system of social deference. This is easier to watch than describe, existing in private smirks at Ascot, little self-abasements at honours ceremonies, and the aura hanging round 'old' families. But it benefits more than the aristocracy, who are richer than ever thanks to huge growth-rates in the value of land, their investments and fine art, even as they face the loss of their seats in the House of Lords. This social system also, in some sort, touches everyone who is a senior 'servant of the Crown', including the Prime Minister. There is a formidably powerful group, stretching from the media, through the Church hierarchy to the higher ranks of the Civil Service and political life, which feels itself threatened personally by any suspicion that the Crown might fall. Tony Blair's swift move to lend his spin-doctors and personal charisma to help out the Queen in the aftermath of Diana's funeral was a sign of this instinct. Add to all this the strong and genuine feelings of many older people about a monarchy which became one of the symbols of British resistance to the Nazi threat in 1940, and it is clear that describing anti-royal feeling in Britain is still tricky. Republicanism, associated in many people's minds with Irish terrorism, is perhaps the only aspect of the ordinary agenda of modern politics considered unspeakable in the UK.

Given the great vested interest in keeping a monarchy, the best guess is that the true feeling of the people is indeed reflected in the polls, which are supportive but far from ecstatic about the business. We do not feel like subjects and we do not treat either Queen Elizabeth or Prince Charles as our Olympian betters. Perhaps the true story goes like this. There once were real kings and queens, invaders from France, and other nations, who struggled to hold their possessions, against not only foreigners but also barons and commoners. They claimed the hand of God was on them and they inspired awe, or more often terror. Then a ruling elite, based on Parliament, tamed these exotic creatures. The Dutch, and then a family of dull Germans, were allowed in to maintain the fiction of royal power, the rule of the Crown, on behalf of the great economic and landed powers of the time. The Crown remained useful as a way of awe-striking the common people on behalf of the establishment.

Now we are in a third phase, when that function too has fallen away. We, the people, are interested in the doings of the Windsors, as with all rich, public and unpredictable families. On high days and holidays, we will use them as an excuse for feeling good about ourselves. Many British people buy the argument that it would be worse to elect a president, because we might end up with Margaret Thatcher, or Tony Benn, or some other boo-figure for the other half. (In fact, it would be the writer Alan Bennett, but not many people know that.) So we carry on, neither much impressed, nor conceding the monarchy any inner grandness.

It is a British institution, the monarchy, not an English one, but it is hard to believe that it is a crucial binding-together force any more. True, the Scottish Nationalists, despite their republican instincts, have been wooed by Prince Charles and have been pinkly chuffed to be so wooed. But the monarchy is less popular generally in Scotland. At one low point, a MORI poll in 1991 showed more Scots in favour of an elected president (48 per cent) than of retaining the Queen (43 per cent) if Scotland became independent. Small nations rediscovering themselves are going to have to think hard about what kind of image they want and this, in the British context, means rethinking the monarchy.

This does not mean that it will necessarily die. It is even possible, I suppose, that 'the Firm' will branch again, and we will end up with rival monarchs once more on two thrones, as in 1600. But that would be a heritage decision, not a political one. Monarchy is a decorative and (for the majority) enjoyable spume on the territory of Britishness; it is not a powerful unifying force. Diana's story was of someone who, at whatever level, understood that monarchy was dissolving into mere celebrity, and who began to play the celebrity game in an English way the German Windsors never quite could. But celebrity is a hard trade, which destroys everyone who tries it.

There are further storm-clouds ahead for the Windsors. One looming question concerns Prince Charles, who is growing to look more like his ancestor, the choleric King George III, so memorably played by Nigel Hawthorne, and whose reluctance to keep his counsel on issues that inflame him is ever more obvious. Charles has recently branched out from his traditional hobby-horses of organic farming and hatred of modern architecture to taking on the government over genetically modified (GM) food, boycotting a grand reception to mark his contempt for doing business with the Tibet-repressing Chinese government, signalling his hostility to banning fox-hunting, and so on. There is no reason in a free society why a man who is well known, thoughtful and intelligent should not express his views, but the prospect of a political King Charles III would give British republicanism its best chance since the Restoration, when Oliver Cromwell's head was exhumed and stuck on a pole by London Bridge.

He is not likely to be able to keep his opinions to himself and has developed numerous ways of nodding and winking when he cannot simply speak. Eventually he would go too far for an elected government on some issue and would be publicly slapped down, or attacked by politicians. This would not be consonant with the non-political monarchy Britain is supposed to have. At the least it would mean calls for Charles to be stripped of the residual powers of action the monarch still possesses, and which are mainly activated when no party has a majority in the Commons – something which would of course become frequent if it shifted to a system of proportional representation, which Labour promises a referendum on at some stage.

If monarchy cannot be considered a core element of modern Britishness, then what about the Church? Protestant religion, after all, was what cut off first England and Scotland, and then Britain, from the European continent. It was one of the original unifiers. But this too can be dismissed, and far more quickly than the monarchy. For a start, the main churches are not all-Britain institutions. Wales has no state church, and a strong dissenting tradition. The Church of Scotland, which confronted the British state and split in the 'Great Disruption' of 1843, was never part of the British establishment, and indeed acted as the voice and semi-parliament of Scottish opinion after 1707. Ireland is overwhelmingly Catholic except in Northern Ireland, where Protestantism takes the form of Presbyterian churches, rather than a dominant Anglicanism.

In England there is a state church, the Church of England, uneasily tied to a state that is not all-English. It possesses no fewer than 16,000 churches, many of them beautiful and ancient buildings, expressing the continuity of Englishness in parishes across the country far more effectively than any other buildings. The Book of Common Prayer, the King James Bible and a body of hymns and carols that go back hundreds of years, with their music, provide an intense and nostalgic sense of English identity. But not British identity. And it is an identity in decline. As one recent commentator on the Church of England put it:

> Fourteen hundred years after the coming of
> Augustine, its membership was so low that it
> decided to stop publishing the figures. The best
> guess is that there are now less than one million
> churchgoing Anglicans. There are more Roman
> Catholics in England, far more Non-Conformists,
> and may soon be as many Muslims, Sikhs and

Hindus. Every year, more people visit Canterbury
Cathedral as tourists than worship in an Anglican
church.[14]

But how long has this been going on? One social history
pointed out that Britain was not a religious society: 'Less than
20 per cent of the capital's population went to church and
those who did tended to be higher in the social scale.' A
Royal Commission argued that 'the churches have come to
be regarded as resorts of the well-to-do.' The tone of Church
of England services 'is opposed to the idea of advancement'
while the average working-class man 'thinks more of his
rights or his wrongs than of his duties ... He is not helped by
calling himself a miserable sinner.' It sounds like Britain
today, though the language is a little starchy even for New
Labour. It is in fact a report from 1901.[15] All of which said,
the idea that the Christian religion can be a unifying force
for Britain in the future looks forlorn; indeed, any British
settlement which was to bind the nations in the future would
look stronger if religion and politics were completely separated, and the remaining state churches disestablished.

If not Crown or Church, what about Parliament? This
runs straight into a main theme, one of the reasons for writing this book, the political challenge to Westminster from
internal and external political forces. But is pride in our
common parliamentary history strong enough to give us a
sense of British identity into the next generation, anyway?
We have already seen that most Britons do not expect it to
be an important force in 20 years' time. Rhetorically, politicians and commentators are particularly apt to speak of the
'English Parliament' and its traditions, rather than the British
one, and it seems likely that if the Scots removed themselves
from Westminster, most English voters would scarcely notice.
The Irish withdrawal is now barely mentioned in popular

accounts of Parliament, except in the context of the bloody and bruising debates that preceded it.

Politics is not, itself, a popular or much esteemed trade. The battle-cry of the anti-Brussels campaigners, that the EU threatens to rob Britain of its independent Parliament, still arouses some kind of worry in a majority of voters; but they spend the rest of the time supremely unimpressed by this institution they are called upon to defend. The lowest moments in recent years may have come with the humiliations inflicted on John Major's 1992-7 government, the 'sleaze' stories, the savage personal abuse carried on inside the then-ruling party and the serial resignations. Tony Blair's arrival in Downing Street signalled a time when the majority of voters were more at ease with their government. But for Parliament itself, the Blair years have so far proved equally testing, if not more so.

In the Lords, the struggle to expel the hereditary peers, which was opened in 1911, was concluded in October and November 1999. There, the third reading of the Lords Reform Bill produced one of those glorious surreal moments which helps explain the long silence of the satirical novelist Tom Sharpe. A young man with a thick beard jumped onto the historic Woolsack, and began ranting: 'This Bill, drafted in Brussels, is Treason. What we are witnessing is the abolition of Britain. Before us lies the wasteland – no Queen, no culture, no sovereignty, no freedom. Stand up for your Queen and country and vote the Bill down.' Then Charles Francis Topham de Vere Beauclerk, Lord Burford, a descendent of Charles II and his orange-selling mistress Nell Gwyn, was hustled away by attendants. The fact that he is obsessed with proving that Shakespeare was too common to have written Shakespeare's plays and is married to a Canadian-born rock singer whose sole hit was called 'One Night in Bangkok' demonstrates why satire finds it so hard to turn an honest penny in modern Britain.

The Lords duly voted by 221 to 81 to abandon 800 years of their history and accept the expulsion of 751 hereditary peers from the chamber, all but 92 who would be allowed to stay on temporarily. Who, aside from Lord Burford, could possibly object? We would not call on Mark Thatcher to lead us, nor James Major. Few Britons really think the hereditary principle has any place in politics and this seems a piece of unfinished business dating back to Edwardian England, when the Liberals made the first serious move towards a democratic second chamber, and were then stalled by war, crisis in Ireland and their own party greed, manifested in the sale of peerages to profiteers. But things are not so simple. The anti-reform group had one popular and potent weapon to fight back with, the failure of the Blair government to come up with a simultaneous plan for injecting any element of democracy into a 'reformed' chamber.

Various worthies, headed by Lord Wakeham, modern Britain's worthy-in-chief, have been gathering advice on a second phase of Lords reform but the preferred Downing Street model would, it is strongly rumoured, be a giant body of place-people, a chamber of political appointees with, at best, a mere fifth or so elected. Since under the British system, prime ministers have engorged the old powers of the Crown and are constrained only by law, treaties and the unity of their parliamentary majority, this 'giant quango' would be heavily influenced by them. Having waited since 1911, people are naturally a little suspicious. An anti-democratic reform would be outrageous and might weaken the standing of Parliament even below where it was with a hereditary house.

The Commons, meanwhile, is suffering the less dramatic but more humiliating fate of slow extinction by boredom. The sheer size of Labour's majority and the highly disciplined behaviour of its backbenchers, dragooned and ordered about by a ferocious mechanism designed to ensure loyalty to the party line, has broken the spirit of the Commons, at least for the time being. Ministers attend far less regularly than they did during the Thatcher and Major years. Prime Minister's questions was reduced from two brisk sessions a week to one by New Labour. The Opposition seems to count for even less. Debates peter out for lack of speakers and, very often, those who are called merely recite pious nonsense. One dissident Labour backbench group, 'the Old Testament Prophets', has instituted a 'golden pager' award for the government backbencher who asks the year's most grovelling question of the Prime Minister. They required much discussion, and a heroic amount of wine, to decide the winner – yet another toadying gentle lob from a senior MP interested in the administration's remarkable progress. In the evenings, when the old Commons was alive with rumour, gossip and argument, with its bars, terraces and corridors humming, and the chamber filling when favoured speakers stood up, we now contemplate a shell of an institution. As numerous recent studies have demonstrated, the Commons has failed to get a grip of the mass of European legislation and is not the effective scrutineer of the detail of primary legislation it likes to present itself as.

Outside London, the Parliament in Edinburgh has its share of unhappy incidents in its early life, including questions of improper influence which sounded all too like the sleaze stories of the Major years. It has a long way to go to prove that it can be the genuinely fresh and attractive alternative to Westminster that Scottish politicians and writers have promised the voters it can be. Yet there is little sign that this Home Rule settlement will ever be abandoned, or of enthusiasm in Scotland for a return to the old days of Scottish committees on the banks of the Thames. If there is to be any serious revival of British identity, then parliamentary politics would have to be at the heart of it. In terms of historic institutions which have moulded the island in the past and whose purpose remains essential for the future, there is nothing to touch the democratic ones. We will return to this later; but for now, it has to be admitted that the current Westminster Parliament is not a likely focus for British self-identification.

Britain continues to exist as a state, of course. All the outward forms are there, intact and apparently untouched. The monarchy, the flag, the Westminster Parliament, the huge state bureaucracy, with its systems for raising and spending money, the armed forces, a 'national' media, the language of the nation-state still half buried and resonant in thousands of everyday signs, from 'British bulldogs' in the playground to Union Jacks on shirts and company logos. When the island's ancient francophobia reasserted itself in a short, loud exchange of insults over the continuing French ban on British beef, it was 'buy British' from the newspapers, not 'buy English'. It is all too easy to jump from sweeping assertions about 'globalisation' to 'the end of the nation-state' when there are many vigorous nationalisms around the world, from the United States to Indonesia, Greenland to Namibia. Nothing in this story is inevitable, or beyond the wit of ordinary people to alter. But it is hard to deny that Britishness, formed in a particular way, with a particular agenda, by the union of northern island nations, has been hollowed out and is under threat. The glue that held us together is dissolving. And the first, most obvious evidence for that is the relationship of the smaller nations, the Scots, Welsh and Irish, to the overwhelmingly dominant one, the English.

3

The Natives are Revolting

It is remarkable that the events of the Dark Ages, when migrations of warrior-peoples and bitter battles reshaped the human stock of the islands, still matter today, in the age of particle physics and hamburgers. But they do. The Welsh, the Irish, the Scots and the English wear the same clothes, shop at the same shops, work for the same companies and ignore the same God. Yet they feel themselves to be different and probably always will, and that goes back to the great invasions of people who came to call themselves English, pushing back the original Britons, the Celtic-speakers, to the west of the main island, and much later invading the smaller island and suppressing its Celts too.

The political effects of that ancient division are still clear today, not only in the two internal borders of the main island and the existence of a separate state in Ireland, but also in a hundred lesser ways – the nationalist parties of Northern Ireland, Scotland and Wales, the separate churches and banknotes, legal differences and the organisation of government, the BBC and many companies. It is still, to a certain extent, a language issue, though Irish, Scottish Gaelic, Welsh, Cornish and Breton, all branches of the original language of the

Celts, have been separate from one another throughout modern history; indeed the first crucial split between Welsh and Breton, on the one hand, and the Gaelic languages on the other may have happened as early as 700 BC. Today's Scotland is not a Celtic nation, in the linguistic sense – hardly anyone is a native Gaelic speaker and the populous centre of the country has been non-Gaelic through most of its history. But Scots identify themselves as Celts; that is, they are part of the loose and unstable alliance of the smaller non-English peoples of the islands. In Ireland, commitment to the Irish language is almost, not quite, an accurate measurement of nationalism, and for many learning Irish at school was a use-less burden. Wales, however, has always clung more tena-ciously to its language and Welsh-only schools are enjoying a revival.

Despite the ragged evidence of language the Celtic ques-tion has been, most of the time, considered a race question. That is, the English – or, in the early days, their Norman rulers – felt themselves better than the hot-blooded, untrust-worthy and unstable peoples around them. The Anglo-Normans were the unifiers, the builders of world-beating institutions, the grown-up race. This belief in superiority, not heard so much now, runs from the Victorian *Punch* carica-tures of Paddy the Irishman as a kind of half-ape, half-African missing link, with a low-slung jaw and heavy brow; the 'Taffy is a Welshman, Taffy is a thief' popular English rhymes and the ferocious Scotto-phobia of the eighteenth century, when Scots were ridiculed as half-starving savages and drunks, pilfering the English coffers.

At times, London rulers have tried to suppress the Gaelic cultures in a systematic fashion. The Penal Laws of 1402 for-bade the Welsh, then rebelling, from gathering together, holding any office or living in their fortified towns; the Welsh 'Act of Union' of 1536 established English as the only official language there. After the 1745 rising, the ferocious repression of Gaelic Scotland included banning the wearing of tartan and the dismemberment of the traditional clan system.

In Ireland, as usual, it was more extreme. Edmund Spenser, the Elizabethan poet and soldier, asked himself whether the Irish should not be 'quite rooted out' before deciding extermination was 'too bloody a course'.[1] Many Irish believe, wrongly, that English hard-heartedness during the Great Famine was an attempt to force a 'final solution'. But more conclusively, the anti-Catholic Penal Laws after the Battle of the Boyne (1690) banned Irish Catholics – that is, almost all of the native Irish – from voting, sitting in Parliament, from careers in the law or university, from keeping schools or sending their children to be educated abroad and even from owning a horse worth more than £5. These laws were described by the great statesman and writer Edmund Burke as 'a machine for the wise and elaborate contrivance for the impoverishment and degradation of the people, and the debasement in them of human nature itself, as ever proceeded from the perverted ingenuity of man.'

English anti-Celtic oppression derived directly from a sense of threat, a national assumption that England was surrounded by natural enemies on all sides. There was some truth in this. Acting on the age-old maxim that 'my enemy's enemy is my friend', the Scots, Irish and Welsh were ready, time and time again, to form alliances with anti-English forces. The Irish were aided by the counter-reforming Spanish and Italians in Elizabethan times. The French fought with them against 'King Billy'. When Wolfe Tone, leader of the United Irishmen who dreamed of an Irish revolution on the Robespierre model, arrived to begin it in December 1796, he sailed into Bantry Bay in a French fleet. The Irish revolutionaries of 1916 sought help from Kaiser Wilhelm's Germany. De Valera kept Eire neutral during the Second World

War, but other Irish nationalists argued vehemently for an alliance with the Third Reich; and De Valera himself notoriously signed the condolence book in the German Embassy in Dublin when Hitler died. Scotland's history as an independent nation was bolstered by the Auld Alliance with France against England. The Jacobite uprising, which reached as deep into England as Derby and produced panic in London, relied heavily on French money, ships and troops. Owain Glyn Dwr, at the height of his great war in the early 1400s, sent ambassadors to Paris and obtained French troops to help him as well as approaching the Pope.

Because England survived and thrived, it is too easy today to dismiss the fears of a succession of English rulers at the alliances formed against them. But the Spanish, French and Germans posed deadly threats. The creation of a United Kingdom was above all an act of security, a way of closing up the gates through which London's enemies could stream. Even today, we hear the faint echo of all this when anti-EU campaigners accuse Brussels of forming alliances with the Scots and Welsh, who inhabit countries small enough to be Euro-regions, for the dismemberment of England, so it can then be gobbled up by federal Europe. If Scotland and Ireland were both members of the euro-bloc that would, in due course, make it still harder for the English to resist.

These are gentler times, however, and the raw hatreds have, with the exception of a few nutters, subsided. Occasional eruptions of anti-Irish racism can be found – cartoons in some newspapers during the years of IRA outrages, for instance – but it is not respectable and not widespread. Today's Irish, uninterested in forcing the pace on Irish unity, richer per capita than the British, are more likely to be admired than despised. The Welsh home-burning seems to come from another age. There are stories of anti-English abuse in some parts of Scotland. But it is a small problem, and in some of the cases, it has been more about rich incomers paying little attention to the community they join. In Northern Ireland, as I write, the peace process, with all its fudges, evasions and inconsistencies, has nevertheless produced a power-sharing assembly and some semblence of trust. The division there remains the worst anywhere in northern Europe; but it is not entirely irrational to hope that the slow anaesthetics of investment and political compromise can, eventually, bring a deeper peace there too.

And yet, in looking at the possible death of Britain, the Celtic national question remains absolutely central. If Britain goes, the first and most obvious cause will be the secession of Scotland from the rest of the United Kingdom. I do not believe this is necessary or desirable but it is, on balance, likely. This is a difficult thing to put your finger on. In elections, the pro-Union Scottish Labour Party maintains its lead over the Scottish Nationalist Party (SNP) for the time being; add the other unionist parties and you have a continued pro-British majority. But there is an underlying momentum to these things that is difficult to resist.

The story of how Scotland won its Parliament is a complicated and fascinating one.[2] What matters is that it was based on a very long-standing and consistent view by Scottish voters that some form of self-determination over their own affairs was needed. It was a view which had existed throughout much of the twentieth century and had led to promises of devolution from a host of British political leaders, including Asquith, Ramsay MacDonald, Winston Churchill, Alec Douglas-Home, Edward Heath, Harold Wilson, Margaret Thatcher, Jim Callaghan, Neil Kinnock and John Smith. In the twentieth century, Scottish nationalism can be dated from the inter-war period, though both Liberals and 'Red Clydesiders' had called for a Scottish Parliament well before that. The Scottish literary renaissance of the 1920s and 1930s coincided with the formation of the National Party of Scotland, as it was first called, but the nationalist breakthrough did not really begin until the 1960s and 1970s, with the discovery of North Sea oil.

Successive SNP election victories turned the Labour Party from a staunchly unionist outfit into a divided party, then a split party and finally a party which was at least partly reconciled to devolution. The first referendum on Scottish Home Rule, in 1979, took place against the background of a failing Labour government, a split Labour party and the industrial strife of 'the winter of discontent'. Though a majority of those voting backed an Edinburgh assembly, the turnout was low, just under 64 per cent and the proposal fell foul of a hurdle erected by Westminster – that 40 per cent of the total Scottish electorate would have to vote for devolution if it was to happen. Some shrewd observers, such as the writer Tom Nairn, now believe that 1979 was the last moment when the British Union could have been modernised and kept securely together. During the referendum campaign, Nairn recalled, 'I was wearing a sticky badge on my jacket, a Saltire with a "Yes" on it, and I found myself accidentally in a house down in the Scottish Borders, full of farmers and gentry who were deeply opposed to the whole deal.' He was

> pounced on, as a curiosity ... and there was great hilarity because they were all basically confident that nothing like that [devolution] was going to happen and that Britain would carry on ... And I suddenly thought, in that context, they don't understand that tomorrow, the day after, was the last day on which it might be possible to actually save Britain, by providing a form of devolution in Scotland with a stronger British framework.

Back in 1979, argues Nairn, the UK was in a stronger constitutional position: 'There was a belief in British identity; there was a mass of unquestioning belief ... which no longer exists.' For Nairn, that was the moment when the breakup of Britain, sooner or later, became inevitable, the last real opportunity to maintain a secure Union being blown. That, in a sense, was therefore the day Britain died.

What followed directly from the 1979 campaign and the election shortly afterwards, however, was an apparent reinforcing and repairing of British identity and self-confidence, with the Thatcher revolution and the return of a certain kind of patriotism represented by the Falklands war, the self-confident revival of the City and the defeat of trade unionism. But during that time, the move towards Home Rule in Scotland spread through Scotland's thinking classes, through newspapers and trade unions, through churches, voluntary organisations and among tens of thousands of families. Far from being a clever exercise in central control, the Tory years simply created a bigger, more serious and more determined movement for Scottish Home Rule than had existed at any time before, even during the first heyday of the Scottish Nationalists in the 1970s. It was partly left-wing hostility to Margaret Thatcher, perceived as snobby, English and out of sympathy with Scotland. But in all honesty, she did Scotland a great favour: she made Scots ask themselves who they were and what still held them together as a country. Her influence, an outside challenge to old assumptions, could even be compared to the effect of the EU on England. Certainly, as a Scot who lived in Edinburgh during the early 1980s, the current mood of unhappy, even neurotic self-questioning among some English politicians and intellectuals is uncannily familiar to what we experienced back then.

The Scottish Constitutional Convention, first launched in 1988, came out of that Scottish self-questioning and unhappiness. Yet it was an optimistic thing. It was a kind of political movement that Britain had not seen before, bringing former senior civil servants, leading churchmen and academics, trade unionists and writers to declare a 'Claim of Right' – essentially, that the Scottish people had the right to determine their own future. That call to basic democratic instincts lured in the Labour Party in Scotland, much of it warily, as well as the Liberal Democrats and smaller parties; the Tories and Nationalists stayed aloof. Over two years of work, it helped create the general assumption that, somehow, a Scottish Parliament would be delivered despite the opposition of Westminster. By the end, despite its holes and compromises, the Convention produced a blueprint for a Scottish Parliament that was not so different from the one eventually delivered, after a successful referendum, by New Labour.

That much history is essential, because there are a series of common English myths about Scottish devolution. The first is that it was basically about greed – the Scots not only had an extra 25 per cent per capita of taxes spent on them, but also wanted to grab more power. They wanted to take English money, refuse any English say over how it was spent, and carry on running England too. Any separation, however amicable, has deep fissures of hurt and anger running through it; the sense that the Scottish electorate is behaving unfairly and ungratefully to England is growing. But it was not like that. The Scots who campaigned for devolution accept that the difference in public expenditure per head has to be up for discussion now there is an Edinburgh Parliament, though the imbalance is shifting slowly against Scotland anyway. And, however much it may disturb the cabinet, the idea that there should be fewer Scottish MPs at Westminster, or even that Scots should cease to play a leading role in London cabinets, does not cause much alarm in Scotland itself. This was not about greed, or about disliking the English; it was about a sense that Scotland wanted things which England did not.

One journalist in Edinburgh, Alan Taylor, executive editor of the *Scotsman*, and a close observer of the Scottish political scene over many years, put it like this: 'I have no resentment towards these people [the English] whatsoever and am extremely grateful for the happy Union we've had throughout all that time, but the time has come to say, well, we must now go off on our own and think about ourselves.' It was caused by a Scottish problem, a time of self-questioning, not by hostility to England or anywhere else. Britain was simply receding as an idea. It was slipping away: 'There doesn't seem to me to be any cohesive sense of Britishness. The only sense of Britishness that there is, is governmental.' Britain was not held together by anything essential and would gradually fade away: 'I feel totally relaxed about it.'

Like me, Taylor had grown up in a British world – 'Harold Wilson and the Everest expedition' was how he summarised it. But it was different for his children; to them 'the key political figures of the time are Donald Dewar and Tony Blair and Alex Salmond.' Unlike me, he has stayed in Scotland. When I protested to him that Britain was useful, he argued that its virtues could be held onto under other labels – perhaps without Scotland, England and Wales would carry on simply calling themselves Britain. But any rate, 'I feel sorry for you, but you know, I don't think we should fashion the country for you.' Or any other exiles, he implied. I had chosen to leave Scotland so, as Britain disappeared, I had a problem about defining myself. But the vast majority of Scots had no such problem. It was a happier country as a result.

Taylor's almost nonchalant acceptance that Britain is over is shared by an awful lot of Scots. That's what the polls show. That's what my conversations over many months showed, too. Indeed, it was hard to find anyone among Scottish intellectuals who thought Britain would survive in the long-term. Tom Nairn told me: 'This process can't be reversed. It's simply gone too far already in Scotland and Wales and, in a different sense, in Northern Ireland.' Many others agreed.

The big question, they thought, was what happened to the English. Alan Taylor dismissed the idea that England would awake in an ugly, nationalistic mood as insulting to the English. Nairn broadly agreed: 'There's a theoretical possibility of it, of a British Balkans and some kind of offended great nation identity, anxious to get its own back for all the insults from the savages on the periphery.' But he did not take it as a serious prophecy:

> It would be amazing if anything like this happened in a country which has boasted of its political civilisation so uninterruptedly for nearly three centuries ... I think that the civic strain in Britain will be as strong in England, among the English, as it is anywhere else.

Again, like Taylor, he thought there was little to be regretted about the disintegration or fall of the British state.

The Scottish Labour Party, still the country's dominant party, does not see things that way. In the first elections for the new Scottish Parliament, in 1999, it was 10 per cent clear of the Scottish Nationalists in the first-preference vote – though its second or 'party' vote was its lowest since 1931. The SNP has not greatly distinguished itself as a party since the new Parliament began with, for instance, one of its leading figures describing the Union flag as offensive, and then having to withdraw. It failed to win the Hamilton by-election later that year, leading Scotland's (first) First Minister Donald Dewar to tease them at the party conference: 'The Nationalists came to Hamilton promising victory. They have been promising victory for as long as I can remember – and now victory for them means coming second – again … Nationalism is unacceptable to the more than 70 per cent of Scots who will not vote for them.'

The Prime Minister, Tony Blair, takes the same view. He thinks that devolution has quietened Scottish anti-London feeling, satisfied the country's aspiration and strengthened the Union. These are the views of heavyweight politicians, at the cutting edge of the political battle. But against them is that indefinable, instantly recognisable, sense in Scotland that the country is drifting away from London rule. The newspapers are different, and now lead, day after day, on Scottish politics rather than British politics. National current affairs programmes such as BBC's *Newsnight* have to be broadcast with Scottish inserts. In private, many Labour people will say they do not know where Scotland is going and believe that the Union cannot last forever.

Many educated, thoughtful Scots, doctors and professors, company directors and trade union leaders, as well as writers, are saying the same thing. In one poll carried out in 1998, 62 per cent of people asked thought that Scotland would be independent within 15 years.[3] Within weeks of the new Scottish Parliament and the Welsh Assembly having started, with feet hardly under new desks, there were three edgy arguments about the impact of devolution. The Welsh voted for a system of support for hard-hit hill farmers which the English farmers on the other side of the border were not immediately offered by London. Scotland debated the abolition of tuition fees for universities, recently imposed across the UK. If that happened it would, of course, not only put Scottish students in a better position than English ones, but also raise interesting questions about the status of students from south of the border attending Scottish universities. Third, though not directly related to the new political system, the health authorities in both Scotland and Wales did not want to go ahead with lifting the BSE-related ban on the selling of beef on the bone as quickly as the English. This all caused predictable anger, particularly from the right, in England. But we will have similar issues month after month, year after year. There will be a constant grating in the new constitution which will fray and eventually splinter the Union unless there a strong determination on both sides to stop that happening. It is not clear that there is.

The next question, though, is harder. What is this new Scottishness about, and how does it differ from Britishness? The conventional self-image of Scots, epitomised by the former Labour leader, the late John Smith, is that they are more community-minded and more naturally democratic than the English. This is traced back to medieval times, but probably owes more to the strong socialist traditions created by mass industrialisation and migration into Scotland's central belt. It owes something to the levelling effect of a strong religious reformation, and a strain of Presbyterianism that emphasised learning for everyone. It may even have something to do with the country's latitude: northern nations, with colder, darker, longer winters, have often developed the mentality of the community before richer, lighter ones. It is difficult to maintain class distinctions when you are huddling together.

In modern times, Scotland has had a higher proportion of public housing than England, fewer selective schools and a much greater propensity to vote for Labour. Even now, the party's main opposition, the SNP, is to its left, not right. Like the Welsh experience of coal strikes, some of Scotland's formative events in the twentieth century were left-wing ones, the industrial and social struggle of 'Red Clydeside' and the later Upper Clyde Shipbuilders' work-in; the intellectual ascendency of Communist miners from Fife in the trade union movement (like Wales, Scotland's Communists were stronger and more influential than the English Marxists ever were); the battles over deindustrialisation in Lanarkshire and Ayrshire. Like Wales, it had had early radical Liberal voting traditions. It did have a majority of Tory and Unionist MPs in the 1950s, but since then the story of Scottish politics has been of Conservative retreat. Like Wales, Scotland returned not a single Tory MP in the 1997 Labour landslide.

However you cut it, Scotland has behaved in a politically distinct way from England. That is, from England taken as a whole: the north of England and Yorkshire, in general, have been more like Scotland than like the Home Counties in their political behaviour. There was a hint of this from Mr Dewar when he wrote in the introduction to the 1992 Scottish Labour manifesto that a Scottish Parliament 'is not an end in itself. It is a means to an end. It will give us the power to rebuild the Scottish economy, tackle poverty and invest in our people. Labour wants to ... renew Scotland as a community. A society based on fairness and justice'.

Trying to dig under the skin of this self-belief, I went to Govan, the industrially devastated little town on the south bank of the Clyde, a short drive from Glasgow city centre. Govan was a shipbuilding place, which once sent its huge steam-turbine ships out across the oceans of the world. Now it is a shell of its former self, hammered by poverty, with the problems of alcoholism and drug abuse, vandalism and hopelessness, that scar hundreds of similar places across northern Europe. It has new housing and new businesses. But its great old pink sandstone buildings, with their lichen and grand Victorian carving, seem like ancient galleons run aground and left stranded. The streets that had once linked them, the bank head office and the town hall, the library and the statue, had mostly disappeared.

In Scottish political history, Govan has also been known

for two famous by-elections, when Labour was surprised by Scottish Nationalist successes in 1970 and 1988; but I had come to see a rather less orthodox political act, in the corner of a camp of caravans and parked fairground junk, where travellers or 'show people' stay. There is a New Age fascination with Dark Age or early history, which you can find across Britain and beyond at the millennium's turn. It probably has something to do with wanting to start afresh, seeking models where there is no writing or inconvenient historical certainty to get in the way. Here, at any rate, I was greeted by a carved wooden totem-pole at the entrance and, inside, by several sunburnt, tough-looking men with dreadlocks, beards and carving tools. They have built a longhouse and a beautiful, immaculate model of an old galley or 'Birlinn' that used to sail the Western Isles. They intend to build a full-scale one – a new kind of boat-building for Govan – and sail it round Scotland. Their mad idea has caught the imagination of everyone who has come into contact with it – ex-alcoholics and recovering drug abusers, the Army, who have helped with transport, local journalists and the council, children and passers-by. It would be easy to make fun of it all – easy, and stupid. The people were eloquent, self-confident and dignified, making a real difference to a battered place. Their carving and their boat are a metaphor, they told me; a metaphor for community and pride in work.

What has all this got to do with Scottishness? A lot, says Alistair Macintosh, one of the inspirers of the trust, and a radical academic. He grew up on the Isle of Lewis with half-Scottish, half-English blood and he argues that identity is not about nation at all but about a sense of place and belonging:

> You have to start with the ground that is
> underneath your feet, and you have to say, is this
> ground being nourished, is the environment

being cared for, and you have to look at the
community around you and say, 'Hang on a
moment, there are people here who are hungry' –
not necessarily physically hungry, but culturally
hungry, spiritually hungry. And you have to start
with feeding the hungry. If in doubt about what
to do, feed the hungry, nourish the earth, and
then the magic will happen. That is what's
happened here in Govan.

He compared it to a chemistry experiment he had done in
school, when he had taken a test tube of saturated sodium
solution and dropped into it a seed crystal 'and the whole test
tube suddenly crystallised solid because it had a pattern and
example to follow.' The trust was doing that:

It's showing what can happen when people
become empowered, when they become in touch
with cultural roots, when they start to rebuild
community and a sense of place, and they do so in
an ethnically inclusive way.

GalGael, the name of the Govan community, is the old word
for incomers to the Gaelic lands, who can become Gaels by
putting something into the community, learning from their
hosts.

There is a wonderful Gaelic proverb Macintosh recites, to
the effect that milk (meaning fostering, not kinship) is
thicker than blood. This was connected, he argued, to 'the
classical Scottish virtues of fostership and hospitality.' People
could be proud to be Scots because of those values. He
thought Britishness was valuable because black and Asian
people could identify with it, it was not too ethnically exclusive. But

the challenge to places like England ... is to say,
what values have you got that you're proud of?
... If the people in the south of England want to
move in one direction politically which is
mutually exclusive to the sense of community and
so on that we might want in Scotland, then too
bad folks, we have to accept we're different and
that means different political systems and so on.

Living in a leafy London borough, where people run voluntary groups for almost everything, collect for charities
door to door and have a strong sense of locality, I have always
been highly suspicious of this. The undoubted wealth and
greater commercial energy of London has brought a crass
materialism and competitiveness in recent decades that many
people throughout the rest of England, never mind Scotland
or Wales, find distasteful. But it is also London which has
absorbed, pretty happily and with a minimum of fuss, a great
number and variety of immigrants and refugees rarely seen in
supposedly more 'decent' northern climes. On the other
hand, the emphasis on community, actually being carried out
with vision and energy in Govan, is at least a clear answer
about values, the flinty bedrock of politics that you can
sometimes see glinting as Britain comes apart. Perhaps this
was an odd place to go looking for new thinking about identity. But the people there were creating more human happiness than a hundred toothpaste factories or credit-card call
centres. They had a sane perspective on identity and would
have found a lot to agree on with some of the angry organic
farmers and local campaigners I met later in England.

In the end, however, the question of whether the Scots
really are more egalitarian than the English matters less than
what they themselves feel. In 1979, a Welsh historian, Gwyn
Alf Williams, made the point in a famous passage about his

country: 'Wales is an artefact which the Welsh produce; the Welsh make and remake Wales day by day and year after year … There is no historical necessity for Wales; there is no historical necessity for a Welsh people or a Welsh nation. Wales will not exist unless the Welsh want it.'

The Welsh condition is different from the Scottish one. Scotland was an independent nation during the several hundred crucial years, from the Middle Ages until the eighteenth century, when most of the usual institutions of European nationhood developed. It had its own Church, its own Parliament, its own royal house, its distinctive legal system, universities and colleges organised on its own pattern and tradition and its own version of English, if not its own language. St Andrew's University dates back to 1412, Glasgow to 1541, Aberdeen to 1495–1505, Edinburgh to 1583 – before then Scottish scholars had tended to head for Paris, Bologna, Louvain, Oxford and Avignon. The writing of the great late-medieval Scottish poets, William Dunbar, Robert Henryson and Gavin Douglas, is recognisably the same Scottish-English as that of modern Scots. The Church of Scotland and its various Presbyterian cousins trace their history to the Reformation, which began properly in 1560 and had a characteristically Scottish tone, driven by the giant personalities of John Knox and Andrew Melville, and notably different from the contemporary religious politics of England. Soon after the self-destruction of the old Scottish aristocratic Parliament, the General Assembly of the Church of Scotland became a kind of second-best national gathering and a great source of patriotic feeling when it confronted the Victorian state and then split. Scots law, codified and reorganised repeatedly from the mid-fifteenth century onwards, and nearer to continental or Roman law than English common law, has its own courts, titles, practices and traditions.

Scotland developed its own sports – golf, curling – and

architecture, public as well as private, its own local aristocracy and its own, admittedly ricketty and corrupt, early party system. The oddness of modern Scottish nationalism, in many ways like the European and South American nationalisms, but a century or so too late, can be put down to the fact that Scotland had developed all these basic underpinnings of statehood, yet missed out on the later nationalist essentials, the national parliaments, armies and liberator-heroes of the nineteenth century. They had Garibaldi, Simón Bolívar, Parnell. Scotland had Sir Walter Scott, in kilt, welcoming George IV in his pink tights, and it was not quite the same.

Wales, though, had been in a far more parlous state for far longer. It spent the entire period of conventional nation-building firmly under the thumb of London, or at least of Norman lords who owed their fealty to the English king. Wales was united under a single Welsh king for all of seven years throughout its entire history. It had had great uniting kings (notably Rhodri the Great and Hywel the Good) from the 860s to the 1060s and major risings thereafter, above all those of Llywelyn ap Gruffudd (1258–82) and of the great Owain Glyn Dwr (1400–15). But the brutal truth was that Wales was too small and divided, with too long an English border, to have a chance at real independence from such a powerful and aggressive neighbour. It had a rich heritage of Welsh law, with distinctive attitudes to inheritance, women and property, which was subordinated to English law from the time of the Statute of Rhuddlan (1284). But it lacked the national institutions for most of its history – no separate legal hierarchy and tradition, no court, no army, no universities until Victorian times, no national church or national religious assembly on the Scottish model. 'Wales' was a territory and a people, a history and a culture – but not a nation. When Henry VIII, in 1536, formally incorporated Wales, the preamble to the Act stated: 'Wales ... is and ever hath bene incorporated, annexed, united and subiecte to and under the imperialle Crown of this Realme as a verrye membre ... of the same.' This was an exaggeration, but not much of one.

Wales did, of course, develop a cultural self-consciousness and distinctiveness. It had a particularly extreme experience of the industrial revolution, through the coalmining industry, and developed a 'chapel' tradition of nonconformism. These things meant that, politically, Wales has been more like Scotland than like most of England – indeed, the only places where Lenin looked optimistically for a British revolution were Glasgow and the Valleys.

But above all, and unlike Scotland, Welshness was held together by language. 'Welsh Wales' may be an apple-core-shaped territory, smaller and more westerly than the country as a whole, but it joins the Welsh from north to south. More profoundly, it has kept them linked together through time, from the medieval revolts, through the industrial revolution to the depression and beyond. Wales is, in many ways, the Welsh language. So, though the Welsh had hoped for 'Home Rule all round' in the early part of the century and, like the Scots, lost that hope because of the Irish war, Welsh nationalism as it later developed was different from the northern version. Plaid Genedlaethol Cymru, the National Party of Wales, was founded in 1924, four years ahead of the National Party of Scotland. It was composed of similar sorts of people – writers, small businessmen and academics. But right from the start, it agreed that its principal aim should be the achievement of a Welsh-speaking Wales.[4] At this time, Gaelic was barely an issue in Scottish Nationalism, and still is not.

So Welsh nationalism was never quite as strong, partly because the language issue excluded a large number of Anglo-Welsh. Its later enthusiasm for devolution was never as strong either. There was no great civic movement to rival the Scottish Constitutional Convention of the 1980s and, after a wafer-thin majority acceptance of the Blair government's devolutionary plan, Wales has, as a result a lesser body, a non-legislative National Assembly, rather than the Parliament that sits in Edinburgh with law-making and tax-raising powers. Plaid Cymru, unlike the SNP, does not aspire to full traditional nation status, complete with armed forces and ambassadors. Indeed, by most measures, it is doubtful whether the 'Welsh nationalists' can really be called nationalist at all. Is Wales therefore less of a challenge to the British state? Strangely, it may have more of an impact on the new politics of England than Scotland will, because it can claim a more modern politics. It looks beyond traditional statehood. It is rooted in culture, not institutions. (Wales, for instance, has been the only part of Britain not to have a state religion, since disestablishment in 1920.) It is more ethnically diverse than Scotland, and than many parts of England – there are more Muslims in Cardiff than there are Welsh-speakers. It has a higher proportion of women in its new Assembly than anywhere in Europe except Sweden. It may seem odd to focus on devolution rather than nationhood, and on an ancient language and ethnic diversity, rather than 'crunchier' political choices. But in a world where countries and peoples are marketing themselves on their flexibility and richness of culture – not one simple industrial skill – and where we are becoming used to layers and levels of belonging – not one single national identity – it is not impossible that Wales is ahead of everyone else.

One of the leading lights in the pro-devolution campaign in Wales argues that the country is indeed at the cutting-edge of a new and post-nationalist Britain:

> In the coming years, it is Wales's difference from
> Scotland, rather than its similarity, which may

> become more obvious. Scotland's flirtation with
> the SNP may or may not be a temporary one ...
> Scotland may be the last example of Benedict
> Anderson's thesis that nation-states are imagined
> communities dependent on the print media for
> their shared sense of cohesion. Wales's sense of
> itself may be more mature.[5]

Very different lessons echo from the third of the major
non-English nations, the Irish. The bloodstained history and
tragic involvement of Britain in Ireland is not within the
scope of this book. But it is a huge mistake to think that Ireland, north or south, does not matter to the future of Britain.
The Ulster Protestants may be the last people in the islands
to identify themselves whole-heartedly with a religious and
traditional Britishness, even though they are not technically
British themselves. They are, in the words of one writer, the
'loyal tribe', the people left behind when the rest of the
country charged headlong into modernity, American con-
sumerism and Europe.

Originally, they had come to the most Celtic and Catholic
part of Ireland, the north-eastern area which looked across to
Gaelic Catholic Scotland. They treated it like other colonists
at roughly the same time were treating North America. They
cut down forests, drained marshes, built forts and fortified
villages and dispossessed the natives. Many were ex-soldiers.
Like the American colonists, they were hardy, self-reliant and
used their religion both as self-justification and a way of
demonising the poor, less advanced natives. But, unlike
North America, this was only a partial conquest. Across the
rest of Ireland, where the 'plantation' never happened, or was
pursued only half-heartedly, the Catholic Irish survived to
grow their own political movements, national identity and
leadership, resulting, eventually, in the ousting of the British

and their withdrawal from the empire to follow another course.

Following their own repression of Irish Catholics unfortunate enough to be coralled into their statelet when the island was partitioned in 1921, the Ulster colonists have suffered a sad fate. To their south is the Irish Republic, run by people they were taught to look down on as impoverished and thriftless no-gooders, now enjoying a per capita GDP higher than Britain's and self-confident about its place in a wider Europe. To their east is the mainland, the place they identify their differentness with – but which, except for small enclaves, has no time for them and frankly does not understand them. When Ian Paisley roars his furious fealty to the Crown, Britain is merely bemused.

The Northern Irish story has had a significant effect on the British state. The Irish problem first produced the idea of a federal Britain, with Home Rule all round, at the beginning of the twentieth century. Then the Ulster revolt and independence for most of Ireland destroyed the idea. From 1919 until 1997, the notion that there could be more than one serious centre of power in the UK was off the agenda – and that was largely thanks to the Irish tragedy. It had a little discussed but significant domestic legacy. Before Ireland left, Liberal Britain had a strong if unreliable bloc of Irish MPs generally supporting the 'progressive' side of politics. Their disappearance from Westminster was a major contributory factor to the Tory dominance of Britain that lasted through most of the century.

In recent years, the Northern Irish 'troubles' have not only cost the UK dear in terms of taxes, but also brought counter-terrorism measures which diminished British democracy. In terms of its own brutal and crystal-clear strategy, the IRA has failed. Its training manual, the *Green Book*, declared

A war of attrition against enemy personnel which
is aimed at causing as many casualties and deaths
as possible so as to create a demand from their
people at home for their withdrawal ... A
bombing campaign aimed at making the enemy's
financial interests in our country unprofitable
while at the same time curbing long-term
investment in our country ... To make the Six
Counties as at present and for the past several
years ungovernable except by colonial military
rule.[6]

The *Green Book* strategy failed. It did so, however, only after
causing British politicians to be surrounded by armed police,
bullet-proof glass and barriers. This has not been good for the
understanding of our politicians. It produced courts which
regularly fell below the standards of the much-prized British
legal tradition and, on several notorious occasions, shamed
Britain around the world by huge miscarriages of justice. It
has been a prime modern excuse for an almost obsessive state
secrecy and for a powerful domestic secret service. Abroad, it
has damaged Britain in the eyes of its most important twentieth-century ally, the United States. This is a formidable list
of effects on the British state.

It is the consequence of hundreds of years of British
involvement in the island of Ireland, that goes back to the
Normans and then the Elizabethans. To come to regard a
neighbouring people as dangerous and almost sub-human, as
many generations of English and Scots saw the Irish, does
damage to the haters too. The lack of proper education in
Ireland, a grossly unfair system of penal laws, badly run
estates and land tenure, the lack of an ordinary, liberal European tradition of reformist politics – all these and more were
caused by London rule. Englishmen who are still revered as

heroes at home, including Sir Walter Raleigh, Edmund Spenser and Oliver Cromwell, are among the prime villains of the Irish story. For the English Crown, and then the British state, Ireland came to represent everything backward and threatening – Catholic superstition, incomprehensible and violent peasantry, sullen hostility to the rationalism and imperial reach of London. The delicate glories of the golden age of Irish history, the time of saints, artists and warrior families, meant nothing to the conqueror people.

Today, bold and risky overtures by both sides are creating the chance of a new politics in Northern Ireland based on peace-making and compromise. The Unionist leader David Trimble and Sinn Fein's Gerry Adams have been speaking and acting together in a way which would have been unthinkable a few years earlier. No one knows whether their historic compromise can work – but so far, it is making them sound more open and modern than many Westminster politicians and this, after decades when their parties were ridiculed as almost medieval.

The people of the so-called Celtic fringes of Britain – I would prefer to say, the Atlantic British – are very small in number compared to the English majority. They have always seemed larger, though, both because of the threat of alternative power-centres in the islands and also because the richer hub of the English south has attracted many of the most ambitious Scots, Irish and Welsh – and still does. London is a large Irish city, with Irish citizens strongly represented in almost all economic sectors, from the City to the media, business to mini-cabs. The cabinet contains not only a Prime Minister who is Scottish by blood and was schooled in Edinburgh, but also a Scottish Chancellor of the Exchequer, a Scottish Lord Chancellor, a Scottish Foreign Secretary, a Scottish Secretary of State for Social Services, a Scottish Defence Secretary and, of course, a Scottish Scottish Secretary. Outside the Home Office, dealing almost exclusively with English affairs, there is not a great office of state which is not held by a Scot.

Scottish voices are well represented in the London media, from the morning *Today* programme on BBC Radio Four, through to *Newsnight*. Though Scotland has its own newspaper market, Scottish editors and writers are strongly represented in the London press. So are the Welsh and the Irish. None of this is surprising. In a United Kingdom, the capital city is everyone's capital, not simply the capital of England; the fact that London is also an important world city, a crossing-point for the global economy, only makes it more likely that people from the non-English nations of Britain will be heavily represented there. The English, sharing their capital, have been tolerant of outsiders and remain so. But these are new times for the constitution. Scottish devolution, if it slowly moves to a clearer independence, poses one obvious threat to the UK. Welsh devolution poses another, rather subtler challenge to a centralised political system. Ireland has deformed the growth of modern British democracy and still does. All this leads us inexorably to the biggest question of all: what will happen to England?

4

The English:
a Secret People

Nostalgia

I have a book beside me which mourns *Vanishing England*. It begins with a lament about the power of progress, the modern 'busy, bustling world' and the bewildering speed of new inventions. Every day, says the author P.H. Ditchfield, 'witnesses the destruction of some old link with the past life of the people of England ... The beauty of our English scenery has in many parts of the country vanished, never to return.' American money is looting English art, rare pictures and books, even houses. Cars, estate agents, speculative builders, commercialism and greed are among the forces ripping away the nation's soul. In an unusual twist to the story, Ditchfield quotes, tongue in cheek, a French newspaper report on the literal 'disappearance of England' through coastal erosion, and notes that another French expert, Professor Stanislas Meunier, 'tells us that the cliffs of Brighton are now one kilometre further away from the French coast than in the days of Queen Elizabeth, and that those of Kent are six kilometres further away than in the Roman period. He compares our island to a piece of sugar in water'. This is the tone, and some of the detail, of many of the books and articles pouring out at the moment about the threat to Englishness. But Ditchfield does not mention the EU or Scottish devolution because his book came out in 1910.[1]

Hand-wringing about the decline of England goes back a very long way. In his fine critique of English cricket, the American socialist Mike Marqusee makes a similar point about England's national summer game: the *Daily Herald* was asking in 1932, 'Why isn't cricket fun any more?'; in 1899, apparently at the noon of cricket's golden age, the England player Vyell Walker was complaining that the game was spoiled – 'There is more self now than there used to be ... there is far too much of the business element in it all around'; exactly the same criticisms were being made in 1884 and in the 1860s, by the novelist Anthony Trollope, while as early as 1833, it was being asserted that the 'modern politics of trickery' had not spoiled the game back in the 1780s.[2] Pained nostalgia about the business-infected nature and the sheer speed of modern life goes far back in England. Ditchfield, writing about a country in which there were only a handful of very slow motor cars, quivers with rage about 'the extensive use of motor-cars and highway vandalism' of Edwardian England where 'the charm and poetry of the country walk are destroyed by motoring demons'. Whether it is cricket, countryside, manners, the conduct of politicians or cars English self-consciousness has been coloured by nostalgia for more than a century.

And the English have in general had something to be nostalgic about. Cricket really is faster and more commercialised; the countryside really has been eroded by the car culture; and, more generally, the English have really been on the retreat for decades. In Ditchfield's England, when Britain was a great world power, much was said and written about the 'genius' of the 'English race'. That has gone out of fashion, and the English, surrounded by smaller peoples rediscovering their confidence, and now part of the European Union, have seemed almost passive, self-doubting, put upon in recent decades. The breakup of the UK? The English must wait for the Scots to decide about that. Europe's federal future? The English follow, or decline to follow; they never lead. Whether it is because of guilt, post-imperial and post-war exhaustion or the bland contentment of a basically secure and prosperous majority, the English seemed to have dropped the politics of identity and self-assertion.

For some time now, England has been going quiet. For two centuries or so, novels have been one of the most important ways a literate part of any community imagines itself. There are, clearly, lots of novels coming out of England – thrillers, historical yarns, romances, comedies, satires – but there are very few gripping, mainstream ones about what life is like in England today. Nick Hornby, clearly. Sue Townsend. But they are the exceptions. Martin Amis has surrendered that territory and other writers produce slim volumes, at best. Book prize shortlists reflect the vitality of novel-writing in Scotland and Ireland, as well as India and America, which seem to be places imagining themselves more intensely than England. And when we do get novels with a strong, fresh sense of England today, who are the authors? V.S. Naipaul, Timothy Mo, Indira Singh, Vikram Seth. Or take film, where England appears as an outdated literary landscape, as in the Merchant-Ivory productions, or a fantasy place of dukes and ancient piles, as in *Peter and His Friends* or *Four Weddings and a Funeral* or, finally, a despairing place in decline – *The Full Monty, Lock, Stock and Two Smoking Barrels*. As with novels, the England where the English actually live is almost entirely absent. It seems to have a very thin sense of itself.

But, at last, this may be changing. The spread of St

George's Crosses at England football matches is only the most commented-upon part of a revival of interest in specifically English identity. Billy Bragg, the left-wing rock singer who rose to fame in the 1980s, points out that footage of the 1966 World Cup Final show England supporters waving Union Jacks. The St George Cross had been revived by England being drawn against Scotland in Euro 96:

> The Scots turning up at Wembley actually
> reminded us of what it means to be English …
> We only notice the difference when the Scots
> come and bring their *Flower of Scotland*. I would
> like to think that if we had our own national
> anthem in England it wouldn't be about defeating
> Scotland in a battle several hundred years ago.

It is not surprising that the return of English flags, hitherto associated only with congregation-less rural churches, should start with football, since this is a world shorn of any complexity about identity. As Bragg puts it:

> There is a beautiful simplicity in supporting one
> team pitted against another. Once a week, home
> and away, we are able to feel and, more
> importantly, to express emotions that most of us
> keep in check. We shout, sing, stand together in
> awe-struck silence, men hug other men –
> practices that would mark us out for ridicule
> elsewhere – all done in the presence of thousands
> of strangers … we feel psychologically at ease
> because we know that what we want as an
> individual is completely at one with the desires of
> those around us. A football match allows us to do
> this because it presents an event onto which a

one-dimensional world view can comfortably be
projected, free of any ambiguities.[3]

This is about how far English nationalism has got. The crowd
had a thought about Englishness, a simple thought which no
one else could express, which produced red and white where
before there had been the Union Jack. Similarly, apparently
spontaneously and without any campaign or fuss, little St
George's Crosses began appearing on the backs of vans, cars
and taxis – to the extent that the London taxi-drivers' association told its members to take them off again.

Anger

There is an English reaction, even an 'English problem',
which ought not to be avoided or ignored. The campaign to
save the pound and resentment about Scottish and Welsh
devolution are early examples of what may become a new
kind of politics. As a newspaper columnist, writing on these
subjects, I get a heavy postbag. Here are extracts from two
letters, taken almost at random. The first is from a woman in
Cheshire:

> In the past, I for one have rarely objected to being
> called British rather than English but the Scots
> have altered all that. I AM English and shall
> remain so to the end of my days. The Union Flag
> is no longer my flag and only last week at an
> open-air performance of opera in the grounds of
> a Tudor mansion I noticed that for the first time,
> the ENGLISH flag fluttered from the roof-top.
> The hearts of 250 English swelled with pride as
> they sang the National Anthem beneath its red

and white … [which one, I am tempted to ask? The one written by a Scot?] I am not a political animal. But Scotland for the Scots and Wales for the Welsh has stirred feelings for my own country I never knew existed … I object to Mr Cook speaking for me in a foreign country. I object to you living in our green and pleasant land if you dislike what the Leader of the Opposition is about. I think that eventually out-of-town superstores will stand empty. Little towns with little shop-keepers will survive and prosper. And so will little countries. Devolution will become world-wide, thanks to the Scots and their ilk. It might be better. It might be worse. But at least I now recognise a long disguised fact. I AM ENGLISH. And proud of it. Chesterton could have been right.

That letter, sent to the *Express* in response to a column I had written warning about the revival of English nationalism, was untypical only in the power of its prose. Another example came from a man in Haverhill, Essex: 'That traitor Blair is the one to blame. He is the one who has broken this country into three and no-one else … everyone knows Blair's cabinet is filled with Scots, well us English aren't going to stand for it much longer. Do get this straight: Scotland for Scotland, Wales for Wales and England for England.'

These sentiments are not echoed by conventional politicians, though they are shared by some Tories, such as Teresa Gorman. But they drive the disparate and small group of campaigners for English rights. What kind of people will lead the new politics? Right-wing nationalists? Fascists? During July 1999 I visited the little village of Shabbington in Buckinghamshire. There, in a compact little brick house and carpenter's workshop, with a huge scythe pinned to one wall and a St George's Cross fluttering from a home-made pole, I met Cyning Meadowcroft – a genial giant of man, in his thirties, with the kind of frank, determined and yet obstinate face that you used to see in sporting heroes – a very English face. This is lucky because he is also an English nationalist, a passionate campaigner for an English Parliament and smouldering with quiet anger about the unfairness of the Scots and the Welsh getting assemblies denied to England. This anger has come to dominate his life, so that he goes every Wednesday during parliamentary sessions down to Westminster Square, to wave a huge English flag at MPs as they arrive for Prime Minister's questions and hand leaflets to passing motorists.

But that is not all Cyning does. 'I've been doing lots of extraordinary things, such as laying seven hundred foot banners along motorways and chaining myself across the London marathon,' he told me. After we'd talked for a while, he said goodbye to his Italian-American wife and young children and set off for a local drive to tack up more posters advertising the case for an English Parliament. It would be easy to dismiss him as a lone fanatic – but when I spent some time with him on his self-appointed political vigil, I was surprised at the number of honks of approval and £10 or £20 notes flung at him by passing taxi-drivers. Cyning is onto something and knows it. One of his earlier campaigns demonstrates it. Incensed at the lack of St George's Day (23 April) cards as compared to St Patrick's Day cards, he wrote to two card companies – Clinton Cards, which is American-owned, and the British company Hallmark. The latter rejected the idea because they would not sell, which infuriated Cyning, but Clinton agreed to try, in 1995, and the line is now successful, with a dozen different cards selling across England; within a couple of years sales were over 50,000.

So where did all this come from? Cyning was brought up in Birmingham until he was five years old, when his mother, now widowed, took him across the border to north Wales. It was at just the time the most fanatical Welsh Nationalists were coming to the boil and Cyning experienced what he felt was 'hatred and terrorising'. At school, his teachers and other children passed comments about English incomers which hurt him horribly. At home, the Meadowcroft family had their door kicked in and were all too aware of the threat of arson against English-owned homes – 'basically living in fear of having our house burned down to the ground because we were English ... just simple English folk trying to live an existence with a widowed mother.' Later, by chance, he ended up working in Boston and was introduced to the strongly anti-English views of the Boston Irish.

Yet, he kept telling me, it was grossly unfair and indeed racist, to label every act by Britain as English imperialism. It was the Normans who invaded Wales and the Scottish independence wars were against French-speaking Norman landowners in England. Later, the English found themselves ruled by Welsh Tudors, Scottish Stewarts and German Hanoverians. As his views hardened, Cyning started to read up on English history, particularly pre-Norman history. His unusual name is not the one he was born with. He was originally Roy Meadowcroft, which he rejected on the grounds that 'Roy' is a French word meaning king, and translated it into the Anglo-Saxon for king, Cyning. So he is King Meadowcroft now, a passionate advocate of Anglo-Saxon values which he defines as fair play and decency. King Alfred, the first English king, made it very clear that 'there should be freedom and justice for all ... I think it is a very English thing to give justice to all and at the moment, ironically, it is the English who are treated unjustly.'

The reader may suspect two things about Cyning: first,

that he is barmy and second that he is sinister. After spending quite a lot of time with him, I am sure that neither is
true. He is undoubtedly passionate in his support for an English Parliament, and unusual in his historical interests. At the
time we were speaking, the papers were carrying stories
about an archeological dig to find the bones of Alfred,
Cyning's great hero. The site in Winchester was, inevitably,
earmarked for a leisure centre, which caused Cyning to
groan. Later, I went back and read my way through writings
by Alfred and noted that, in his will, he called himself not
English, but 'King of the West Saxons'. History that early has
very little to teach us. But, after all, is there anything inherently barmier about this Anglo-Saxon interest than there is
about the Scottish Nationalist obsession with *Braveheart* or
the Battle of Bannockburn in 1314; or the Welsh Eistedfodds;
or numerous versions of romantic Irishry, from people as
notable as Yeats – or any other attempt under pressure, to
fling back to a purer, simpler version of national identity?
Cyning is a self-conscious name, a propaganda name: but the
same goes for Irish Republicans who have Gaelicised their
names. He is only doing, in some sort of way, what other
kinds of nationalists in these islands have been doing at the
English for long enough.

Cyning did not strike me as racist. There was, he admitted,
'a tiny, tiny minority' that spoke against blacks, 'and they're
just rubbish and they'll never have any power … I will fight
it tooth and nail, just as most English people would fight it
tooth and nail.' Could black people and Asian people be English, I asked. If England became independent of the other
British nations, could I, as a Scot, be English? 'I don't think
anybody can be English by simply living here, but I do think
you can be English by being born here. That is your
birthright, it is your clear right … if you are black and you are
born in this country then your national identity is English.'

What he wants is fairness, not pogroms. All my arguments for the reasonable compromises of a state in which the English, as the overwhelming majority and the richest part, accepted home rule for smaller nations inside Britain, moved him not at all. At one point he brandished the Scottish Constitutional Convention's 'Declaration of Right' which helped launch the drive for a Scottish Parliament. He had crossed out 'Scottish' on page after page and written 'English'. There, he said, thrusting a finger at the grand declarations of sovereignty and democratic tradition, 'that's what we want.' What Cyning represents is not going to disappear. It is going to grow – many English have been provoked by devolution – and more, perhaps, by decades of subtle slights, from Hollywood's enthusiasm for English villains to the general American preference for romantic Irish republicans rather than stiff-backed English politicians. Speaking personally, as a Scot, I am with the English in all this.

Eloquence

Radical English self-assertion has, of course, a long history. Cyning chose his hero well, since without Alfred the Great, it is perfectly possible that the English would have been defeated and swamped by the Norsemen and Britain would, today, be speaking a language much more similar to Danish. If Englishness is identified first with the language, then Alfred's translations of Latin into his native tongue may be taken as the first self-defining act of Englishness. A second near-catastrophe happened to the English with the Norman invasion, imposing a French-speaking elite on the country. For nearly 300 years after the Battle of Hastings, no English king spoke English. French was the language of power and Latin the language of religion. To be English under the

Normans can be compared to being Irish or Gaelic Scots at the time of British government repression. It was the language of the peasants, the poor-speak, the mouthing of the defeated. That it turned its great mouth around and gobbled up the French of the conquerors was a credit to its flexibility, as well as the sheer numbers of English-speakers compared to the small crust of knights.

Today it is a world language, more influential by far than Chinese, Spanish or Arabic, its nearest competitors. The story of the language is also the story of the people. A history of English puts it this way:

> When Julius Caesar landed in Britain nearly two
> thousand years ago, English did not exist. Five
> hundred years later, *Englisc,* incomprehensible to
> modern ears, was probably spoken by about as
> few people as currently speak Cherokee – and
> with about as little influence. Nearly a thousand
> years later, at the end of the sixteenth century,
> English was the native speech of between five and
> seven million Englishmen and it was, in the words
> of a contemporary, 'of small reatch, it stretcheth
> no further than this iland of ours, naie not there
> over all.' Four hundred years later, the contrast is
> extraordinary.[4]

It is so because of politics and luck; the British Empire started early in America, which became the world's superpower. But not only that: English has also proved to be an extraordinarily absorbent language, with enough rules to function but too few to prevent it constantly receiving and adapting other usages. It is a usefully flexible language, more so than German, which some early American politicians suggested be adopted as the USA's official language. There are some

500,000 words listed in the *Oxford English Dictionary*; French has fewer than a fifth of the number.

The openness and gusto of the English was never greater than during Elizabethan times, the last moment of entirely independent English statehood, when the greatest English person of all time, William Shakespeare, was delightedly rifling its word-hoard. Shakespeare has been credited by the American scholar Harold Bloom with 'the invention of the human' because of the interior monologues and emotional complexity he revealed. That is a rhetorical eye-catcher; but it is certainly true that Shakespeare had a major hand in the invention of the English sense of themselves. His English history plays, his images of a jewel-island, his elevation of Falstaff into an emblem of so much the English would like to think themselves, all had effects on the nation.

In terms of the language, the great change came with the spread of the London and southern dialect to the rest of England as the official version of English, breaking down the thick hedgerows and impenetrable thickets of other dialects, which were often mutually incomprehensible. Even in early Tudor times, many English people living in different parts of the country would have been as little able to understand one another as monoglot Europeans today. That was ended by the decision of the patriotic Henry V to use London English as his official court language, and by Caxton's use of the southeast dialect in his printed works.

No people on the planet have had a greater literary tradition, producing more transcendent poets, brilliant novelists and mighty orators. Chaucer, Shakespeare, Donne, Milton, Marvell, Pope, Johnson, Fielding, Gibbon, Blake, Wordsworth, Coleridge, Keats, Byron, Austen, Dickens, Thackery, Trollope, George Eliot, Tennyson, Hardy and D.H. Lawrence ... and those are only the top team. Most of us who read have lesser-known favourites without whom life would be thinner, duller, bleaker – I would not surrender Herrick, or William Cowper, Crabbe or Clare or Surtees, or Adrian Mitchell. English literature was, and remains, the single greatest and lasting achievement of the English people, which is why its currently rather subdued state is so eerie and worrying. In politics, English self-assertion has been made in ringing language, from the patriotic speeches of Shakespeare, to Milton's muscled prose, the writing or speeches of Wilkes, Cobbett, Dickens, Orwell, Churchill. There is a possibility that now, reaching across the world and attracting second-language status everywhere, English is becoming simply too successful to be as useful to English national identity. The Scottish novelist A.L. Kennedy argues that English may become the Latin of our age and suffer the same fate, breaking eventually into many tributaries, as Latin became both an official church language and a number of popular romance languages. Will we end up one day with an official, business version of 'classical English' and romance-Englishes, Korean-English, Germlish, Nordlish, Spanlish? The interconnected-ness symbolised by the Internet suggests a more complicated pattern than that, but also suggests that the influence of English on the thought-patterns of billions of people who do not speak it as a first tongue is bound to increase, infecting their imaginations and word-hoards.

What does this mean for 'English-English', the original island version of the coming world language, and the people who speak it? That language is certainly not ossifying. The English people are not becoming a community of declining Romans, with a decaying tongue spoken amid moss-stained marble ruins. On the contrary, the latest major revision of the *Oxford English Dictionary* is crammed with new words from around the world, from Asia, the former colonies, America and Japan, pouring in and restocking the sensibility of the English too. American English is the most powerful influence, for obvious reasons, and many people will lament the death of dialect-words and rhythms, the preserved nuances of language trapped for centuries in small folds of Wiltshire, or Lancashire villages, but now wind-blown away by the success of world English. Better that, though, than a language that shrivelled. Better that, than an island of linguistic antiquaries, of fastidious word-curators; if the state of English as a living thing is any guide, then the English themselves, outside politics and constitution, remain as open to change and the rest of the world as ever they were.

How, though, do these loquacious people picture themselves? This is a hard question to answer simply because we have to rely on those tiny number of English who committed themselves first to reflecting on English identity, and then to writing down their reflections. Early English writing is, in general, not much help. The first chroniclers are interested in holiness and have little real sense of national difference. Asser or Bede are writing in the context of Christendom and its fight against heathens, rather than about England in the national sense; the medieval writers are interested in story-telling (the *Gawain* poet), religion (Langland, Gower) and the classes and types of people (Chaucer) rather than in national identity. There are anti-Scottish and anti-French themes in Tudor writing, and then the flashing defiance of Elizabeth I, an early Euro-sceptic: 'I know I have the body of a weak and feeble woman, but I have the heart and stomach of a king, and a king of England too; and think foul scorn that Parma or Spain, or any prince of Europe, should dare invade the borders of my realm.' But none of this gets us much further; royal anger and national consciousness are rather different things.

Shakespeare's English patriotism is a better starting-point, not only in the famous speeches of John of Gaunt, Henry V and other individual characters, but also in the story of

English advancement built up in the entire body of his history plays. Shakespeare gives us the single most important example of how the English began to see themselves as a blessed people, betrayed by bad kings but riding an upward curve to national greatness. But even in Shakespeare, English patriotism is an essentially martial, expansive phenomenon, glittering words and royal progress, impressive but in the end less interesting than the engaging anti-heroics elsewhere. Indeed, the most vivid 'Englishness' in Shakespeare is the folk-Englishness, the songs and sense of natural magic in *A Midsummer Night's Dream*, *The Winter's Tale* and *Twelfth Night*; the peasants and comic characters of many other plays; and the boozy anarchism of 'plump Jack' Falstaff and his companions.

Green England

No proper discussion of Englishness must start anywhere but the strange, intense knot of feeling that connects land and countryside to freedom. If anything is 'essentially English' it is the retreat from authority, hiding behind the hedgerows. What we do not get explicitly in Shakespeare is the popular myth of the free England before the Norman conquest which animated early rural protesters against the enclosure of land (riots which began while he was still alive). Forty years later, during the English revolution, we find it in the writings of the English revolutionary Gerrard Winstanley, who was arguing after the execution of Charles I that 'the common people of England, as well as some of the gentry, have conquered King Charles, and recovered themselves from under the Norman conquest ... everyone upon recovery of the conquest ought to return into freedom again' otherwise the English would have no more freedom 'than we can have in Turkey or France'.[5] Shakespeare had little sympathy for rural rebellion – in *Henry VI, Part 3* he mocks Jack Cade, who makes the glib politician's promises of 'seven halfpenny loaves sold for a penny; the three-hoop'd pot shall have ten hoops ... All the realm shall be in common ... there shall be no money; all shall eat and drink on my score, and I will apparel them all in one livery, that they may agree like brothers and worship me their lord.' (A satire that twentieth-century Russians or Chinese would recognise immediately – though perhaps a larger cheer would have gone up in Elizabethan London at Cade's follower Dick's response: 'The first thing we do, let's kill all the lawyers.')

The popular belief in an earlier, freer England, the communistic dream mocked by Shakespeare, erupts not only in direct rural rebellions but also in the ballads of Robin Hood, the outlaw – though since these were often regional ballads, we must be cautious in assigning them national significance. The sense that the English were once unusually free, and had somehow been tricked out of that freedom, can be found in the poignant Robin Hood story that King Richard was a good, almost Christ-like figure upon whose return the country would be freed from John's wicked tyranny. This is not so different in emotional impact from the Levellers' belief that it was the Normans who stole English common freedoms and that all that was needed was a restoration of Anglo-Saxon freedom.

Freedom: betrayal: restoration. Robin Hood, Arthur, the Once and Future King. This pattern carries on as a subversive element into Chartist rhetoric and thinking unaffected by industrialisation. Samuel Bamford, the nineteenth-century radical leader, for instance, recalls being told the Robin Hood tales by an old woman in his boyhood, 'And I was quite delighted with the idea of a free life in the merrie green-wood.'[6] We get echoes of the same instinct in Blake's writing, including *Jerusalem* itself, though in the vision it is

Christ himself, not some kingly local substitute, who treads in ancient time upon England's green and pleasant land. Freedom and greenness and insularity are intermingled forever in the English imagination. And – alongside that – is the necessary belief that the continent, from France to Turkey, was a place of tyranny and unfreedom.

Perhaps the most significant single act of the forging of a separate, independent English nation had been Henry VIII's break with the Church of Rome – an essentially selfish act by an unstable and vandalising monarch, it nevertheless separated his country from Catholic Christendom and therefore began the tradition of English difference from continental Europe that lasts to this day in the protests of many against 'Brussels'. That difference was said to be about England's organic and dispersed power, ancient institutions that worked and habits that had lasted 'for generations'. Given the violent history of dynastic struggles, revolts against Crown power and religious feuding that composes England's pre-British history, that is a difficult argument to sustain at any length. Magna Carta is, to modern eyes, a very strange document indeed. But there is something in it.

Despite the feuds, England was rich in pastures and soil, easy to defend and composed of a mix of peoples and traditions that fused together, after several centuries, very successfully. They valued those fusions and traditions – common law and the rule of law, the language and later the distinctively English church and limitations on royal power – which seemed to offer a happier contrast to the absolutisms that could rage across borders on the continent. It might be the terror of the Counter-Reformation, or revolutions, or despotisms; but a sense that 'them over there' were flighty, unstable and dangerous is deeply rooted in English identity.

There are other ways of reading and interpreting the story. The English, after all, launched the first European revolution, which was surrounded by more than enough political-religious theory and ideology to satisfy the most enthusiastic French philosopher. England's Cromwellian revolution was not separate from the story of the continent and the French revolution, but was an early version of middle-class power and a precursor in its tragic trajectory, from anti-tyranny to tyranny, that France followed later. From painting to music, architecture to politics, food to clothing, English adaptations from continental Europe have been intimate, constant and long-lasting. Eighteenth-century noblemen went on the Grand Tour to learn how to be civilised in Rome and Naples and the better-off English now flock to the south of France and northern Italy to mimic the lifestyles of the locals. Yet all countries have myths about themselves which are only fragments of the whole truth, yet which matter because they bind people together, warm in the snuggle of the common illusion – even when they 'really know' the illusion for what it is. What matters is how the English saw and understood themselves; which bits of the story they liked and elevated to myth.

In this mixing of greenness, freedom and insularity, the English claimed themselves from early on as a people famous for fair play, plainness and a sturdy resistance to abstract ideas. The true English ate simply, drank honest beer and enjoyed a birthright of freedom from tyranny. They were slow to anger but, once roused by unfairness, they were utterly formidable. Oddly, they prided themselves on not being great thinkers. Given the English achievements in science, technology and language, never mind the empire, this is – yet again – a little hard to justify. But there we are. The true English did not hold with hierarchy or fancy words.

These themes are all present in the life and work of England's most celebrated artist, William Hogarth – in his satires and in the sturdily patriotic 'Sublime Society of Beefsteaks' (later the Beefsteak Club) he set up with friends in London in 1735, where they damned Whigs and foreigners and sang Fielding's song which contrasted the appetites, wealth and freedom of the English, with their continental enemies:

> When mighty Roast Beef was the
> Englishman's Food
> It enobled our Hearts and enriched our Blood;
> Our Soldiers were Brave, and our Courtiers
>   were good …
>
> Then, Britons from all nice Dainties refrain
> Which effeminate Italy, France and Spain;
> And mighty Roast Beef shall command on
>   the Main.
> Oh the Roast Beef of Old England
> And Old England's Roast Beef.[7]

Beef-eating, though it also had contemporary resonances as an anti-Whig activity, goes far back in the English sense of themselves. When Hogarth was painting his great *Gate of Calais*, a ferocious satire on the French after he had had a very unhappy jaunt round Paris, he used a huge side of beef gleaming amid French poverty, to symbolise English freedom and prosperity. The beef cult went back earlier than that: in Sir John Fortescue's *Governance of England* in 1467 the English were shown as gluttonous beef-guzzlers; again the implication was of a richer, freer, simpler people than the French, if not quite so quick on the uptake. You find it in Dr Johnson's great dismissive Tory voice, and in the patriotic poets of the eighteenth century and, running on towards modern times, in the work of writers such as G.K. Chesterton, in his poem called 'The Secret People':

> Smile at us, pay us, pass us; but do not

> quite forget.
> For we are the people of England, that never have
> spoken yet.

These were the lines referred to, I assume, by the letter writer to the *Express* quoted above and Margaret Thatcher has used them too. The secret, unspeaking Anglo-Saxons are clearly beef-eaters, their faces reddened by excessive quantities of meat, their minds slow, their anger terrifying. Chesterton, though a Catholic and anti-Semite, had a better feel for the emotional pitch of Englishness, the curious combination of swagger and self-pity, menace and modesty, than many greater writers. He was also responsible for the more good-humoured lines about the rolling, reeling rambling road 'the rolling English drunkard made', in which the curves of old shire roads become an emblem of England's anarchical spirit, again connected by myth ('Before the Roman came to Rye …') to an earlier and ideal free Englishness:

> I knew no harm of Bonaparte and plenty of
> the Squire,
> And for to fight the Frenchman I did not
> much desire;
> But I did bash their baggonets because they
> came arrayed
> To straighten out the crooked road an English
> drunkard made.

Good, decent, beery English drunkenness, an entirely different matter from the disgusting behaviour of Scots near whisky or French swilling wine, is an image that runs right back for centuries. John Bull drank beer and consumed beefsteaks and was not, we can assume, a keen reader of complicated sentences. In an editorial article in *The Economist* in 1848, the paper congratulated itself on the 'slow, reflective, phlegmatic temperament' of the English. Today, in one of the few expressions of rising English consciousness in book form, from the right-wing journalist Simon Heffer, we find them characterised as decent and kindly, but not very bright. While they are a cheerful people, says Heffer, they have 'only limited awareness that they are English'; they suffer from 'an incipient fear of asserting themselves'; they suffer from various 'stupidities or carelessnesses' and have 'a national characteristic of taking too much for granted'.[8]

In Hogarth, Chesterton, Heffer and many other writers, there is an essentially conservative reading of England's mild anarchism. But these are images that go beyond party. Mid-Victorian England saw a revival of interest in old Englishness, which was as much progressive in tone, as reactionary. There was a revisiting of Anglo-Saxon history and early island stories, a great popularising of Arthur and Hereward the Wake through painting and fiction. Folk customs were recalled on the verge of their death, for instance in the novels and poems of Thomas Hardy. The Commons Preservation Society was formed in the late 1870s and in 1877, horrified by the Victorian restoration of the local church in the Cotswold village of Burford, William Morris founded the Society for the Protection of Ancient Buildings. In architecture, simple rural designs, untreated oak and 'honest' brickwork were championed by people such as Norman Shaw, and then popularised and vulgarised in the new suburbs. By 1899, Cecil Sharp was collecting English folk-dances and in 1903 he began to collect folk-songs too.

Many of the people involved were progressives, either guild socialists, or in various brotherhoods and sisterhoods, or Fabians. Organic 'green Englishness' was an inspiration across the political spectrum. Think, for instance, of William Morris, the pioneering artist and socialist, writing about

Kelmscott Manor, the Oxfordshire home he adored. Kelmscott was, said Morris, 'a house that had grown out of the soil and the lives of them that lived on it.' It was, in the words of his biographer Fiona MacCarthy,

> doubly organic, deeply rooted in its landscape and connecting with, embracing, a long local human past ... Morris came to see himself as living at the centre of a country of immense beauty and complex interconnection ... Morris's view of the countryside roamed far outwards from the grey stone villages of Oxfordshire and Gloucestershire to all the variations of land and architecture that made up the mixture of England as a whole.[9]

For William Morris, as for the creators of early new towns and model villages of all kinds, this was a call to action, summoning him to work for an England which could be enjoyed in its greenness and freedom by all the people, not a mere pre-industrial remnant. He wrote in a communistic vein explaining this to Louisa Baldwin, a friend who was also the mother of the young Stanley Baldwin.

In a famous speech to the Royal Society of St George in 1924 the later Conservative leader asserted that

> To me England is the country, and the country is England ... The sounds of England, the tinkle of the hammer on the anvil in the country smithy, the corncrake on a dewy morning, the sound of the scythe against the whetstone, and the sight of a plough team coming over the brow of a hill, the sight that has been seen in England since England was a land, and may be seen in England long after the Empire has perished.

For Baldwin, the sight of wild anemones and the smell of woodsmoke 'strike down into the very depths of our nature and touch chords that go back to the beginning of time … These are the things that make England and I grieve for it that they are not the childish inheritance of the majority of the people today in our country.' From Levellers and Chartists through Victorian Socialists to a Tory leader in the 1920s and, in some ways, environmentalist conservatives today, there are threads of thought that wind back like the smell of woodsmoke.

Politically, the countryside is a complicated place, scored with ancient divisions and battles. Yet somehow, the conservative image of England summoned up by Baldwin, and decades-worth of magazines like *The Field* and *Country Life*, smooths out to nothing that complexity and rebelliousness. Outside the 'alien' towns, it replaces the real history with immemorial title-deeds, quiet acres and rural hierarchies. It uproots the folk and substitutes property. The fact that those acres have been the scenes of violent peasant protest, clearances of villages and the seizing of common land, unceasing rural guerrilla war between haves and have-nots, under the anodyne-sounding names of poaching and gamekeeping, matters not a whit. This is the nation engaged in an act of collective amnesia, ethnic forgetting. In rare moments of cynicism, tramping round a grand country house and trying to stifle a rising sense of proprietorial pride in somebody else's ancestors, I reflect that this instinctive, conservative view of England has been greatly helped by the simple fact that the buildings remain, and the people die. The National Trust (by far the country's richest charity, with assets in 1997 of more than £509 million) is able to represent to the modern English, and millions of tourists, a country of wood panelling, brick towers, vast avenues and a few peach-cheeked families as seen by Gainsborough and Reynolds.

There is no national trust for the vanished people in all their turbulence and complexity, the people with strong ideas but few possessions. The countryside matters more to the idea of Englishness than towns, where almost all of them live – it is where the secret people go to hide in their minds, particularly during moments of stress. The English suburb, a place unlike anywhere else on earth, with its neat gardens, brick walls, fake Tudor homes, allotments, tree-lined streets and local parks, is surely the town-dwellers' tribute to that mythic green past, to the lost England of Morris and Baldwin. This explains the huge popularity among the urban English of essentially rural organisations like the Trust and the RSPB. And surely the national English obsessions – gardening and dogs – are the private protest of a people who secretly consider themselves farmers and animal-tenders, against the speed and gloss of modern urban life?

The more urban the English became, the more defence of the English countryside mattered to them. One of the first big national arguments, in September 1939 as Britain went to war, was not about Spitfire production or who was to blame for appeasement, but about a decision to build speculative housing across a swathe of the South Downs outside Brighton, between the villages of Keymer and Ditchling. Southern Sussex is territory which has long been special to the English, the richest home in the Home County imagination. Shelley grew up thereabouts. It was where Kipling set Pook's Hill in his magical children's history, *Puck of Pook's Hill*. In it, Kipling's children go fishing

> in the bed of the brook that for centuries had cut
> deep into the soft valley soil. The trees closing
> overhead made long tunnels through which the
> sunshine worked in blobs and patches. Down in
> the tunnels were bars of sand and gravel, old roots

> and trunks covered with moss or painted red by
> the irony water; foxgloves growing lean and pale
> towards the light.

In this landscape, the children are introduced by Puck to a story of an England washed by waves of migrants and passing peoples, all leaving something to mark the country. It is a story already touched with melancholy, for Puck had seen the Old England of 'giants, trolls, kelpies, brownies, goblins, imps; wood, tree, mound, and water spirits; heath-people, hill-watchers, treasure-guards, good people, little people, pishogues, leprechauns, night-riders, pixies, nixies, gnomes, and the rest – gone, all gone! I came into England with Oak, Ash and Thorn ...'

This south Sussex landscape is also the territory where Virginia Woolf sought refuge in wartime, listening to the sound of the guns of Flanders across the Channel on long nights, then later tormenting herself with the fear of imminent Nazi invasion before filling her pockets with stones and drowning. Between those wars, she loved walking the Downs. She says in her diary for 5 September 1929, for instance, that she needs 'space to spread my mind out in ... to breathe in more light & air; to see more grey hollows & gold cornfields & the first ploughed land shining white, with the gulls flickering.' A different sensibility from Kipling's – the two passages could stand almost as an explanation of modernism – but the same intensity.

In the same month as Virginia Woolf was striding between Seaford and East Chiltington, thinking free thoughts, fears for the future of the English countryside led to the creation of the Council for the Preservation of Rural England, the CPRE – though its name was later changed, in a tacit acknowledgement that it was losing the fight, to the Council for the Protection of Rural England. By 1939, ribbon development was eating deep into the counties and the CPRE took a stand to fight for Ditchling village, with the support of newspapers. As the war began, the Ditchling case was one of the catalysts for a remarkable artistic project, jointly supported by the Ministry of Labour and the American philanthropic Pilgrim Trust. This was called 'Recording Britain' and the idea, originated by Sir Kenneth Clark (later creator of the *Civilisation* television series and father of the Tory diarist, Alan Clark) was that under-employed artists, some of them conscientous objectors, should be sent around the country to draw and paint it before Nazi bombers and Whitehall planners finished it off. Clark suggested the paintings should be of 'fine tracts of landscape which are likely to be spoiled by building developments ... towns and villages where old buildings are likely to be pulled down'; parish churches, and country houses which 'will be largely abandoned after the war and will either fall into disrepair or be converted into lunatic sanotaria.'[10] It is a resonant fact that, admittedly partly through lack of funds, 'Recording Britain' ignored Scotland altogether and was scanty on Wales.

It was perhaps the last great English romantic project. The names of paintings and drawings give an idea of its tone. Ditchling is there, of course, in a fine watercolour of Anne of Cleves' house. Then also: John Piper, *The Tithe Barn, Great Coxwell* and *Chancel Arch, St Peter's, Stanton Low* and *The Temple of British Worthies, Stowe, Gloucestershire*; Barbara Jones, *The Hop Castle, Chieveley*; Stanley Roy Badmin, *Flooded Meadows at Olney* and *Stoke Bruerne, Northants*; Kenneth Rowntree, *The Smoke Room of the Ashopton Inn* (complete with stuffed trout in glass case and darts-board) and *Underbank Farm, Woodlands, Ashdale*; A.S. Hartrick, *Breast Plough at Tresham,Wotton-under-Edge, Gloucestershire*; Raymond Cowern, *Cottage Gardens, Dalham, Suffolk*. And on, and on, a huge visual Domesday recording of townscapes, London streets, industrial sites, but above all villages and churches, threatened meadows and huddled, organic-looking lumps of old stonework and thatch, caught in brilliant, flickering hogshair brush, dots of China White, jumps of graphite pencil and gentle washes of blues, before oblivion. At a moment of looming national catastrophe, this was what England thought of England.

It is nostalgic and backward-looking, of course. But it is also real, it fits. The English have never been among the world's great musical nations. As Sir Thomas Beecham put it, they 'may not like music – but they absolutely love the sound it makes.' Their painting and sculpture does not rival the productions of Italy, France or Germany. It has been said that native English cooking leaves something to be desired. But the English are, in certain ways, undoubtedly artistic and visual. They have a gentle, and occasionally soaring, tradition of building, not only the Gothic and Classical native adaptations of styles invented in France, Germany and Italy, but also the domestic architecture – the stone churches, the brick palaces, the roofs and shapes of rural farms and villages that could stand nowhere but England. The particular agricultural history and shape of many parts of England, from the soft leaf-green humps and deep crannies of Devon to the stony, flattened ridges of Derbyshire, have produced a man-made landscape that has become the most secure, simple emblem of England.

It was those images that politicians turned to, as well as the artists, again and again, during the wars against Germany. In the Second World War, alongside the 'Recording Britain' team, popular poster-artists were creating less specific bucolic idylls, with teams of horses ploughing, beeches and oaks, square church towers and the glint of the sea, to remind people what they were fighting for. All this matters. The core English aesthetic is still about being outside, about soft light and rain, the sharp colours of spring and thick tangles of forest: Constable and Turner, the Pre-Raphaelites, twentieth-century painters like Ivon Hitchens and the modern romantic inheritors, such as Richard Long, with his photographed walks, or Andy Goldsworthy, with his sculptures of leaves, ice, sticks and mud. The urban art traditions, from Hogarth himself, to Blake, the Camden Town school, Bacon and Freud, and the new wave of installation and video artists, are English in another sense. They are rude, crude, raw, full of the pain of dislocation and the shock that is also what England has gone through, ripped from an agrarian society to the world's first city and industrial one in only a few generations. But the emotional pull of the rural idyll is more general and, still, deeper.

So what of Ditchling, that little village threatened so particularly in 1939? It is still there, though much changed. But 60 years on, it is threatened again, more seriously, by the new housing pressures on England's green and pleasant oases – pressures brought to a head by the leak of a government document advocating the abandonment of planning controls on prime agricultural land. Maps of the English south showing the areas most likely to go include Ditchling and its whole surrounding space, as the spread of urban Britain continues, great fuzzy blobs of development, first surrounding old towns and villages, then appearing between them, then joining them up. The writer Simon Jenkins, who has recently completed a massive survey of *England's Thousand Best Churches*, has written that, since 1980

> built-up Britain has increased by 50% and an area
> the size of Bristol has gone under bricks and
> mortar each year. My beloved churches seem to
> wave despairingly as they sink under a sea of vivid
> red roofs and concrete drives … All of rural

> England should be regarded as greenbelt. There is
> too little of it left … Shrinking the protected
> countryside to areas of national park and National
> Trust land would be vandalism on a millennial
> scale. Southern England in the 21st century
> would become a vast dormitory, its residents
> fleeing in their millions across the Channel at the
> weekends and for holidays.[11]

Now clearly, in all this, there must be a split English personality: the English want both to live in sight of the countryside, and to have it preserved. Their ideal mode is to be
invisible, immaterial country-dwellers, seeing but not seen,
enjoying but not affecting. This is not given to corporeal
bipeds, who must live somewhere, dispose of their rubbish
and sewage, move around, shop and make a certain quantity
of unnatural noise. The English countryside, prime traditional source of English self-understanding, is threatened
above all by the English desire to live there, and not in towns.
You always kill the thing you love. There are solutions,
involving public money, the reclaiming of urban centres, and
planning laws, which are blindingly obvious but outside the
scope of a book about national identity.

What matters more in this context is the politics of the
English countryside today. It is conservative, in all sorts of
ways, of course, and hypocritical to the extent that the anti-
housing lobby contains many recently arrived ex-urbanites.
But at its core is a sense of being besieged by an uncompre-
hending enemy. Some of the farmers whose businesses have
been ravaged by the catastrophe of 'mad cow disease' or BSE,
and by the high pound, will now become multimillionaires
by selling their land to developers. But more, and the people
who should concern us more, are the farmers who are trying
to stay on the land, preserving it and maintaining it for future

generations of English. They, and the communities around them, have had a hellish time. Good sheep change hands for less than the price of a packet of crisps. There have been scores of farming suicides. Land which has been in one family for hundreds of years has become utterly uneconomic. Some of it is likely to be simply abandoned, turning back to scrub. As a result of this, and the campaign to make fox-hunting a criminal offence, many rural people now feel worryingly alienated from the rest of the suburbanised, Americanised nation.

I felt this when I visited an agricultural fair north of Leeds and heard the bitter anger about the new government from people there. I felt it a few months later when I was reporting the Labour conference at Bournemouth and saw, on two successive days, rallies by farmers and by supporters of fox-hunting, winding through the little town streets to pass the fortress-like centre where the Labour delegates were gathered. The farmers, with their weather-beaten faces, Viyella shirts and flat caps, carried bitter messages – 'If all Farmers were Buggers, Blair would Care' read a not-untypical one. The pro-hunters, with their exotic costumes, horns and angry exchanges with saboteurs, seemed like a different race from the smooth New Labour people inside. 'Listen to us!' they chanted, uselessly. Just as with the miners and their supporters, who marched past Conservative conferences during the 1980s, these people looked very like a doomed minority, who could protest and express anger and pain, but who were on the losing side in British politics and had no redress. This too is about Englishness, its tone and temper in the future.

One of the first signs of the rural revolt, which has become semi-organised as the Countryside Alliance, organisers of marches on London, was a controversial BBC decision to drop a show called *One Man and His Dog*. (That a TV programme about the behaviour of sheepdogs could cause quite such a furore is, in itself, a very English phenomenon.) The man most associated with the show, a farmer and writer called Robin Page, has become one of the most articulate voices of the new rural politics. He and his brother have an unusual stretch of land a little west of Cambridge, which I visited in September 1999. Not the best time of year to see the attractions of a sustainable farm, supported by the Countryside Restoration Trust, perhaps; but even then I noticed the quantities of insects, birds and rich plantlife around the borders of the fields. Another observer, who has written a major account of the condition of British farming, described the same farm in summer:

> Wildflowers have begun to appear in the wet
> meadowland which now lines the stream's banks
> – ox eye daisy, lady's bedstraw and birdsfoot
> tretoil. Nearby a grass field blazes with the flowers
> of meadowland, while a wheat crop is speckled
> with cornflower, corn cockle and the rare
> shepherd's needle ... Here beside the Bourn
> Brook the wild flowers are returning, and with
> them many of the indigenous birds and animals
> that once made up our glorious wildlife heritage.
> Clouds of butterflies drift on summer breezes.
> Reed buntings, yellow wagtails and grasshopper
> warblers dart amongst the willows. Otters haunt
> the stream and banksides.[12]

It sounds very like Kipling's Pook's Hill. On the day I visited him, Page led me round those same fields and then down to where a herd of beautiful grey-blue cattle were grazing. A round, ruddy-faced man with whiskers and an engagingly schoolboyish smile, he let me enjoy it all before explaining that all the mothers, these glossy, healthy cows, were heading for the incinerator, a casualty of the rules that followed the BSE disaster. Hogarth's patriotic roast beef had been brought low in one of the worst psychological reversals to hit English self-belief – worse even than the performance of the national cricket team.

'We have not had BSE, we can't have BSE, they eat food produced on the farm, these are your environmentally friendly cattle, and because of the BSE cock-up, every single cow that you can see here will be burned … Mounds of ash, and it's obscene, it's disgraceful and it's pathetic.' He is literally shaking with emotion, and goes on to talk of the bureaucratic nightmare and the gravy-train that BSE, caused partly by a loosening of government regulations in the Thatcher years and partly by some industrial farmers' greed, has brought in its wake – in his words, 'a mixture of bureaucratic incompetence and industrial farming'.

The government, he complains, is interested only in cheap food for the urban punters, not with sustainability or the English countryside. Page, though, quickly expands his attack. His 'rant' (his word, not mine) deserves to be quoted at some length because it stands for the boiling anger of so many others. Neither the Tories nor Labour had listened to the country, he said: 'It's absolutely desperate. People losing money, losing their self-respect, losing their hope.' There was a wave of suicides, which would get worse if people lost hunting, their sport and release-valve:

> I said to a huntsman's wife, 'What will you do if hunting is banned?' and she said, 'Don't talk about it, Robin, because he says he will hang himself the next day.' And I can't see how a government who came in saying it wanted to bring people together is actually driving this wedge in, and it's a cultural wedge, and it's an economic wedge, and it's a

rural/urban wedge. And I think it is callous, I
think it's disgusting, hypocritical and it's cultural
cleansing ... and with the suicides, I think it's
almost ethnic cleansing.

He did not want a CD player or a computer, he wanted to
enjoy the rural life – 'I like my way of life, I don't want to be
improved ... when Mr Blair goes off to enjoy the rural life of
Tuscany, why doesn't he admit that there is a rural culture of
Britain.' But, he continued, with rising rage,

We're an embarrassment, and they don't want us
... We're dispensable. You know, we don't fit in
with the image. If you want to be the first
president of Europe, then you don't want people
like us and you don't want people chasing foxes
with dogs. You want to be part of [ineffable
contempt] 'Let's go and drink wine in Tuscany.
Oh, let's go to the [even ineffabler contempt]
Bistro. Let's go and earn five hundred pounds an
hour' ... And so you're getting Blair and his wife
on this huge salary, prancing about like little
emperors, and you've got farmers who can't get
tuppence a fleece for their wool. There is
inequality of democracy, there is inequality of
economy.

There would be a massive reaction, including 'civil disobedi-
ence on a scale that hasn't been seen in this country for a
very long time.'

There, in all its rawness, is the desperation of the English
countryside, pressed in from all sides and losing its patience. I
did not agree with him. I eat in bistros myself. But I heard the
voice of Hogarth. It was olde, greene England speaking. As I

write, there have been demonstrations but nothing worse, while the French ban on British beef has produced a big 'buy British' backlash and farmers' blockades of some ports, suggesting that perhaps they are beginning to learn from continental farmers' tactics. There are questions about England here. Who are the English? Are they their rural ancestry and the composite images that it provokes, the ideas the English return to in times of crisis? Or are they the materialistic, suburban, TV-drunk and electorally mighty new middle classes, in thrall to huge supermarket chains and their cars, that Robin Page fears and detests? Both of course, but they are more the latter. If it comes to a bare-knuckle political fight, there is no serious doubt about which side would win. The 'forces of conservatism' would be pushed back to the edge of Page's Bourn Brook, and then right into it.

The new middle-class suburban England is politically fickle and hard to admire. As Simon Jenkins put it in the article quoted earlier, Tony Blair had come to power on a platform of communitarianism:

> That platform is fast vanishing under developer
> pressure. If unchecked, England will indeed be …
> a continuous suburb, leafy but without
> community, church or focus, dependent on cars
> and scornful of neighbourhood. Such introverted,
> atomised societies may suit the politics of control.
> They were never the politics of provincial
> England.

This suggests that there is a vanishing, defeated Englishness, doomed by urbanisation and politics to become a folk-memory, and that it is conservative in almost every aspect. But there is another force of protest equally present in the countryside, and just as intimately tied to the urban consumer agenda – the environmentalist movement, recently grouped around anti-road protests and the struggle against genetically modified food. It shares perhaps only one thing with the conservatives of the Countryside Alliance – a strong, suspicious instinct about the relationship between Labour in government and corporate power.

Percy Street in Oxford is a row of small terraced workers' cottages, now feeling like some kind of south-English radical fantasy, the house-fronts painted sky blue and ox-blood, little gardens overflowing into one another, bicycles propped up everywhere. On the lamp-posts are stickers complaining about nuclear weapons, calling 'Save the Pound' or demanding 'Stop GM food'. This is where George Monbiot lives, a man who is becoming a kind of guru to radical environmentalists and someone who should be listened to alongside Robin Page, for the differences and similarities. He is a professor in different universities, a *Guardian* columnist, trained zoologist and leading anti-GM campagner. He is handsome, charismatic and eloquent. The previous day he had been speaking to a group of anti-GM food protesters who had invaded fields of modified oilseed rape at Watlington, ripping them up until arrested by the police. He was gleeful about the political failures of Monsanto, the American GM giant which was busy losing the battle for hearts and souls in Europe and perhaps not so far from giving up. I asked him why these attacks on law-abiding farmers' fields were going on. They were happening, he replied, 'because the Labour government has demonstrated on this issue, as on quite a few others, that when it comes to a choice between listening to what the electorate wants and listening to what big business wants, in seems to side with big business every time.' It is clear, literally, where Robin Page stands in opposition to this. But where does Monbiot stand? What is his identity? For, after all, environmentalists are engaged in a struggle that often takes place in and about the countryside, yet they are also a world-wide network, helping each other across national boundaries. Monbiot himself was brought up in Oxfordshire and looks and sounds very English but, as his name suggests, he is a mix of many races – French, Jewish, Peruvian and Norwegian as well as English. He sounds traditional. His concern with organic farming and the fate of the countryside can sound traditionalist. Yet he describes himself as an internationalist campaigning against globalism. So what is he?

> I feel very clearly that I belong to East Oxford, to this little part of the town where I live. I have a very strong sense of that, a very strong sense of neighbourhood, a strong sense of belonging. I'll go round to the bakery in the morning. I'll meet lots of people I know there, I'll buy bread from the baker I have bought it from every morning. When I come back from travelling ... I have very much that feeling of coming back home.

He also feels fellowship with people whose struggles he has witnessed or helped, all round the world. For him belonging is local, and then about belonging to a group who share values and hopes. 'As for feeling British, I don't really have a sense of pride or engagement with the concept of nation.' English? 'No, I don't really feel that either ... I'm clearly an Englishman de facto but I don't really feel much identity with the concept of Englishness or the concept of British-ness.'

What about traditional British values? 'They send a shiver down my spine. Because what they seem to be saying to me is, there is only one set of values which British people can subscribe to and if you don't subscribe to these, you don't deserve to be part of this nation.' These values 'are tied up with colonial conquests, perhaps being rather anally retentive, a public school sociopathy ... that really admits very little tolerance, admits very little diversity.' But what about the countryside, the fields, the essence of the English romantic self-image? Monbiot is derisive, describing the values of the Countryside March as reactionary and sentimental – the armed wing of a Tory party redefining itself as a particular kind of rural party which believed in the right to hunt, but not the right of the 'urban proles' to range freely over the land; that spoke mistily of the country, but was actually happy to butcher it with motorways and out of town shopping developments.

Blood and soil is the old and dark way of defining identity: Monbiot noted in passing that modern British fascists had tried very hard to recruit and associate themselves with the rural revolt. So if not Britain, if not England, what? This East Oxfordian wants to see more power devolved right down to the community level – every group of streets having some say in their own planning decisions, for instance – while other, big battles, such as over hormone-treated beef or fair trade, require international politics. Nations can survive in some way, Monbiot concedes. But he thinks that national identity in the old ways is slipping away – and rather than feeling horrified by that, or threatened, is delighted:

> it can be extremely positive. I think it can lead to a flowering, an opening-out. It can lead to us, just on the individual level, recognising that we have far more potential than sometimes we've been told. We can be the thing we want to be. We don't have to be straight-jacketed by this concept of Britishness, or this concept of Englishness.

The Other England

Green England and liberty, or green England and tradition, are essential parts of the English mental picture. Rural English heritage inspires strong feeling, which will in turn affect the politics of the twenty-first century, as the country struggles to hold onto the last fragments of its past. But any proper discussion of Englishness has to move quickly on, to the realities of the crowded and intensely urban country of modern times. Like Britain as a whole, England is also the creation of empire and industrialism. Its self-image does not stop with the bucolic ideas discussed so far. 'Green England' excludes most of the English, not only the metropolitans but also the midland urban English and the northerners – it is no coincidence that the villages and writers I have so far mentioned are almost all from the south. Many of the leaders of opinion who live in the leafy suburbs of London, or the Home Counties, and who have weekend cottages in Oxfordshire, the West Country or Norfolk, seem to regard much of the geographical area of England as not really English at all. The massive urban estates of Leeds, Manchester, Birmingham, the Black Country, Liverpool, Newcastle, Sheffield, and the web of red-brick housing that connects them, has been 'another country' since before the industrial revolution.

The midland and north were first Danelaw and then, in Norman and Plantagent England, the territory of marcher lords, independent baronial families who paid little heed to London, except during outbreaks of dynastic warfare. In Tudor England and beyond, the north was Catholic long after the south had become Anglican; in the civil war, it was more intensely Royalist, while the south was more Parliamentarian.

During the eighteenth century, the north was simply cut off from London's colonial growth by poor communications and the huge economic importance of the court. Then came the industrial revolution, the defining moment in the severing of one-nation England, if such a place had existed before. It is not fanciful to think that the metropolitan and landed English saw the industrial northerners as a race apart. (Indeed, because of the huge influx of Irish labour before the famine, they were at least more heavily Celtic than the south.) In the north, self-help, industrialisation and nonconformism created an urban ideology which looked down on the southern English as soft, effete and old-fashioned, divided still between snobbish landlords and dim peasants, while Manchester and Birmingham were being transformed by grit, hard work and practicality.

There was a lot of truth in this. Manchester Cotton Exchange, extended in 1838, had more dealers and floorspace than the London Stock Exchange; Manchester Town Hall, begun in 1868, was larger than the House of Commons. The historian Raphael Samuel also noted that Manchester 'conducted its own foreign policy, backing the Free Trade treaty with France in 1860 and siding with the North against the South in the American Civil war (Ashton-under-Lyne and Stalybridge took the other side).'[13] This northern nationalism later produced the great reforming radical administrations of so many great cities. In British political history, both the defeat of the Corn Laws and the successive waves of parliamentary reform can also be seen, however crudely, as the triumph of the midlands and north over the south and west, a victory solidly based on their economic power and their greater vitality as human societies.

It was not, however, a victory bought at a small price. A succession of southern writers, politicians and journalists portrayed the northern industrial zone as enemy territory, a place of barbarism, inhabited by almost sub-human factory and mine serfs, and their flat-vowelled overseers, thugs in wool coats and top hats, as far removed from the ideal of the English gentleman as any foreigner. The north was ruled by swaggering parvenus, without education, whose faith (if they possessed any) was the degraded merchant Christianity of nonconformism, not the true Anglican religion; who possessed no fine sensibility and who gloried in 'brass' not breeding. It contains a flickering cultural echo of the contemporary US division between Confederate south and Union north; though in England, the Confederates won.

Disraeli, who as a young novelist had popularised the idea of 'two nations' and drawn vivid attention to the social troubles of northern industry, finished his life as the Earl of Beaconsfield and the set-designer of imperialism. It was somehow symbolic. Social criticism of the north became mingled with southern snobbery, and the two are found in Dickens, Ruskin, *Punch* and lesser sources. The north/midlands might respond with other eloquent writers, including Mrs Gaskell, George Eliot, Arnold Bennett and D.H. Lawrence, but the dominant, political English imagination remained in the south so long as industrialisation divided England. By the time George Orwell set off towards Wigan Pier, he was describing a foreign country to most of his readers. For J.B. Priestley, like Orwell a writer of the left, the north was a horrific, hellish landscape of exploitation and pollution.

Almost all nations, of course, have significant internal divisions and many are, on the face of it, more significant than the English one: Scotland was long divided between Gaels and the southerners; Belgium is two different language communities; Germany has the Catholic south and the Protestant north. What is curious about the English case, however, is just how successfully one part of the country, and arguably the less hardworking part, overshadowed and denigrated the other. The north was about class war, ignorance, squalor and dirt, a sub-England best ignored, and that is how the south saw it, even when it was also the world's workshop, the crucible of British modernity, alive with progressive and democratic ideas, the part of England most galvanised by optimism! England was exemplified by broad acres, gentlemen, the City, even when the industrial money of the north was challenging the southern Conservative elite on its home ground, buying into Home Counties families and taking peerages by the dozen. For a century, it seemed, the north was England's dirty secret.

In modern times, when first the Depression and then the deindustrialisation of the 1980s and 1990s hammered the north, all these southern prejudices were simply confirmed. Social-realism films, television dramas and the work of successive angry writers kept the voice of the north loud and insistent. But it was never, somehow, the essence of Englishness; bit by bit the industrial history of the country, not fully embraced at the time, was forgotten and the north was seen as the land of local authority corruption, empty factories, retreating trade union romanticism, work-shy Trotskyist wide-boys and those immigrant communities who were obviously failing. The north responded in kind. Incomprehension faced down incomprehension. The journalist Robert Chesshyre, who returned to Britain in the mid-1980s after a four-year posting in Washington, and wrote a brilliant, bleak account of the country he found, entitled a chapter based around Easington Colliery in County Durham, 'My wife would never leave Surrey'. In it he anatomised the north–south incomprehension, quoting a miner:

> I've got a sixteen-year-old son. I would chain him
> by the ankles and nail him to the floor before I'd
> let him go down south. Not into that

exploitation. Lads who go to London for jobs fall
into vice and everything else – homosexuality
and rentaboy. A boy down there would become a
servant to the people with money and high
qualifications.

Chesshyre also quoted a Liverpool professor protesting about
the 'almost racist' view of the north held by the London-
based political elite. The north was not only a different
world, but also inhabited by troublesome, irritating people
who 'are all tarred with the same brush, all are somehow
responsible for the crisis and all can be left to stew in their
own juice … We are not a United Kingdom. We are deeply
divided.' In Chesshyre's own summation, the north in the
mid-1980s was 'being run like an overseas colony by a complacent establishment of Sir Humphreys and Sir Roberts and
by hard-faced politicians, with braying didactic voices.'[14]

Things have changed, of course, since Norman Tebbit was
telling the north to get on its available bikes and report for
duty in Essex. Whatever one's opinions about New Labour it
is certainly a party with a strong north of England base, and
many of its ministers are northerners, or sit for northern
seats. Whether this government can bring enough investment into the north remains to be seen; there is a strong
drive within Labour for more 'go-it-alone' regional assemblies, which could work directly with the EU and, in a
vaguer way, embody northern values and pride. My guess is
that a stronger northern political identity is likely and is right
– the place just feels different, from the way people talk to
you, to the quality of the light, the sharpness of the air, the
architecture and the shape of the world when you look
around from Yorkshire or Northumberland. But it is a long
way from there to saying, as some would, that therefore England 'does not really exist' as a single nation, and that English

national feeling is bogus. To me, as a Scot, Newcastle and Liverpool feel more like Scotland, in bad ways as well as good, in diet and cigarettes and pessimism as well as solidarity, warmth and humour, than they feel like London or the Home Counties. But they are English nevertheless, not Scottish, and even now, nations exist and cannot be ignored without serious risk. Manchester may well be a stronger political centre in a generation's time – indeed, it would be a disaster if it was not – but will not be once more running its own foreign policy, any more than Basildon will be. Local and regional identity in England needs to be restored and cherished after decades of casual centralising vandalism; but this does not mean the English question is therefore resolved.

What a northern infusion adds to the English brew is a dose of realism. The English popular experience is not simply about rural liberties and empire. It is, much more, about trauma. It is about the enclosures of the common land, waves of agricultural and industrial revolution, a forced march to the cities, and lives blighted by hellish working conditions and bad housing. Some English, the ones lampooned abroad, did very well out of the empire. Many of the great aristocratic estates, swollen again in money value thanks to the stock-market booms and growth in land prices in recent years, are the booty of empire; tens of thousands of well-paying City jobs, subsidising expensive Home Counties homes and private school fees, would never have come to London had it not been for the empire; the imperial experience has created an English-speaking Atlantic business and cultural elite which well-educated English people exploit with great wit. But how has the imperial experience benefited the lives of middle-class English families today who depend upon manufacturing jobs in the West Midlands, or managers in Liverpool, or teachers in the West Country? Are they better off, richer, happier than their equivalents in

countries without an imperial history – than middle-income
Danes, Swedes, Italians or Irish? Not at all. For a large majority of the English, inheritors of trauma and the human cogs
of the grand corporate project of empire, it has brought them
nothing much.

Hence, I suggest, the cross-class, cross-political appeal of
'Jerusalem' – the harking back to an ancient time – and the
note of self-pity in so much English popular culture. Hence
also the English swagger, the aggression for which, despite
their middle-class self-image as patient, put-upon types, the
English are also known. In its nastiest side, this swagger is the
brutality of the English football yobs, a horrible and disgraceful sight, lauded by the late Alan Clark as good fighting
English. And, much more generally spread through history, it
is the violence of the English crowd. In a famous essay at the
time of the Brixton and Broadwater Farm riots in London,
the writer Neal Ascherson pointed out that despite the gentle
wartime pieties of writers like George Orwell 'Rioting is at
least as English as thatched cottages.' There had, throughout
history, been countless violent outbreaks. The 1780 Gordon
riots killed more than 200 people in London and the London
police were issued with firearms as early as 1883.

> This country was torn by violence in 1919 ...
> First came the race riots against black seamen,
> which flared around all the major seaports. Then
> came the outbreak at Luton, when crowds burned
> the town hall with petrol; there were over 100
> casualties and troops had to be brought in. The
> next month, the police went on strike in
> Liverpool and there followed days and nights of
> fighting and looting, put down with troops who
> had to charge with the bayonet while tanks
> moved into the Scotland Road area.

And on Ascherson's record went.[15] In an age when the poll tax riots helped bring down Margaret Thatcher and when the country was ravaged by violence during the miners' strike of 1984–5, it is hard to fully understand the deep English belief that they are an almost unnaturally docile people.

This is the Other England – the violence, revolt, swagger and at times the racism of a suppressed people. This is the England barred from the rural inheritance, locked out of that Eden dreamed of by Winstanley, and William Blake and William Morris. This unEngland has become the country of high rates of crime and a passion for prisons, of gangs burning police stations and the raw race-hate and yobbery of the 'Ingerland' football crowd at its rampaging finest. It has never heard of the writers quoted in this chapter and knows almost nothing of history. It is the England which could rediscover its nationalism not in any green or optimistic mood but as ugly and violent. Like the spirit of the English countryside, it is always there, always waiting, a Bad Arthur, sleeping but available for reawakening.

Out from under

How do these different ideas of England connect, if at all? Despite its small geographical size, could it be that England today is simply too diverse to have a national character of any kind – that between Home Counties ruralism and northern self-help, inner-city unemployment and the new rich of the City, there are divides too deep to be covered by any identity? Certainly, despite the continuities described in this chapter, the English idea of England has also been a state of constant flux. *Beowulf* is the Germanic poem of a Germanic people, light years away from the sensibility of French-influenced medieval England. A Catholic people became a

Protestant people who became an agnostic, materialist people. The empire made English self-images more aggressive and vainglorious – all those humourless stone lions and nasty-looking bulldogs. Nor did most English people necessarily have a similar view of Englishness at any one time. What links the radical-revolutionary impulses of the early Romantic poets, the Corresponding Societies and the nonconformists with the provincial patriotism of the army and navy families drawn by Jane Austen? Not a lot. As between the English described by Hogarth as simple and plain to the point of being dim, and the English described by Milton as 'a nation not slow and dull, but of quick, ingenious and piercing spirit, acute to invent, subtle and sinewy to discourse, not beneath the reach of any point the highest that human capacity can soar', there is a great empty space of mutual incomprehension. The emergence of a large public-school elite produced an idea of England, the Rupert Brooke Englishness, which was actually opposed to the England of the majority of the people. Today, the europhile, sundried tomatoes and a holiday in Provence English have a strongly different view of Englishness than northern working-class consumers of almost purely American culture.

Most nations have inconsistencies and discontinuities in their idea of themselves, however, and the traditional way in which these are bundled up, gathered together, is statehood. A bloodline of monarchs, a republican constitution, an army, a tune, a common history of defeat and revival – these have been used as a blanket to cover the underlying differences between rich and poor, urban and rural, mountain-dweller and valley farmer, even left and right. But the English do not have this, not quite. They have been world-beaters, but also a people controlled by others – by foreign monarchs who could not speak their language, or by Scottish cliques, or by an imperial ruling class that included Germans, Welsh and so on – and latterly, by powerful American and continental corporations. The English, as the English, were never consulted about the Union with Scotland or the imperial destiny, any more than the Scots were. In modern times, they were never asked about immigration or about federal European Union.

As a people, they have both triumphed and been semi-submerged in the visions of others. The rulers of England have never been as English as the rulers of France have been French, or the rulers of Germany, German. Today the cabinet is dominated by Scottish politicians; England's trade position is championed or undermined by French, German, Italian and Spanish politicians; its towns and counties have very little say. Many English with a sense of history would remark, not having an English expression handy, '*plus ça change* ...'

English democracy is not old, and at some level the English have never quite taken responsibility for their extraordinary story as the dominant part of the British nation. They were connected to it so long as the armed forces, the manufacturing and trading wealth and the needs of administration gave millions of English people a direct pay-out from imperialism. But no longer. The comment that they obtained the empire in a fit of absent-mindedness is one way of putting it. The truth is that throughout the British experience, and despite constantly confusing the two terms, the English have kept some part of themselves aloof from Britain. The Scots have been rightly mocked for reinventing themselves as a put-upon, exploited people, and conveniently forgetting their role in empire. But many of today's English feel the same. The empire never belonged to them anyway. Nor, yet, does 'Europe'.

To achieve the benign patriotism of the best of England's self-image, a tolerant and ironic nation, it will be necessary to have an England which feels basically happy about its own place in the world and its political identity. England will never, as Ditchfield and many others have suggested, vanish or be abolished, however many housing estates and super-markets mushroom on farmland. In potential, it is a hugely powerful place. This is the same country which has 85 per cent of the UK's votes, most of the MPs and ministers, and wields, through Britain, considerable power both inside the EU and in world bodies such as the United Nations Security Council. England is heavily urbanised and composed of many different communities, is international and outward-looking in business and culture. England is perhaps more open than any other in Europe to new ideas and new influences.

There is, in short, a huge mismatch between the real activities and lifestyles of the English and the way that influential groups of the English see themselves as put-upon and besieged. But as the sudden eruption of nationalism shows when the French ban English beef, or the Scots challenge British laws, the politics of grievance can be ignited very easily. The themes of this chapter – English nostalgia, English eloquence, English rural passion, English rebelliousness and England's darker self – are all clues to the kind of England that may emerge if Britain dissolves. Unfairness is the fuse. And unfairness is a constitutional, democratic question. Who gets to come and live here and on what basis? On competing rights, on taxes, who decides? And who gives them the right to decide? On planning and the countryside, juggling between the need for new, decent housing and the cause of protecting green land, who makes the call? Can the shire or borough dictate, or is to be a regional government, which might seem as far from the needs of village or suburb as Westminster? These are questions for the English. They are practical political questions, and the answers we give will set the temper of England in the decades ahead.

5

The New British
and the World

It is time to leave the 'heart of England' and travel instead to
its dynamic edge, the area of Britishness which most touches
the world. It has become one of the dullest commonplaces
that we belong to a global economy. Globalisation can be
overstated. Much of what we actually consume and work
with comes from close to hand. Even so, by almost any measure we can think of, the volume of real and virtual trade
around the world is growing at a staggering rate, and Britain
is intensely, inextricably involved. We come fourth in the
league table of the world's biggest traders, behind the US,
Japan and Germany, with 6.6 per cent of the total of world
exports. When it comes to invisible trade, we are third, ahead
of Germany, with 9.7 per cent.[1] The British industries and
utilities bought by foreign-managed firms, most famously
the car companies, are a well-understood part of the story.
Less well-known is the massive growth in the overseas assets
of the British, a portfolio which has swollen even faster than
foreign investments here. Foreign investment in the UK has
grown from a little over £10 billion in 1979 to £415 billion
in 1997, but UK investments overseas in the same period

have grown from £12.6 billion to £574 billion, giving a net asset growth from £2.2 billion then to about £160 billion now.[2] These are mere figures but they represent an inter-twining of economies with profound cultural and political consequences. They are the solid residue of all the investment and trade in 'invisibles' that carries on in the City, the prime symbol and engine of British internationalism as well as the result of British companies buying directly into other economies.

This globalism infects a wide range of policies – the deadly moral dances in Whitehall over arms sales and inter-national mergers; competition policy; the arm-wrestling inside the EU over deregulation of German banks and French nationalised industries; wage bargaining, the limits of taxation, monetary policy, the curriculum in schools.

Global power is inside the products that are inside our houses and inside the computer-web that is now inside our heads. It is made flesh in our manufactured goods. As one observer put it, of the slinky new Ford Ka, it

> is manufactured in Spain by an American
> corporation using components sourced from
> Basildon, Belfast, Bridgend, Dagenham, Enfield,
> Halewood, Leamington, Treforest, Berlin,
> Cologne, Saarlouis, Wulfrath, Genk, Bordeaux and
> Valencia. It was designed in Essex and Cologne by
> a team of individuals sourced from more than
> twenty different countries.[3]

There is the same eclectic mix of people from round the world in the management consultancy offices of McKinseys in London, in the big banks, in the major industrial groups (though less so) – and, of course, on the streets of the larger cities of the UK.

It is a great error to think that global markets must mean the end of the nation-state, or democracy; in fact, they demand more effective political power, to protect the social foundations without which markets cannot work – the education systems, the infrastructure, the law-abidingness, the sense of community. But it is as great an error to assume they do not have a major effect on how democracies function and at what level. This chapter is about the internationalism of Britain, the people, technologies and policies that have an abnormally important impact on the country's future.

The City is the obvious place to start, with its mind-numbingly boring streets and its mind-dazzling statistics. Its square mile-plus of glass-plate offices, marble reception areas, taxi-crammed streets, winebars and pubs, carved from the flattened ruins of the post-Blitz city, is the home to no fewer than 555 foreign banks, more than any other city in the world. Of the 300,000 City workers who struggle in each morning by tube, bus, car and bicycle, more than 40 per cent work for foreign companies and many of the dealers, managers and lawyers themselves are American, German, Japanese and French. The London foreign exchange market is the largest in the world, with a daily turnover of $637 billion, a third of the world's total and more than twice as much as New York. London is the world's largest financial management centre, too, with $2.2 trillion under management. The London Stock Exchange is the world's largest centre for trading foreign equities, taking 63 per cent of the business in 1998. More foreign companies are quoted there than in any other stock exchange. And so on ... It is a staggering achievement.

The reasons for it are deeply rooted in the colonial history of the country, from the merchant banking of the early British empire, to the development of the joint-stock company ahead of rival nations, the subordination of money-raising monarchs after the creation of the Bank of England and the new forms of money-raising forced upon London by wars and overseas expansion. It is partly the creation of the United States, in that the dominance of America made English the world business language. It is partly a matter of chance. But in recent times, it can also be credited to a series of far-sighted gambles that pitched British finance early and hard into the new global market.

As moments of destiny for the modern British story, alongside the Maastricht Treaty and the formation of NATO, two financial decisions stand out. The first was Geoffrey Howe's, announced to the Commons on 23 October 1979, to abolish the system of exchange control on sterling which had been erected as a temporary wartime measure in 1939 and had stayed. It shocked the political world. It caused the immediate redundancy of an entire department of the Bank of England of 750 people. Later, Sir Geoffrey described it as 'one of the most important achievements of my chancellorship, and certainly the most fraught with worry ... It still stands as the only economic decision of my life that caused me to lose a night's sleep.' In the event, the timing was right, since the pound was buoyant and outflow of capital was relatively modest and it set the stage for the success of today's City – and the overseas asset figures quoted at the head of this chapter. Its success can be seen from the fact that apart from Howe himself, both Nigel Lawson ('I persuaded him – somewhat nervously – to agree') and Margaret Thatcher ('I took greatest personal pleasure ... "Steady on!" I was told') take credit for the decision in their memoirs.

The second moment came seven years later, in October 1986 when the London Stock Exchange abandoned its restrictive monopoly on securities trading, causing a massive reshaping of the City – the so-called 'Big Bang'. This in turn produced an almost hysterical period of poach and counter-poach as firms bought up individuals and then whole teams of brokers, investment analysts and jobbers. A sense of the gold-rush tang in the London air, which created some 500 millionaires in a very short space of time, is given in one account. It brought about, says Dominic Hobson, a permanent alteration in the manners and morals of remuneration in the City of London:

> This extraordinary upheaval ... was preceded by a scramble for talent. Foreign and domestic banks bid against each other ... A huge weight of capital was brought to bear on a limited number of people as the member firms of the London Stock Exchange were bought by foreign and domestic banks. The total outlay, of roughly £1.5 billion, put a price of exactly £1 million a head on the 1,500 people who happened to be partners at the time. In the race to purchase talent, people doubled and trebled their salaries as they hopped from firm to firm ... During this period Golden Hellos and Handcuffs were invented to prise people away from firms or persuade to stay ... It was a good time to be a partner in a stockbroking or jobbing firm. Decades of goodwill were sold by a single generation, at prices driven by a timetable nobody could halt.[4]

This has carried on, with the Western stock market boom, and despite mergers and closures and the Far Eastern meltdown of 1998, ever since. The effects ripple outwards, on luxury goods prices, the car market, the modern art scene and property. My London suburb, whose residents comprise a wide range of middle-class and working-class people, running everything from small shops to local Internet businesses, has seen the best houses rocketing in value by more than a quarter in a year. One local accountant tells me there are plenty of anonymous-looking chaps, not in top jobs, taking home more than a million in a 'not very exciting' year. The City draws in more and more people whose livelihoods depend, often very indirectly, on the honeypot of high finance, putting further pressure on housing and the entire south-east.

The effect of all this on the democracy that supports and sustains it is hard to measure. There are the obvious political impulses from a high-earning City, on which so many jobs and so much personal wealth depends, when it comes to finance-related decisions. A proposed EU 'withholding tax' which would have damaged City business was fiercely resisted by the new Labour government, alongside a ferocious press campaign, which suggests that a vital national interest was at stake, and that investment was to modern Britain what wine was to France. The City is not unanimous on the question of whether or not Britain should enter the euro, but if it sees the beginning of a flight of capital to Frankfurt, the pressure on Westminster's 'local' politicians to persuade the rest of the country to go in will be immense.

More generally, though, a hyperactive and high-earning dynamo like the City, however welcome, is unsettling for the rest of the country. It exaggerates regional differences, it injects a plaintive note into any discussion about money in the ordinary economy and it increases the hold that London has over the rest of the UK. Most economic migrants to Britain are white, male, American or European, and are coming here 'on business'. They are rarely stopped by Customs officers. Their Mercedes are not often pulled over to the side of the road so police officers on motorbikes can ask: 'This your car, is it sir?' All these things may be a price worth paying for the wealth that the City brings, but they have not made Britain, as a whole, either happier or more tightly bound together in social solidarity. In terms of Britishness the City has loosened, not unified. And in that it is a good example of globalisation at work.

But it is not the only one, nor the newest. Not all American money sloshing into Britain is coming through the City. The Internet, rapidly becoming the developed world's prime communications and information system, and shortly to begin to fuse with digital television and mobile telephony, provides another way of analysing Britishness. We are nowhere near the American experience, an e-commerce-driven economic revolution which many observers think helped keep the US economy growing during the final Clinton years. No one can match the US in the number of Internet connections, the optimism of its capital markets and the ingenuity of its first-generation cyberspace pioneers. Nevertheless, as an open, risk-taking, English-speaking economy, Britain has been perfectly placed for the second wave of Internet development.

The Net owes its origins to many sources, from the US military computer network between universities, to a cluster of scientific geniuses working at Massachusetts Institute of Technology. But the acknowledged father of the World Wide Web is an Englishman, Tim Berners-Lee, a man as modest as Geoffrey Howe himself, who works at the European Centre for Nuclear Research (CERN) in Switzerland and who wrote the programs for a 'web' of interconnected links to enable CERN scientists to keep track of the huge amount of information and argument swilling around that huge, publicly funded body. Essentially, what Berners-Lee did was to turn the Internet from a community of egalitarian technicians into a tool for everyone to use, with the system of browsers and servers that we know today. He did it in just over a year, and the Web finally went public on 15 January

1991 – a day which, with the signing of the various world trade deals, the fall of the Berlin Wall and financial deregulation, will go down as one of the defining dates in the history of the contemporary world.

As in the City, London attracted an array of foreigners to work alongside the home-grown entrepreneurs. Self-regarding, painfully young and over-serious, the Net community is nevertheless a significant and energetic addition to New Britain. A survey of some of the young e-millionaires in London, carried out for the *Guardian*, listed, among others, Eva Pascoe, the Polish director of the home-shopping business Zoom; Abb Hardoun, educated at George Washington University, of 'Magic Moments'; Ernst Malmstem and Katja Leander of Boo.com, who had met in Sweden; the American, Valparaiso-educated Julie Meyer, who set up the e-people's networking group First Tuesday. Then there was Ziad Salem of Beirut and Future Internet Technology; Serena Doshi of Liv4now.com. There is the South African, Brent Hoberman, running an online ticketing company, and the American Don Hersov, of Sportal. Ernesto Schmitt of peoplesound.com is half-German and half-Uruguyan. And on it goes. Apart from the well-known British players and investors, there were already a clutch of big American firms looking for start-up businesses in London. Circling it all were global tycoons such as Rupert Murdoch, with e-ventures, and the Frenchman Bernard Arnault, who runs Louis Vuitton.

It may sound an entirely irrelevant little metropolitan bubble. Not so. These businesses, or some of them, will touch all our lives within the next few years. A fifth of the British are connected to the Net, either at home or at work, and 70 per cent of students are. The multinational clutch of people in London trying to build and dominate the next stage of electronic commerce are today's version of earlier waves of entrepreneurs and business-people, the latest generation of Bonaparte's dismissive '*une nation de boutiquiers*'. As with the City, Britain has a kind of national beachhead, rammed hard into a new world market; London happens to be the place where a large number of e-commerce hopefuls, from across the continent and from the US, want to meet and do business. Language, availability of capital and trustworthy, but not excessively heavy, company laws are all reasons for this. The Net is bringing people, money and profits (so they say!) into Britain; they are coming here as a little, alternative America.

What might the Net mean for our sense of national identity and the power of national governments? This is too big a world event for anyone to lay down the law so early in its history, except to say that it is likely to flatten old hierarchies, link groups of people who could never speak before, and may make many of the basic weapons of the nation-state, such as censorship, reliable taxation of consumers and the restriction of official information, almost impossible to maintain. The Net allows easy transfer of information out of societies which are naturally open, above all the US, into the American societies which traditionally made a fetish of state secrecy, including Britain. It is possible to quickly compare what governments and large corporations are saying in one place, and what they are telling other audiences. Commodities of all kinds, from music and film, to tickets, drugs rationed by the state, property and investments can be bought and sold electronically, in some cases easily bypassing national value-added or purchase tax regimes. If Amazon, the online bookshop, decides to sell Hitler's *Mein Kampf*, contrary to German law, there is nothing Germany can do about it. Holocaust-deniers, black separatists, extreme anarchists and oddballs of all kinds can find a home on the Net more easily than they can find a physical base in most countries. Bomb-making, fascism, child pornography ... however many blocks are put up by individual governments and legal systems, there will always be more groups ready to supply a demand. If they are not based in the US, they will be based in South America. If not there, Eastern Europe or Africa. International banking arrangements, the ease of hiding financial flows and the openness of the Web on all sides makes censorship all but impossible. We have the whole world in front of us now, the nasty bits as well as the rest.

One of the earliest adventurers in the new world is a former Soho advertising copy-writer, highly successful, who has semi-retired to a rambling house near East Grinstead in Sussex. Indra Sinha, a large, gentle-looking man, has been longer and deeper into this world than most people and has become a kind of guru on these matters. His book, *Cyber-gypsies* (Scribner, 1999) describes how he stumbled across the Net in 1984, when most people had never heard of a modem and long before the Berners-Lee Web, and then plunged head-first into a strange world of electronic role-playing and political activism, which nearly cost him his marriage. Sinha's home is surrounded by thick, almost primeval, woods and is lush with fruit trees and foliage; he spoke to me in what he described as his 'magic circle' of herbs in the middle of a lawn whose view stretched for miles. Sinha's style can be glimpsed from his romantic description of his own early engagement in cyberspace:

> The night is full of invisible pathways, criss-crossing the globe, bounced off the stratosphere by orbiting comsats. They're thronged by clouds of insubstantial travellers, the restless folk who ceaselessly wander the electronic pathway ...
> They are the computer gypsies, as ragtag a crew as ever roamed the 'real' world we can taste and touch.

For him this is a glorious adventure of the mind, a great human advance that challenges everything from our idea of narrative in ordinary novels (in cyberspace, you can take part in stories, and change them, through complex role-playing games) to the political structures around us. He told me:

> I wonder sometimes whether the American
> government, had it realised how the Net would
> grow and what it would make possible, would
> ever indeed have supported it and helped it;
> because when ordinary people make contact with
> other ordinary people in other parts of the world,
> they do transcend their nationalities, respond to
> each other as human beings first and foremost.

He himself had become heavily involved in campaigning for Kurds and for the victims of the Bophal chemical factory disaster in India. 'The way I'd like to put it is that it's deeply subversive of all kinds of tyranny, whether of the media moguls, the corporations, or governments.' He could raise money, pass on information, subvert attempts to hide the truth. It was a world-wide shift of political power:

> If people are campaigning for corporations to be
> held more accountable, and for them no longer to
> be able to evade responsibility for their actions by
> hiding behind national boundaries then the Net
> becomes a very important tool for that ...When I
> hear governments talking about sovereignty, it
> always strikes me as faintly ludicrous, when one
> considers that just about everything from their
> agricultural policy to their foreign policy is
> dictated by the needs of huge corporations.

As more people come onto the Net and begin to voice their view on GM crops and other issues, 'it'll be a challenge to the way politicians conduct themselves and their politics. I think that if we have leaders in Westminster who want to listen to what people actually want for a change, then the Net is going to help them.' But it would also radically free up information, ending the idea of the state as a repository of wisdom forever:

> pronouncements from on high must be dead,
> really … when so much information is available
> to so many people freely, it becomes impossible to
> tell lies, really. Politicians have worked through
> traditional media – they will use a particular
> newspaper or television programme or whatever
> to air their views. But of course, when people can
> get the information directly from the Net, all
> those things are completely subverted. It has, of
> course, immense implications for the media
> industry as well.

But, Sinha insisted, this did not mean that politics or nations would simply become redundant, as some Net-theorists have suggested:

> Given that we live in a real world with grass and
> trees and houses and roads, we are never going to
> be other than in the place where we live. That
> place will always have to be administered and it's
> administered in nation-states at the moment –
> though Europe is becoming so regionalised we
> see already that the idea of the nation-state is
> coming under question at the moment.

Despite the overarching power of the City, and the growing popularity of the Web, the globalising of Britain is more
obvious through what might be called the populist businesses. Take football, for instance, which not only is a major
business – its publicly quoted British clubs have a total value
of over £1.74 billion, while the English Premier League
enjoyed a turnover in 1998 of £433 million – but also has
been a key part of male identity, both local and national. The
international character of football, the huge business it does,
both for itself and television companies, and the emotional
impact it can swing, have combined to make it one of the
most interesting arenas where questions of identity, as well as
mere games, are played out.

In the winter of 1999, for instance, with Scotland and
England drawn against one another in the European Cham-
pionship play-offs, there was much debate in the Scottish
press about the team for this most resonant of fixtures. Craig
Brown, the Scotland coach, made an approach to a 23-year-
old striker from Ipswich Town, David Johnson, the leading
scorer in the English first division, with 48 goals in 100
appearances to his credit. There is nothing surprising about
that; as footballers travel more widely from club to club,
national sides are almost always composed of club players
from all over. Except this time, it was a little different. David
Johnson is Jamaican. He has both a Jamaican and a British
passport, but his connections with Scotland are nil – not even
a Scottish granny. He had played for the England 'B' side
against Russia and was picked by Wales too. But none of this
inhibited Brown from approaching Johnson and suggesting
he think about signing up for Scotland. The footballer, meanwhile, was keeping his cards close to his chest – he had 'the
whims of a dancing bear' when it came to his football
nationality, one friend said. In the end, the deal was never
made. But what, you might ask, could be more of a blow to

Scottish patriotic pride than having to beg Jamaicans playing for English clubs to nip up and give them a hand? The answer, of course, is obvious: being beaten by England. Which did, sadly, happen. Winning is what counts, and Craig Brown was only making the kind of hard-headed assessment that happens daily in any other business. There followed some nasty racist stuff in the Scottish press, but most fans seemed in no doubt; what mattered was getting the best team.

Whether it is about management skills, capital, technology or branding, patriotism today takes second place to quality. Football is different from other businesses only in that it relies unusually heavily on the raw talents of young men from a wider range of countries than you would find in, say, banking. A quick selection from a recent alphabetical list of top players with English clubs shows the result. Under 'A' there are 18 players listed, and half are from overseas – Samassi Abou, West Ham's man from the Ivory Coast, via Cannes; Manuel Agogo (Sheffield Wednesday, Ghana); Philippe Albert (Newcastle United, Belgium); Niclas Alexandersson (Sheffield, Sweden); Bernard Allou (Notts Forest, France); John Aloisi (Coventry City, Australia); Andreas Andersson (Newcastle, Sweden); Nicolas Anelka (Arsenal, France); Pagguy Arphexad (Leicester City, France). The list continues down the alphabet in the same way, painting a true picture of English club football as a sport full of stars from continental Europe and further afield, where the big names and heroes are as often Italian or German as British. Chelsea, managed by Gianluca Vialli, had its players rated by performance and all-round ability. The top four were: Frank Leboeuf, Gianfranco Zola, Roberto Di Matteo and Tore Andre Flo. In some key games, there is hardly an English player on the pitch. It does not seem to matter to Chelsea fans, nor most of the fans of the scores of other clubs heavily dominated by bought-in talent; racist chants abound, but are generally directed at the other side. As with Craig Brown in Scotland, winning matters more than the national composition of the team. It is the same for the Rover Group, the management accountants, and other international businesses.

In art, too, Britain is part of a fast-moving international market, in which overseas players mingle with native-born players in ways which bemuse traditionalists. The 1999 Turner Prize show, like many before it, produced excellent news stories in a swirl of hype and mutual exploitation. Tracey Emin, an artist who describes herself as 'Mad Tracey from Margate', had been shortlisted for a rumpled, stained, unmade bed, surrounded by tampons, condoms, a Vodka bottle and so on. Then two half-naked Chinese artists, Jian Jun Xi and Yuan Cai, leapt onto the bed and jumped all over it, threatening to indulge in 'critical sex' before they were arrested and led away. (Another, more anonymous and heroic woman from Swansea arrived and tried to tidy the bed up because she thought it her 'duty' to 'keep things nice'.)

At the exhibition of the Turner-nominated artists, you can see huge numbers of foreign visitors from the US, Europe and Asia; silly it all may be, and certainly a long way from careful watercolours of Swiss mountains, but these art-jokes are an international success, part of the lure of contemporary London.

How does this odd new art world work? It begins in the art colleges, London's contemporary schools for scandal. Among the most influential teachers is a sharp, clever artist called Michael Craig-Martin, a professor at Goldsmiths College, London. He was born in Dublin and raised and educated in the United States. Among the people who went through his hands are Cathy de Monchaux, Julian Opie, Anya Gallaccio, and Hong Kong-born Fiona Rae. The greatest collector by far of the 'Brit-Art' movement they belong to is the Iraqi-born Charles Saatchi, described as being to late-twentieth-century London 'what Cosimo de Medici was to quattrocento Florence'.[5] Among the other figures swirling round this world are the sculptor Anish Kapoor, Susan Hillier of Nevada, Paula Rego, the great Portuguese painter, Willie Doherty of Derry, Jake and Dinos Chapman, who in turn used to work for Gilbert and George, themselves half-Italian, Chris Ofili of Manchester, and curators and dealers with names like Klassnik, Logsdail, D'Offay, Schubert, Fleissig, Franck and Starkmann. Around them are a circle of cut-glass English dealers and artists, from the cabinet minister's son Jay Jopling to curators who sound as if they are reincarnations of Quentin Crisp.

'Brit-art' is undefinable: it is a catch-all name for a huge variety of artists working in every medium from videotape to body fluids, pottery to texts. At its heart there is a strong group of mainly London-born artists whose trademark is a cocky, jokey, commercially savvy brand of lateral thinking. Questioners, icon-smashers and sometimes phoneys, they bear a similar relation to traditional fine painting as the punk rockers of the late 1970s bore to nineteenth-century string quartets; they behave and promote themselves accordingly. They have been fabulously successful and they have greatly brightened life in the English south. Yet like the Internet start-up boom, or successful Premier League football, the 'Brit-art' movement would not have been possible without the rich, complicated irrigation of different nationalities and cultures into the UK. It is at least partly, as the names above make clear, a branch of world art, which looks to Europe and the United States as much as to traditional English art history. Its leading figures form one of a large number of free-wheeling, unclassifiable new British tribes who have given the country at the turn of the millennium its strange, sharp flavour.

But there is a more serious, more familiar aspect to globalism which also needs to be pondered and which has been, so far, a less optimistic story. The Britain of the immediate post-war years was profoundly racist. This was an inevitable inheritance of the empire, and also because racism had been a normal part of the furniture of every Western country. 'Racist' is a word that applies to the treatment of white non-English groups too, particularly the Irish and Jews. Irish migrants had arrived in large numbers during the industrial revolution and, as we have seen, came carrying a great cloud of anti-Catholic and anti-Gaelic prejudice against them. Even such observers as Marx's collaborator on the *Communist Manifesto*, Friedrich Engels, showed himself profoundly anti-Irish, describing them as

> people who have grown up almost without civilisation ... rough, intemperate and improvident, bringing all their brutal habits with them ... Whenever a district is distinguished for especial filth and ruinousness, the explorer may count upon meeting chiefly those Celtic faces which one recognises at the first glace as different from the Saxon physiognomy of the native.

Anti-Jewish sentiment too was deeply embedded in English and Scottish thinking, reflected in a huge amount of casual reference in writing and politics. Edward I had expelled England's Jews in the 1290s, a few years before Philip the Fair expelled them from France, and they were not readmitted to England until the 1650s by Cromwell. A century after that, however, Britain became one of the first countries to give its Jews, by then numbering around 30,000, full civil and legal rights, except for the right to sit in Parliament, which followed after battles by a member of the

Rothschild banking family in the 1850s. Yet as late as the 1930s, anti-Semitic thinking was very powerful in Britain. It could be found in popular novels by people such as 'Sapper'; in the writings of the modernist trio, Wyndham Lewis, T.S. Eliot and Ezra Pound; and in the actions, or inactions, of the Foreign Office when the first evidence of the Nazi extermination plan began to leak into London. Indeed the Foreign Office has always been profoundly 'Arabist' and suspicious of Zionism throughout the post-war period – ambiguous, compared to America, about the founding of Israel.

In every case of racism there were exceptional fighters and campaigners on the other side. The long battle against slavery in the British Empire, led by the Christian evangelist William Wilberforce and the Quaker Thomas Clarkson, began publicly with the formation of the Anti-Slavery Society in 1787 and culminated in an Act abolishing the trade in British possessions which came into effect in 1808, followed by British naval support for the 'free town' in Sierra Leone. Anti-Irish racism was partly countered by the movement for Catholic Emancipation in the early part of the nineteenth century and the growing support for Irish Home Rule among British Liberals under Gladstone in its later decades. The basic assumptions of anti-Semitism were challenged not only by the arrival of Benjamin Disraeli, who had been converted to Christianity by his father, as the leader of the Conservative Party, Prime Minister and chief architect of British imperial pomp, but also by the writings of some powerful literary figures, such as George Eliot. These names are worth honouring because a mood of simple-minded self-chastisement is unhistorical and forgets that England has had a strong liberal, nonconformist and radical tradition of human equality for centuries before political correctness was dreamed up on North American campuses.

Attitudes to racism in the modern world were formed by

two closely related events. The first was Hitler's 'Final Solution', which meant that the casual racist attitudes, particularly towards Jews, became steadily less respectable across the West afterwards. The second was the fact that, in prosecuting that war, Britain had virtually bankrupted itself and emerged in the 1950s with her empire visibly falling away, India and Pakistan free, and a desperate shortage of workers at home. We all live in the moral shadow of the years from 1933, when Hitler came to power, to 1948, when on 22 June, a crammed old troopship, the *Empire Windrush*, arrived at Tilbury Docks on the Thames with what the press called 'the 400 Sons of Empire' – Jamaican men looking for work in Britain.

It is rightly seen as a turning point in modern British history, though at the time government departments were confused and worried. The Labour Colonial Secretary, Creech Jones, put the legal position clearly when he said that they had British passports and must be allowed to land, before adding, 'There's nothing to worry about because they won't last one winter in England.' Though there are complex questions of labelling and self-definition involved, from the first few thousands arriving in austerity Britain, there are now more than 1 million Black British. With Asian and Chinese Britons, the 'visible minorities' make up nearly 6 per cent of the population of England and, across the whole UK, account for some 3 million people.

The official view of all this veered between the complacent and the hostile. During the last of Winston Churchill's administrations, in 1953, the Home Office working party which was seeking ways to keep 'coloureds' out produced a nakedly racist report, asserting that black men were physically unsuited for hard work and potentially violent, black women were 'said to be slow mentally and the speed of work in modern factories is quite beyond them' while Indians were 'mainly hardworking though unscrupulous'.[6] Searching for ways of keeping out coloured migrants while, in the words of the official report, 'avoiding the appearance of doing so' led to the first Commonwealth Immigration Act in 1962 and the growth of a large apparatus of controls intended to keep Britain white.

The history of each migrant group is different. The Pakistani migration, for instance, took off during the early 1960s, heading for the textile mills around the Pennines, and was based on employment vouchers; when they stopped in 1965, direct Pakistani immigration fell sharply too. Pakistani traditions of marrying among cousin groups mean, however, that they are far likelier to return to Pakistan to seek spouses and therefore to marry overseas partners. Bangladeshis, with a different tradition of marriage, are more likely to look for partners in Britain but, with large numbers of young children, are likely to double as a community before stabilising. The Indian population began arriving in the late 1950s and their fertility rate is now little more than the indigenous whites. In fact, the Indian population, like the British Chinese population, may actually be falling, partly because of out-migration to other countries, notably the United States and Canada, by highly qualified professionals who feel they are excluded by racism in Britain.[7]

To generalise wildly, there have been three phases of modern immigration to Britain. The first was the post-war phase, described above and curtailed in the 1960s, though with a 'tail' of marriages and family members arriving long after that. Rights of entry were progressively stripped away, though not for people with UK-born grandparents – the overseas whites of the Commonwealth. The second phase came with the expulsion of East African Asians from Uganda in the 1970s. They make up a heavy proportion of the highly successful South Asians of modern Britain, who, as Bhikhu Parekh, professor of political theory at Hull, has put it,

represent just under 3 per cent of the population
[but] provide about 16 per cent of the total
number of GPs, nearly 20 per cent of hospital
doctors, and about 12 per cent of pharmacists.
They own just over 50 per cent of the 'cash and
carry' shops and just over 55 per cent of the
independent retail trade ... they comprise 300 out
of Britain's 18,000 millionaires and the top
hundred of them are estimated to be worth
£5 billion.[8]

If those two first phases were caused by the end of empire
and its consequences, the third phase, the current one, was
caused by the end of the Soviet Union and the movement of
peoples around the world following the end of the Cold War
as old 'client states' engaged in civil war and cheap air travel
made getting away easier. Vietnamese boat people, Eritreans,
Somalis, Tamils and Kurds were followed by refugees from
the Balkan conflicts and from Eastern Europe, whose countries could no longer keep their people in. Many were fleeing poverty rather than persecution and 300,000
asylum-seekers arrived in Germany in a single year. In
Britain, groups as diverse as Albanians from Kosovo and then
Roma, or gypsies, from Central Europe, have been claiming
asylum. There have been violent clashes in Dover and the
immigration service has entirely failed to cope with the
backlog of cases needing investigation – as I write, the
number is close to 100,000. The free movement of people
inside the EU not only allows would-be migrants to pass
more easily from continental countries to Britain, but also
encourages moves to create a higher wall around the EU as a
whole, the so-called 'Fortress Europe'.

These flows of people into (and sometimes out of) Britain
make for some hard questions about what kind of country

we are, and want to be. The raw numbers of 'visible minority' people in Britain are not enormous. Some communities, such as the Chinese and Jews, are falling in numbers. There is a significant, but not yet quantified, trend among some Black British to return to the Caribbean. And in some ways, of course, Britain has always been multi-ethnic. One observer I spoke to pointed out that for him 'Anglo-Saxon' contained the hyphen which refuted the myth of English purity right from the start. Since then, influxes from France, the Netherlands, Scandinavia, Germany, Russia, Spain – the Basques who settled in Wales – and Italy, quite apart from the Chinese and Black or 'Lascar' groups in English ports, have made Britain more complex than outsiders usually realise. But there is no doubt that the scale and visibility of post-war migration has had a greater and more dramatic effect than any previous movements, including the large French-Protestant one; it is simply bigger and more obvious. Its importance, however, is about more than size or colour.

We live in a densely interwoven world market in which non-white people from Britain are making an impact which is disproportionate to their numbers. Add to that the greater numbers of Asian and Black British there will be in the population over the next 25 years. In the context of lower and lower levels of reproduction among white groups, they will provide Britain with much of the labour force for the next generation that would otherwise simply not be there. Add to that the fact that Black, Chinese and Asians are heavily grouped in London and a few other metropolitan centres, whose influence over the whole country is notoriously disproportionate, and you have a picture of non-white communities who are bound to matter more in modern Britain than even their considerable numbers would suggest.

I am not suggesting that incoming groups are already some kind of super-class, more important to the economy than white people. There are groups of new British doing well and others doing spectacularly badly: Bangladeshis are lower than any other group by measurements of educational disadvantage and social exclusion; the Irish-born are near the bottom of the economic heap; some 38 per cent of African-Caribbean young people are unemployed, compared to 12 per cent of young white people. A melting pot, or a 'community of communities', does not mean that the main ingredient, the soup in which the rest swim, has suddenly evaporated. But migration and a sense of the wider world, plus a cultural background which means you naturally speak two or more languages, has to be a help for people trying to make their living in a global economy – and therefore for the country in which they live. It is very striking that at my son's school so many of the prize-winning boys are Asians. Their families push them harder than white parents push their children and it shows. If these islands are going to thrive in the twenty-first century, it will be partly as a result of attracting and keeping the best and most motivated people around, and by strengthening, not weakening, our reach into new markets such as India and China. So, for much the same reason as Britain has benefited from its American links, it can benefit from its new, unintended status as an island of many communities.

But this poses political questions: how do we balance the demands of Islam, so vivid during the Salman Rushdie *fatwa* affair, with the rights of secular people to criticise religion? How do we make sure more of the best people in the Asian and Chinese communities stay, rather than going to the US or (as many of the richest, most driven Hong Kong Chinese did) to Australia and Canada? All experience suggests that, over time, today's new British will slowly mingle with the old British, but the rate of intermarriage is still tiny; for the foreseeable future, we are talking about different communities with different instincts. How do we acknowledge them, while maintaining a culture of individual rights and of free speech? How many of the new refugees, economic or political, should we take? Would it be fairer and better for the UK to operate an open, above-board quota system, which assessed how many people from different backgrounds we could find space and education for, and let in a certain number each year? But if so, how can that be reconciled with our duties under asylum agreements? Most seriously of all, how would the breakup of the British union affect the groups of New British still putting down roots here?

'Britain' has, after all, offered a relatively loose national identity, a commodious overcoat beneath which all sorts of minority groups can be themselves. In a state which includes Scots and Welsh, Jews and Irish as minority communities, it is easier to be 'just another community'. Yasmin Alibhai-Brown, a writer and journalist, puts it forcibly:

> Even though I've been here 27 years, and it would
> be fair to say that I don't feel quite at home, in
> the last three or four years I was finally beginning
> to feel that this thing called Britishness meant
> something to me … I started saying 'we' when I
> meant the British, instead of 'you' when I meant
> the British.

It had taken a long time to have a feeling of ownership and belonging

> and it does feel enormously frightening, almost a
> kind of huge betrayal, that just when we started
> feeling comfortable by calling ourselves British,
> and feeling that this was a nation we were going
> to change and make our own for the next

century, along comes devolution and little bits of
it are grabbed away from us and really quite
frightening original ethnic identities begin to be
spoken about.

To talk about Britain as a country of four nations 'immediately excludes all of us, because those four nations have a particular history, a particular ethnicity, which really doesn't
include us.' Alibhai-Brown pointed out that the Scottish Parliament and the Welsh Assembly were all-white. 'Well, what
does that mean? That means that all the fears I was expressing
before devolution actually took place are absolutely borne
out; that this has become an issue of ethnicity, of an ancestral
connection to a Scottishness which we can never buy into.'

    Most Scottish politicians would protest, indeed splutter
with protest, at this. Scottish Home Rule was heralded at one
giant demonstration in Edinburgh, as the creed of the 'bas-
tard people of a mongrel nation' who felt themselves to be
more conscious of equality and fairness than the English
south. But Alibhai-Brown's fears are widely shared, including
by many Asians living in Scotland. More widely, south of the
border, there is a feeling among many blacks and Asians that,
as she also said, 'I don't feel myself to be English, I never will.'
Britishness may be on its sickbed but that leaves the large
number of Asians and Afro-Caribbeans in England with a
problem. Do they change the hyphen from Chinese-British
or Black-British, to Chinese-English or Black-English; and
in doing so, does the hyphen turn into a non-sequitor?

    A good place to ask about where the end of Britain might
leave the smaller communities is London's Brick Lane. It
stands at the heart of a warren of ancient streets which have
been irrigated, generation after generation, by different
waves of arrivals. The earliest buildings include houses and
churches put up by the French Protestant Huguenots, fleeing

Catholic persecution. After them have come Russian and Polish Jews, Bengalis, Somalis, Bangladeshis. As one group comes in, previous ones have tended to move on, leaving only a few inscriptions or bagel shops behind them. So the Huguenot church became a synagogue and the synagogue became a mosque. The latest invasion, caused by the swelling prosperity and space-shortage of the City, is likely to be of American and European Yuppies, looking for flats in converted eighteenth-century townhouses, themselves once used for sweatshops.

Within a few hundred yards, you can journey from the old East End, with jellied eel and whelk stalls, elderly men in 1950s-style suits, junk shops stacked with old shellac records and moist, moulded furniture, to the London of the 2000s, with coldly trendy clothes stores, cutting-edge new Asian restaurants, impossibly fashionable cafés and walls covered with Indian film posters. On busy days, the air is full of Bangladeshi, American, French and Asian voices. The massive old Truman Brewery, in the middle of Brick Lane, has been bought by an Iraqi who is turning it into a set of new media, film, PR, design and arts spaces, the cutting-edge businesses of modern London.

One shop-owner is Bashir Ahmed, who described himself as a 'street intellectual'. He was exhibiting an elaborate painted wooden sculpture loosely based on the Union Jack on the street. With its swirls of colour, it was articulating the idea that British culture was an amalgamation 'taken from all over the world, for hundreds of years, and the red, white and blue is now mixing, and it's not so clearly red, white and blue. It's about the multicultural landscape of Britain. It's the changing face of Britain.' So how would Bashir define himself, I asked. There was a long pause. 'I'm a British-African-Asian,' he said. And what about the idea that Britain was over? 'It's not over, it's just changing ... It's in transition. The whole world is changing and everything is being redefined. And it's just a process, and it's not 'Britain is over', it's just a new Britain.' How would he describe it? Bashir barely paused: 'For me, it's about a diversity of culture, it's about creative regeneration – encouraging people to look at themselves in different ways, encouraging them to participate, and get together and do things in ways that wasn't around before.'

A few hundred yards further west, I spoke to another Ahmed, Mukheem Ahmed, who is an older man, with the gloss of success on him. He has lived in Britain for 25 years, longer than he lived in Bangladeshi and says: 'I classify myself as a British Bangladeshi ... I would not go back to Bangladesh.' Mukheem is a highly successful businessman who owns, among other things, the Café Naz, which has a Conran style to it and specialises in new-wave Indian food. He began in the East End and talks knowledgeably about the Huguenot and Jewish influences, but moved his family out to Kent some years back. His children thought of themselves as British and 'we are not totally English, not totally Bangladeshis, you see; we are in between, in a new sort of nation, a new culture'. This could be seen in the new cooking, including the British invention of chicken tikka masala, and the new Bangla music of younger British-Bangladeshis. His ambition was to try to create 'Indian dishes to the standard of French cuisine' and he said he felt relaxed about being British or English, using the words more or less interchangeably. On the Norman Tebbit 'cricket test' he supported Bangladesh when they were playing, but increasingly supported England and was particularly enthusiastic as the English team fielded more Asians.

Behind the self-assurance, however, Mukheem had been close to the centre of racist reaction. He was in Brick Lane with his wife and 5-year-old daughter when the 1999 nail bomb attack happened. When the bomb went off,

> in that split second I thought the building
> collapsed on my wife because she fell, you see, the
> thrust of the bomb was so much ... I felt a big
> pressure ... I looked around towards the direction
> of the blast and I saw the boot of the car where
> the bomb was. It went up in the sky, at least
> 15–20 feet and a big cloud of black smoke came
> out of it, followed by a ball of fire. We were all
> terrified.

His daughter had nightmares and had to be kept off school,
but Mukheem said he, like the rest of the community, was
determined to show that 'we are not going to be beaten by
this; we tried everything to show to the bomber, look, we are
not frightened.' He had the restaurant open again in ten days.

Remarkably, he said the incident had made him feel more
secure and more British. The wider reaction

> really pleased me immensely. I received a lot of
> letters from a lot of customers and friends. We had
> the Home Secretary, Jack Straw here, and William
> Hague here as well ... you know, the British
> people are all united together, and we are also
> British, and it made us feel good. I felt personally
> that the British nation was supporting us – it was
> a good feeling.

Just as his cooking was being infused with European influences, so he personally was a different kind of person by
living here:

> in physics terms, if the iron is with the magnet, it
> gets some of the properties of the magnet, so
> obviously, when I've lived here, I have acquired a

lot of good things … you get infused by the
surroundings and it leaves prominent marks on
your personality.

The most emotional way he could put this was that, unlike
the earlier generation of Bangladeshis who came to Britain
and were sent home for burial, 'I would like to be buried in
England'.

Back down the road, where an Asian protest music band
was preparing to play, younger men had a rawer reaction, but
as he readied himself for anti-racist songs, 'Dr Dass' of the
Asian Dub Foundation was making a remarkably similar
point.

To me, Britain is not a white place, it is all these
different communities and has been for a long
time. And this is the consequence of Britain's
colonialism, all right? We say we're only here
because you were there. All these communities
come back to the so-called mother country and I
would say that's the only good outcome of
colonialism. I now have an opportunity to mix
with people and cultures thousands of miles
removed from where I might have been, which is
India.

For him, British was a legal term: 'Why do people have to be
squashed into one small box? I'm English as well, I think, and
speak English. I'm Bengali, West Bengali … Hindu by birth,
but I don't practise that any more … all these are parts of my
identity.' He found it difficult to relate to people who were
hung up on one single identity, adding mildly, 'the *Anglo-
Saxons* are immigrants to this country. They try to forget.'

The end of the empire has also been the start of a new

kind of country here, one with special advantages which can be salvaged and exploited. It has left us as an abnormally internationalist island, with a network of overseas links, the world's prime language and a rich mix of people. We are ourselves a WWW – a world-wide web. Most smaller communities will fit into England, or Scotland, if they have to. But their arguments for multiple identities, and not singular ethnic ones make sense. They apply to the rest of us, who can be Cornish-English-Europeans, or Jewish-Welsh, or York-shire-Chinese, not simply 'English' or 'Scottish'.

Through history, multiple or complex identity seems to give people more cultural richness and more 'go'. It is not simply Ugandan Asian refugees now on the list of Britain's millionaires: how many of the great minds, the world's creative business people and its best leaders were not of a simple uni-cultural extraction? Disraeli has already been mentioned, but any such list would also include Andrew Carnegie, Albert Einstein, Gandhi, the exile Joyce, Joseph Conrad, Picasso, De Valera, Churchill (half-American and recently claimed to have Cherokee blood), Handel, half the people who created the nuclear age, the Rothschilds, the Saatchi brothers … the list would go on for pages.

There are no rules about such things: they are too intimate, chance-touched and vague. But quite a few of the people who are going to shape our lives over the next 50 years are children today who do not speak English as their first tongue and are struggling in inner-city schools. There will be, somewhere out there, a Black Thatcher, an Albanian Mick Jagger and a Chinese David Hockney – and maybe, if we are very lucky, a Bangladeshi Bill Gates. This is a question of faith, but faith based on history. I would rather be a citizen of a mixed Britain than of a purely white one: an obsession with ethnic purity is not only bad in itself but also a sign of a retrograde country, turning its back on the outside world and settling for stagnation.

Some critics of modern Britain – such as the French educators whose textbooks present the UK as sunk in inevitable decline, class-bound and insular – simply do not see the opportunity the islands have in a more open world market with a more diverse population. Although the long list of denationalising influences described earlier does undermine the nation's old sense of itself, it is hardly a phenomenon which is unique to Britain. Whatever is going on here is going on through much of the rest of the world. If Britain, the nation-state, seems rather fragile, the same is true of most of the nation-states of the north and the west of the world. They are losing much of what bound them together. The strongest nation of all, the United States, is riddled with self-doubt and nostalgia. The rise of Spanish-speaking Americans is reshaping its political and cultural map; the earlier heroic myths of the Wild West and the frontier which shaped white Americans' sense of themselves have been replaced by revisionism and guilt. Most of its traditional industries are in decline, from steel to automobiles, and it is forced to use China as a giant offshore factory, producing everything from 'classic American' clothes and shoes, to its children's toys, books and electronics. Its traditional urban neighbourhoods have been taken over by drugs and eaten out by poverty. Its historic promise to make every citizen proud and part of the American dream has failed, certainly for most blacks. But at least the US has a strong, vigorous, 'can-do' culture which has produced the brilliant science and the business ideas behind the new industrial revolutions in electronics and the life sciences. The US has a vitality and power which every other country simply envies.

For the also-rans of the nationalisms of the past 300 years, life has been harder. The United States's northern neighbour, Canada, struggles to hold onto any sense of itself. Any fragile sense of an independent Canadian economy is already submerged by the North American Free Trade Agreement

(NAFTA); some observers believe that it will not be Quebec which goes next, but the Canadian dollar. In Europe, every significant nation has cooperated in a massive retreat from national independence, by joining the European Union. Countries like France, Italy and Germany, which entered the twentieth century intending to rule great world empires, have lost almost every inch of soil beyond their borders and have smudged those borders, most dramatically and recently with the euro. The EU is meant to counter the huge power of the United States. Yet even inside it, American and Asian influence is vast and growing all the time. The French economy is far less 'French' than it was even a few years ago – less state-interventionist, less of a 'fix' run by a highly educated, closed elite, more like the economies of Britain and America. Large tracts of France, for instance the pine-forested coasts of the south-west, with their trailer camps, car culture and pizza bars, or the light-industrial sprawl round most French cities, linked by highways and retail parks, could be American.

Ask what is French high culture today, in the sense of something living and important, and you are hard put to answer – except in the most obvious sense of language and food. Even here, basic French traditions are under heavy assault, through the rise of English and new European laws, for instance on hunting and the preparation of foods like cheese. France is a country with 800 branches of McDonald's, Disneyland Paris – and a profound conviction that it stands bravely alone against American culture. All this has had noticeable effects on the way French people regard their state, their nationalism. One respected French commentator made the subtle but important observation recently that 'French decorations such as the Légion d'honneur, may be sought after as much as in the past, but there is, at least in Paris, a tendency to wear them less, as if to demonstrate one's independence vis-à-vis the state.'[9]

Germany is a more obvious, dramatic example still, because it has had to reinvent itself after the disasters of 1914–45, becoming (thankfully) a blander, copy-cat country with a federal, almost anti-national, political system and a fervent belief in European Union. The German state is reasserting itself gingerly – the move back to Berlin, the new Reichstag, the growing insistence on more use of the German language in the councils of the EU, the first German service personnel in action in the Balkans. The same is true with Japan, now pushing its old Rising Sun flag and rebuilding its armed forces quite substantially, as the US leaves that area of the Pacific as a major military power. Perhaps there is a natural timescale to defeat, shame and reassertion. But no one today expects a revival of German nationalism or the German state as a powerful independent force in the world. Or, outside the poorest housing estates of former East Germany, wants it. Germany's way of life, economy and culture is heavily Americanised and becoming more so, not less.

Both France and Germany have some big international companies. But they do not influence the world much as independent nations any more. So much for Bismarck and Napoleon. Smaller nations have even less independence, most of them. The bundled-together world economy and the rise of a world culture threatens their very existence. In 50 years, will places like Canada, Denmark, Peru or Jamaica exist as independent nations, or will they have been drawn into regional blocs entirely? In a century's time, how many people will still speak Dutch or Irish? If Britain is going through a time of self-doubt, if we are questioning who we are and what we stand for, then we are in good company.

One way of looking at this is simply to applaud it. The military, expansionist and often racist Western nationalisms brought misery and danger to millions and badly distorted the development of many other parts of the world. Where there is still strong nationalism, in Asian nations, for instance, such as Indonesia or Thailand, it has not brought the people anything but danger. And there are, in the West, benefits in post-nationalism as well. There are the economic regions straddling old national borders which have a life and culture of their own, which people who live their profit from and presumably enjoy. Obvious examples include the elongated semi-circle that runs from Catalonia through south-west France to northern Italy, a Mediterranean region which worries traditionalists in the French foreign ministry and in Madrid, but which now has a semi-autonomous feel. Then there is the rising region of the North American Pacific, stretching from Silicon Valley south of San Francisco, through Seattle to Vancouver in Canada. Here micro-electronics and e-business are the driving forces but, again, there is a distinctive and unmistakable common culture, which could be defined by the mingling of European, Chinese and Japanese people, the coffee-bar casual style, the architecture and political liberalism. National histories and boundaries make little impact on these regions. They threaten nobody and have no military power or single political centre. But, for whatever reason, they 'work': their reach and grip on the imagination of the rest of the world is impressive.

Then there are the megacities of Asia and the city-regions of Europe and North America. They have economies which are often distinct from and pursuing alternative economic interests to, other parts of the nations in which they exist. Finally, there are, existing under and alongside the various supranational groups, treaties and organisations, plenty of examples of sharp-witted small nations, which have found ways of using their residual identity to great effect around the world without armies or jingoism. Take Ikea of Sweden, whose stores now dot the globe. Ikea sells what? Chairs, rugs,

cheap office furniture, glassware, sofas ... But more important, Ikea sells an affordable dream, the middle class (rather
New Labour) dream of bright, cheerful, clean living, in space
which is uncluttered and optimistic. It is a democratic dream
– Ikea tells its customers that everyone deserves to be able to
buy a good sofa, and that its flat-pack, self-assembly system
has brought well-designed things in everybody's reach. It is
the vague image people around the world have had of
Sweden itself, something which Ikea, painting its stores in
the state's yellow and blue, and using Swedish names everywhere, consciously reinforces. These Swedes have decided
their national identity includes things which are attractive,
marketable and universal, and are busy making a good living
out of that. Across the world, in a rather less organised fashion, hundreds of thousands of Irish people are doing much
the same thing, marketing Ireland's reputation for music,
talking and booze in theme pubs and bars. They are exploit-
ing national difference, travelling light. National culture in
this sense remains valuable; in the tiny crinkles of difference
between similar peoples is a world of commodities, symbols
and mental pictures to live off.

The nations who are having the hardest time and are most
threatened are the post-imperial ones – England, France,
Russia, Belgium. Being 'top nation' means, in part, that you
define yourself by your political and military strength, rather
than by lifestyle or culture. So when the strength goes, there
is less to fall back on. That may just be too bad. But it is
harder for Britain than almost anyone else. At least the
French and the Portuguese, the Germans and the Dutch,
have languages that are special to them and define the edges
of their belonging. They may be under threat. They may have
to learn extra languages to participate in the world economy.
But linguistic separateness is a powerful source of basic
human identity which is not available to British English-

speakers. They find themselves strangers in their own language, colonised imaginatively, in their heads, as foreign usages and ideas float back into the British islands.

One example from my own background can serve as an example of the effect. Those war comics I read were made for children looking for heroes. When I was back in Dundee, researching this book, I met one of the writers of such comics, an engaging, post-1960s man called Pat Mills, who explained: 'At the end of the day, a comic reader wants a power image; they want a powerful hero. So it's reasonable to draw on their fathers and grandfathers. So you have these traditional comics like Commando, War Picture Library and so forth, which I think catered for that need for heroism during the 1950s and 1960s.' In that first wave of comics, Americans were largely kept out of the story; or if they were included, it was to point up British characters like 'Union Jack Jackson' who joined the US Marines and showed them how to fight.

Mills drew for the next generation of comics, produced outside Dundee, such as *Battle* and he noticed that by the mid-1970s, interest in the old stories was waning. So the comic writers upped the ante. One story that made Mills particularly embarrassed was called 'Sergeants Four', an Englishman, an Irishman, a Welshman and a Scot, who went around doing ludicrous things like tying knots in German tank-barrels. (This, of course, follows the conscious use of Welsh, Irish and Scots people in wartime British films, to help create a united national feeling – and is a distant, mutant cousin of the Celts who play bit-parts in Shakespeare's *Henry V*, itself a key wartime film.) As readers seemed to become steadily more bored, Mills and his colleagues began to take bigger and bigger risks, introducing a German hero ('Helmann of the Afrika Corps'), using the grimmer imagery of Spaghetti Western violence or the 'Dirty Dozen' films and even, by the late 1970s, drawing comic strips about soldiers' mutinies in the First World War. The drawings, which had been done with meticulous attention to detail by Scottish and English artists, were farmed out abroad, so that Spanish graphic artists began to get the uniforms wrong. The ambient culture, in other words, was infecting the old, simple war stories. The industrial strife of the 1970s, the growing international market, the lust for more realistic and gorier images, ate into the strong-jawed Douglas Bader world of the earlier stories. In the end, says Mills, the whole Second World War comic strip market collapsed and 'all the top artists, top writers and so on moved into science fiction.'

Mills himself is still working on the same stories, only transmuted into the fantasy and science fiction world. For male comic readers,

> it's a rites of passage experience. Somebody is disempowered and they overcome various obstacles and become empowered ... it's the same thing whether they're dressed in Second World War khaki with tin hats, or whether they are dressed in outer space gear or whether they're dressed in tights, it's the same basic function.

So you could take the old war picture stories 'and change it to a planet on the other side of the Galaxy, and change the uniform and it would probably be very popular.' Indeed, Pat Mills is now writing stories for the 'Warhammer' stable, which produces detailed models of fantasy warriors, mutants, Gothic fighters, in a melange of outfits rifled from Japanese Samurai, sci-fi films, Vikings, dinosaurs, Teutonic knights and twentieth-century armour. They are the contemporary equivalent of the model soldiers, tanks and Spitfires small boys played with when I was young; indeed my son collects them, and spends time with his friends in Warhammer shops where spotty teenagers play long and abstruse games, and seem remarkably like the old consumers of war comics. All that has changed is the national context and the historical pride. That has been stripped away. Is this story not a small but neatly glued-together and accurately painted scale model of the more general effect of globalisation on old nations?

6

Intimate Enemies – Britain in Europe

Margaret Thatcher was an effective pro-European. As Prime Minister, she took Britain further and deeper into the European Union than ever before. But she hated what she felt she had to do and let her feelings show in private and, later, in public. In her old age, she has become our most vivid anti-European politician. She was always particularly hostile to Germany, to the extent of initially opposing its reunion after the fall of the Berlin Wall. In her memoirs, she describes Germany as 'by its very nature a destabilizing rather than a stabilizing force in Europe'. Being against the return of East Germany to the rest of the country was a particularly odd line for her to take since she prided herself on her own role in the defeat of the Soviet Union and her staunch support for NATO which had, since the days of the Berlin airlift of 1948, constantly supported reunification.

Indeed, as she said herself, when she met President Gorbachev after the fall of the Wall, 'I explained to him that although Nato had traditionally made statements supporting Germany's aspiration to be reunited, in practice we were rather apprehensive.'[1] Politically incorrect and backward looking she may be, but Lady Thatcher speaks for a large number of British people who feel pulled in different directions by cold interest and hot sentiment, many of them connected either directly or mentally to the wartime generation. Throughout her career she has played up the connection, even referring to Churchill, the greatest Briton of the century, by the familiar 'Winston'.

It is salutary, therefore, to remember that 'Winston' was himself an early advocate of European union. In 1930 he wrote that 'Every step taken to that end which appeases the obsolete hatreds and vanished oppressions, which makes easier the traffic and reciprocal services of Europe, which encourages nations to lay aside their precautionary panoply, is good in itself.' Given what was about to happen in Germany, this might be regarded as getting history stunningly wrong, just like Thatcher's misreading of Germany after the fall of the Wall. But Churchill was thinking along the same lines during the war, even contemplating a European supreme economic council to deal with currency questions and a supreme judiciary too. He wanted Britain and its empire to be involved but not compromised, yet after the war was quickly proposing a Franco-German partnership including 'a spiritually great Germany'.

Again, speaking in Zurich, he used the resonant phrase, 'a United States of Europe'.[2] Winston, in short, has a great claim to be represented as one of the founding fathers of Europe. It is a part of his thought and achievement which has been ruthlessly excised by his so-called followers among the right of the Conservative Party today. Churchill was not alone. An array of British politicians, historians, economists and thinkers argued for euro-federalism throughout the twentieth century. William Beveridge, founder of the British welfare state, called for a federal Europe with power over defence, foreign policy, currency and trade, during the

darkest days of 1940, while Ivor Jennings, arguably the greatest constitutional writer of the period, wrote a federal constitution himself and baldly stated: 'The desirability of
replacing international anarchy by international government
is so generally recognised in Great Britain than it needs no
demonstration.'[3]

The European continental politicians who stood looking
at the ashen waste of their continent after the war took these
ideas with utter seriousness. Today, among the anti-European
writers in Britain, these visionary continental politicians are
tarred with a totalitarian brush. It is suggested that European
Union is an anti-democratic conspiracy based on pan-European thinking developed by the SS; that because the fascist
leader Oswald Mosley became a passionate Europeanist in
later life he, and not Churchill, is the secret guiding spirit;
and even that because the founders of the EU were mostly
staunch Catholics, it is 'really' a grand Catholic conspiracy to
reinstate the Pope as Europe's true authority and to put
down the minority of Europe's Protestants. It is true that the
Nazis dreamed of a single European home, with its own economic, financial and agricultural systems, as well as a single
European army, all dominated by themselves. Mosley became
a fervent campaigner for a united, white Europe, and the
founders of the European Community were indeed largely
devout Catholics.

But to conflate from all this a grand series of anti-British
conspiracies is mad; about as mad as seeing vegetarianism as
inherently Nazi because Hitler did not eat meat, or declaring
the Union Jack a fascist emblem because Mosley saluted it.
However wild, these theories are gaining currency in the
heightened, almost hysterical mood about European Union
that exists in Britain today. They are contained in books published by respectable firms and passed round among the
growing and utterly fervent cadres of English resisters of

Europe. They are the far-out end of a wider spectrum that sees Europe as essentially conspiratorial and subversive of democracy. But before we can have a proper argument about whether we should stay inside the European Union, it is essential to understand, in a non-emotional way, where it came from and what it is intended to do.

In one sense the Nazis were indeed the founders of the European idea, along with the Stalinists; but only because they destroyed the old order, smashed down pre-existing national boundaries and threatened to end freedom and democracy for the continent's citizens. The Europe which has slowly developed into today's EU was conceived as the answer to those dark times, a bulwark against Soviet communism and a way of ensuring that war between the European states became impossible – exactly the Churchillian dream mentioned above.

France was in the most difficult position. On the one hand it had been invaded by the Germans three times within a lifetime, in 1870, 1914 and 1940, and had been comprehensively beaten and occupied in two of those wars. France had more reason than any other European nation to desire to bind the Germans in. Yet at the same time, as Charles de Gaulle understood very well, France was a historic unitary nation which would find it horribly hard to subordinate itself to any other authority. In the end, the French looked out at the world, saw the huge power of the United States from the 1940s onwards, and the Atlantic link, and decided that its identity and future were best served by a close, unbreakable link with Germany. There has always been an element of French self-deception in its European project; Paris has assumed too blithely that it would be the dominant diplomatic and political leader, with the Germans and others providing the easily-led economic power. One nation to think; the other to do. But having made that choice, the

French have pursued it with a remarkable single-minded determination, swapping civil servants, subordinating the Banque de France to the old Bundesbank before monetary union and doing everything possible to reconcile themselves with 'les Boches'.

Germany, meanwhile, started the peace in a devastated and divided state, but with two huge advantages. It was protected from the Soviet Union by NATO, and it had been given a (British-made) federal constitution. These, when cemented by a powerfully anti-inflationary and economically liberal government, headed by some of the most forward looking leaders on the continent, enabled the Germans to concentrate on rebuilding their economy and turning their country into one of the great success stories of the second half of the century. European Union was not a post-Nazi plot, by which Germany regained through federalism the dominance it had tried to snatch on the battlefield; it was a way of a resolving and loosening its nationalist past. It is hard to see any other route that could have been taken, short of breaking the Germans into cantons and teaching half of them Italian, French and Dutch instead.

The European story contains, clearly, the national ideas of a dozen other nations, some of them great ones; but it could not have come about without the Franco-German alliance, and its meaning today is inextricably linked with that. From the first, the French and the Germans had wanted Britain there too, for obvious reasons. For France, it would have weakened the British–American alliance and ensured that a resurgent Germany would never be able to dominate. For Germany, it would have tipped the balance inside the community away from the protectionist Mediterranean countries and towards a free-trading, more free-market northern bloc. It would have been one of those rare marriages that works better with three partners than with two.

But from the first, Britain was reluctant and, again, for obvious reasons. We had an empire, parts of which were clearly going, but leaving behind a Commonwealth which, many British people thought, would keep our privileged position in the world. The white Protestants of Australia, New Zealand and Canada mattered much more to the post-imperial British than the European continent. As late as 1961 the Labour leader Harold Wilson was saying that if there had to be a choice between the Commonwealth and Europe, 'we are not entitled to sell our friends and kinsmen down the river for a problematical and marginal advantage in selling washing machines in Düsseldorf.'

British superciliousness about the European project is best encapsulated in the famous story about the Foreign Office official sent by London to the great conference at Messina, a nondescript town in Sicily where, in 1955, the modern 'Europe' was born. It was a moment when Britain could probably have created the European Union it wanted, on at least partly British terms. But there was no interest and, according to the legend, the British official dismissed the whole thing: 'Gentlemen, you are trying to negotiate some-thing you will never be able to negotiate. But if negotiated, it will not be ratified. And if ratified, it will not work.' It is a wonderful legend, which tells an important truth about British arrogance and blindness when confronted with Euro-pean 'dreamers'. Hugo Young, who has written the best account of Britain's long agonies over the EU, has investi-gated and doubts its truth.[4] What is not in doubt is that it was an important lost opportunity for Britain.

Another story, rather more solidly based, is about the cre-ation of the European Coal and Steel Community in 1950, the moment when France and Germany merged control over the industries that had, up to then, been essential for war-making; an act of visionary peace-making which led in due course to the EEC itself. The first British reaction was, in the words of one official, that it would not work and 'we shall have to do what we can to get them out of the mess in which they have landed themselves' but – dammit – they went ahead anyway. Eventually, the question of whether Britain should admit defeat and take part in this early version of 'Europe', or ignore it, could not be avoided any longer by a Whitehall that really wanted the whole thing to go away. Robert Schuman, the politician who had created the community, the 'Schuman plan', had bombarded London with requests for an answer. Eventually his last ultimatum ran out, on 2 June. By then the Prime Minister, Attlee, was on holiday in France and did not wish to return, and the same went for the Chancellor, Stafford Cripps. The Foreign Secretary, Ernest Bevin, was in hospital. Eventually the deputy Prime Minister, Herbert Morrison, was tracked down to the famous Ivy Restaurant in London's theatreland, by a civil servant, Edwin Plowden. They retired to a back passage where some tables and chairs were stored and Morrison pondered the historic question. 'It's no good,' he finally replied, 'We can't do it. The Durham miners will never wear it.'[5]

Consider what might have happened to modern history if he had said yes. Ponder, too, on the extraordinary self-confidence of a government and party which put the happiness of coalminers in the north of England ahead of the future of Europe. Wrong, but somehow rather magnificently wrong. In a curious postscript to this tale, Peter Mandelson, Morrison's grandson, is now one of New Labour's most vigorous promoters of European Union.

So far as the anti-Europeans are concerned, there followed a long conspiracy by different British leaders, from Eden and Macmillan to Heath and Major, to get Britain into the EEC without ever telling the British people what they were signing up for. This was a superstate in the making, which the mere populations of the European nations had to be led quietly into, since they would never go willingly. In the rival pro-European story, what followed was a series of cata-strophic missed chances. After the Ivy Restaurant and Messina came desperate attempts to join, then the Heath referendum, then a pulling-back again under Margaret Thatcher, and then the refusal to join the euro in the first wave, thus giving Britain a second-class place.

There are elements of truth in both stories. Some in Heath's government certainly thought that the EEC would lead to political union but preferred not to advertise the fact, and considered, in any case, that it was an unlikely pipe-dream. It is also true that Britain has played its hand badly, time after time. But the fairest assessment of what happened would be to say that, utterly confused about its role in the world, and never quite believing the full ambitious scope of the European project, Britain has followed a policy of unen-thusiastic membership under successive leaders, while a North American-owned press, with its own reasons to be hostile to Europe, has helped keep the people suspicious.

It was Margaret Thatcher who approved the Single Euro-pean Act, one of the most integrating measures of the EU. As a political correspondent from the mid-1980s until the mid-1990s, I watched as first her government and then John Major's destroyed themselves over Europe. That story has been well told elsewhere, but the bitterness, despair and exhaustion of the struggle cannot be underestimated. It was a melodrama which veered from knife-edge votes and hys-terical denunciations on the floor of the Commons and energy-draining marathon negotiations in Paris and Bonn and Maastricht. Now, with Labour committed to a referen-dum on joining the single European currency when the (flexible) economic tests outlined by the Treasury are met, the UK is committed as a nation to the next phase of this argument. Declining to join would be a decision as momentous in its way as Herbert Morrison's in the Ivy. It would exclude Britain from key meetings about the economic and therefore the political direction of Europe. It would certainly be impossible to be at the heart of Europe (John Major's phrase) or to lead in Europe (Tony Blair's phrase) if we were not in the single currency.

So the referendum will about the European Union, as much as the single currency itself. If Britain joins it will have taken a profound and hard-to-disentangle step into a genuine union of formerly independent nations, whose people are, today, very similar in their lives and assumptions but which lacks a proper functioning democracy. If we do not, we put ourselves outside this large and rich union on our wet doorstep. We will be obliged to work more closely with other countries, above all, presumably the United States. So this long struggle which has dominated news programmes, party meetings, Whitehall and the pundits of Westminster, while rarely gripping the people of Britain, may come down to a simple-seeming question which every one of us can think about and give a personal answer to: do you feel more European, or more American? With whom, in the end, do you wish to stand?

This argument is conducted at two levels. One of them is highly abstract – sovereignty, harmonisation, pillars, and so on – and the other is almost vulgarly concrete – straight bananas, bans on our beef, and the rest of it. Both these ways of thinking have their place, but they tend to elbow out the realities of daily life in a country which has, however reluctantly, taken the European road so far. The arguments of the politicians are by now familiar territory; so are the passions on both sides of the euro campaign. It is the ordinary business experience of Europe that tends to be excluded largely because it is, though

important, detailed and dull. None of the people I inter-
viewed for this book can be seen as 'typical' of British opinion, and there is indeed no such commodity. But it seems
worthwhile to try to put back into the argument some of the
sub-political life that ought to inform it. Often, it seems that
the only voices missing from the European debate are those
of the people at the sharp end of daily life inside the EU.

Cardiff Bay was once the greatest coal port in the world,
as good a symbol as you would need of British might at the
height of the industrial revolution. Today, it is quiet and
empty. A few tall, graceful buildings, in silver and white,
metal and glass, are clustered around the brackish water. It has
become a kind of place you can find across Britain and
indeed the rest of Europe, for which there is no name, but
which are all much the same – regenerated urban places,
which have been devastated by the withdrawal of industry to
the Far East or its collapse for other reasons, and which have
been sandblasted, part-demolished, part-rebuilt with public
money and subsidies. They mix 'leisure' with expensive flats
and turn what had been the plain ornaments of money-
making into bijou 'features' – merchant names, stencilled on
the sides of buildings, ornate corners and twists on old ware-
houses, working-class pubs spruced up and selling wine. You
find these places in every post-industrial city of Britain, from
Edinburgh's Leith Docks to the canals of Manchester, from
the 'Merchant City' of Glasgow to the old seafront at Liverpool. And this is Cardiff's version. Like the others, it is meant
to bring new money, hope and jobs to gutted places. Like
most of the others, it has succeeded, a bit, though like them,
it still seems curiously empty. This is not a sentimental place
and why should it be? Money and jobs are what counts.

Among the new headquarters there is the anonymous-
sounding insurance group, NCN. But this company is, in
miniature, a picture of what is happening to the British state.

It used to be a major part of a British government department, the Export Credit Guarantee Department (ECGD),
originally set up to help British exporters with insurance in
new markets. After financial deregulation, it found itself
competing in a much tougher world against ordinary commercial insurance operations. Its civil servants became con-
vinced that if they stayed inside government, they would be
destroyed so, in the dog-days of the third Thatcher government, they lobbied ministers and asked to be privatised. They
were bought by NCN, a Dutch company, in 1991 and were
then bought by a Swiss reinsurer, Swiss Re. It is now a
Dutch-managed, Swiss-owned, English-speaking company
working all round the world but with a major presence in
Cardiff. And it is highly successful: Gary Hicks, one of the
directors, told me the sale had been 'Not ideological but
driven by the market. It was a privatisation that really worked
… we now insure £38 billion of world trade, whereas when
we were in government it was only £13 billion.'

Hicks, like tens of thousands of others, has made the jump
from the old British state into the global economy. He started
out as a parliamentary lobby correspondent, joined the government information service and then the ECGD. It was a
safe, predictable world. He says he loved getting away from it.
'Fantastic. Recommend it to anyone … A liberation.' Hicks's
liberated world is hectic. He lives in Cambridge, works part
of the week in Cardiff and part in London, commutes to the
continent and so do his colleagues:

> People move around, we go to Amsterdam, the
> Dutch come here, the Japanese come over to
> learn about credit insurance. People go to
> Baltimore; people go here, there and everywhere.
> In this building we've got Dutch, French –
> Chinese were trained some time ago.

And what, I asked him, does it all mean for Britishness? There was not much left of the old civil servant in his answer:

> The way the market is going, it will inevitably
> mean that there will be a diminution of the
> nation state, that is the logic of it. Whatever the
> Little Englanders think, that is what's going to
> happen for the benefit of the state and its
> customers, and the economy … what is an export
> any more? An 'export' is almost a misnomer. An
> export is a sale in Europe across national frontiers
> in the home market.

He sees Europe developing not largely through the actions of politics, but business – 'cross-board alliances and business practices'. Gordon Brown, he mordantly notes, described the original privatisation as a shambles and ferociously attacked it in the Commons. But he feels as if he is living in the future, and it works.

He is part of a new class, the international business class, the inhabitants of exclusive airport lounges. Hicks is unusual only in coming from government service. But the big banks, US and European corporations and the world-wide management consultancies are a culture almost to themselves now. Go into many of their offices and you will find people of a bewildering variety of nationalities who have, at least in their working lives, come close to leaving their national origins at the door. They read publications like the *Wall Street Journal* and *The Economist* and they travel, travel, travel. They may be suspicious of European bureaucracy but, by and large, they see supranational organisations as a good thing and the merging of currencies as 'the way the world is going' – which is not surprising since they work for supranational bodies too. In the battle over Britain's future, they are an immensely powerful group whose influence on politicians, subconsciously and directly, is constant. Once ambitious people dreamed of working for the state. Now they want to work for private corporations, where the status, money and power is greater.

There are of course many businesses which are hampered by the costs and bureaucracy that the EU has brought in its wake – abattoirs have been put out of business, cheese-makers have been tied in red tape. But, aside from the bigger businesses represented by Hicks, there are smaller firms and operators who are committed to the EU. Their voices are heard less often. Derick Nickolds, a lorry-driver, is an example of one such firm. He is every pro-European intellectual's vision of the enemy – the working-class Basildon man in person. Except that they would be completely wrong, for Derick describes himself as European, as well as English. He would be perfectly happy to see the arrival of the euro. He has no nostalgia for sterling: 'Whether it's called a pound or the peseta, or a franc or a euro, money's money. If you spend it, it buys goods for you. So no, I wouldn't have a problem with that at all.' He does not flinch from the word federalist and thinks the Commission should be stronger.

To understand why Derick thinks as he does, you need to know two things. The first is hard-nosed and commercial. His two trucks were built in Belgium by a Swedish company. He then bought them in Germany, saving some £12,000 each on the cost. The same story applies to his French-built trailers. Because road tax for each of them would cost him £5,750 in the UK, he has registered them in the Nether-lands, where it costs £660, so they have Dutch plates along-side his Union Jack, and have their MOT in Holland. He is a self-employed English driver, but he works under contract to a Spanish-based company, taking goods to and from Madrid and Barcelona. Like all other cross-Channel drivers, he fills up on diesel in France, where (again for tax reasons) it is less than half the price of British fuel. Another driver I spoke to later on told me it cost him about £450 to fill up in Boulogne, against more than £1,000 in England. For him, it was the difference between profit and bankruptcy. Though he is a British driver, therefore, Derick's business has directly depended on Sweden, Belgium, the Netherlands, Germany, France and Spain as well as Britain – seven EU countries in all.

That is only half the story. There is a more emotional side to it. Derick thinks Europe should be like America, with few boundaries, if any. In some ways, he is typically British: he has been driving across France and Spain for 20 years but hardly speaks any French or Spanish. Yet early on, he began eating in the French truckers' favourite Les Routiers restaurants, and noted how friendly they were:

> You would sit down maybe with a load of French
> lorry drivers. But never did I feel that I was out of
> it at all. They knew you was English, didn't speak
> the language. But when they poured their wine
> they would pour wine for me. When they handed
> the bread round, they would hand me bread.
> When they was talking they would look my way,
> even though I couldn't understand what they
> were saying. They would still look at me, smile,
> and I felt welcome all the time.

He has had the same experience with German, Italian and Spanish drivers. So, while some British lorry-drivers keep their food in the cab, never mingle and long to be home from foreign parts as soon as possible, he and other drivers make a point of mingling. 'They are just the same as us,' he says repeatedly.

It has been the small, personal things that made the most impact on his politics – breaking bread with other Europeans, sharing problems over fuelling and laws, helping out with maps and directions. In that he can stand for millions of other British who have been on school exchanges, bought French or Italian houses, work in pan-European businesses or simply go on holiday to the continent. None of this means that Derick is an unabashed admirer of the EU as it is today. He finds the different interpretations of European law infuriating. For instance, no issue matters more to lorry-drivers than the hours they are allowed to drive, monitored by the tachograph, or so-called 'spy in the cab'. But because the UK and France have subtly different takes on the EU law about them, British drivers can find themselves pulled up by French cops and arrested, for punctiliously following the Department of Transport advice. Some French police officers accept the British version. Others do not. This can lead to on-the-spot fines of several thousand pounds. If British drivers refuse to pay up immediately, they can be held in custody for weeks, with their lorries impounded, until their case comes up in a hostile French court – ruining them. This can feel like the arbitrary justice of a police-run state. Or again, France bans lorries from its roads between 10pm on Saturday and 10pm on Sunday. British lorries caught in France then have to pull over at the nearest layby and wait for 24 hours. French lorry-drivers try to be in Britain on a Sunday, where they are free to keep working.

It is clearly unfair. But though I doggedly questioned Derick about whether this made him feel anti-European, he equally doggedly denied it. It made him want a better Europe, he insisted – one where the Commission was more effective at banging the national governments' heads together, and where legal remedies were surer. National opt-outs were the menace. He sounded like a real federalist. Yes, he said, he was. You have to look to the future, not the past. The old history of wars against France and Germany did not bother him – except that he hoped the EU meant they would never happen again. Derick looks like the kind of guy who would sign up for the UK Independence Party. He sounds like Roy Jenkins's ideal trucker, a small businessman who is pro-European by commercial and personal experience.

None of this would apply to the man whose ferry we loaded onto at Folkestone. The neat, clean-looking *Purbeck* is the last ferry running from the port. She is a comparatively old ship, built in 1976 and strictly for freight traffic only. After their massive rigs are secured in the hot, diesel-fume-filled-hold, the French, British and Spanish drivers congregate upstairs, where they are offered plain but excellent British food served by white-uniformed stewards. Looking on proudly was the man responsible, a short, fat Mancunian called Ian Longdon, managing director and chairman of Falcon, a freight company with 70 lorries. A one-time Navy man, Longdon is quite a character. 'Three heart attacks, one multiple bypass, four wives,' he tells me proudly. His latest wife, Tracy, is a blonde many years younger who is a hard-working director of his company and is shortly expecting their first child. 'Yes,' he says, 'I'm starting again. I'm a bit of a character in haulage.' A series of larger companies have tried to make a success of ferries out of Folkestone and failed. The Channel Tunnel is clearly a formidable competitor and the French run a state-subsidised service of three vessels. Longdon calls the *Purbeck* the greatest gamble of his life and last year, it made a substantial loss. This year he will turn a good profit, but every day seems a close-run thing, wholly dependent on the lorries he attracts to the ship. He does it by offering good food, personal service and flexibility – sometimes the ship will wait for a slightly late lorry, if the driver is a frequent customer. And he is making a success of it – a great example of old-fashioned British grit and commercial enterprise taking on the odds and succeeding.

Longdon is no fan of the EU, or the French in particular. He considers they do not play fair and are out for themselves, but laughingly admits to being 'a bit to the right of Genghis Khan' and perhaps old-fashioned. He has been operating for 18 months and so far, hundreds of illegal immigrants have been found hiding on lorries on the *Purbeck*. Yet he is running a Bahamas-registered ship, crewed by Spaniards, taking French drivers to and from the UK. He takes us to the bridge and is momentarily deflated to find the British captain is off duty and Henri, his French skipper, is in charge. 'But he's a good bloke, Henri,' says this classic English entrepreneur, only a little reluctantly.

These businessmen are not representative of anyone but themselves. It is just that their views of the EU are gleaned from their daily working lives, rather than the newspapers or party manifestos. Politicians would make the argument against them that they fail to see the wider picture – the Euro-sceptics saying that there is an unsustainable supranational dream animating the continental elites which Britain simply cannot participate in without losing its essential independence. But again, rather than stay at the level of constitutional theory, it makes more sense to look at the hard, daily, evidence of what this might mean.

This could involve interviewing other business people with other experiences but, since their campaign covers a lot of such traders, I chose the British Weights and Measures Association instead. The BWMA is one of the very rare examples of a British organisation created as a direct result of American politics. It was founded in the late 1860s. In the aftermath of the American Civil War, the US government was looking again at the whole question of which system of measurements they should use – the British one, the imperial measurement, including pounds, ounces, miles, yards and so on, or the metric system, originally developed by revolutionary France. American metrification would have been a serious threat to the trading position of the then-dominant British Empire, which relied on common measurements for the export of huge quantities of manufactures. The BWMA was formed to lobby Parliament to repel the metric arguments. America never did go metric, and still uses quasi-imperial measures today; but the BMWA, after a long period of dormancy, is back and fighting once more. This time, it is fighting a desperate rearguard action against the British government itself, which has – in its view – treacherously colluded with the EU to force metric measurements on the British people by criminalising, by the end of 1999, the tried and trusted imperial system.

Vivian Linacre is the kind of man government officials loathe and fear, and have done since governments were invented. In his sixties, an Edinburgh-based surveyor, he knows more about weights, measures, parliamentary procedures and the workings of the EU than any civil servant working anywhere. He is livid, witty, brimming with energy and mischief. Compulsory metrification and the criminalisation of pounds and ounces is, he argues, a constitutional abomination, driven through in secret and against the pledges of four successive Prime Ministers (Wilson, Heath, Callaghan, Thatcher). He sees this as an exercise deliberately designed to damage British businesses, since the former German Commissioner, Martin Bangemann, part of the disgraced ex-Commission, had admitted to him that he wanted Britain to go metric because the country had an 'unfair advantage' over the rest of the EU when it did business with the non-metric United States.

But a lot of his anger is directed at British ministers and

MPs. The proposal was first adopted at an EC ministerial meeting in December 1988, with three British ministers, Douglas Hurd, Lady Chalker and Francis Maude. Little was made of it and nearly five years passed until the measure was nodded through a Commons committee, without a vote, in 20 minutes flat. The Hansard record of the meeting shows there was no serious discussion, merely good-natured banter and jokes. After that came various formal delays and exceptions – miles are not covered by the weights and measures rules, and the pint of beer was exempted for the time being, ditto the pint of milk in a glass bottle, on the grounds that this would be too much (or rather just right) for voters to swallow. Now, though, despite the broken promise of a 'complete reappraisal of metrification policy' from Labour, pounds and ounces are going. Again, the relevant announcement was sneaked out on a particularly quiet parliamentary day, 23 July 1999, while MPs and journalists were heading for their holiday breaks. Linacre promises that, since it is impossible to challenge the measure's legality – he thinks it wrong in law and 'a constitutional abomination' to make only one system of measurement legal and everything else illegal – the BWMA is going to go further. It has ready 'martyrs' – ordinary grocers, mainly – queuing up to break the law by selling fruit or cheese by the pound. In the words of one of those present, 'we are going to force the government to jail an Englishman for selling a pound of apples to another Englishman'. Linacre made it clear he wants the Blair government to face the most politically embarrassing court case possible, deriving from a silly, ideological law. The words that most spring to mind when watching him speak are relish, determination and anger.

With Linacre when I met him was a pale-faced, formally dressed man in his thirties, a former Tory and a financial trader. He can stand as the opposite to the pro-European Gary Hicks

from Cardiff. Nigel Farage is now also a Member of the Euro-
pean Parliament for the UK Independence Party and every
Frenchman's caricature ideal of an Englishman. Unlike the
Tory Euro-sceptics, who he despises, he believes that Britain
must leave the EU, because it is an oppressive superstate which
will take away our liberties and destroy the nation-state itself.
To my surprise, he quoted Roy Jenkins, the grand old man of
British Europeanism, with approval. At a recent conference on
Europe organised by the *Daily Telegraph*, Jenkins had said he
thought there were only two honest positions on the EU.
Either you had to accept it, for all its faults, and try to influence
it as a committed member, or you had to leave.

Quite right, says Farage. It cannot be reformed or radically
changed. People (like me) who want it democratised and
slimmed down or those like William Hague, the Tory leader,
who want some of the treaties reconsidered, and all those
who think you can take the EU without the euro, are wrong.
It is a straight choice. Farage thinks that the euro-referendum
will certainly be lost by the Europeans. If not, Britain is dead,
'and I accept that there is a threat that it could just disappear.'
He rejects the idea that he is an extremist but, in the year
when an Austrian admirer of Hitler won second place in that
country's elections, gives this warning:

> I think that you're beginning to see resistance
> movements against the EU … my fear is that they
> will not manifest themselves in nice decent
> middle-of-the-road political parties. My fear –
> and this is where, as an ex-Conservative, I find
> myself in total agreement with Dennis Skinner
> and Tony Benn – my fear is that that if you strip
> people of their nationality, if you strip people of
> their individuality, the reaction to that is likely to
> be a lurch towards extremism.

He makes a strong point. (Note, however, that he conflates individuality and nationality, an elision which millions of his fellow citizens would reject.)

The hardest question here is what 'stripping people of their nationality' means in practice. There is no proposal to abolish nations, but yet the EU is a thoroughly ambiguous organisation, a series of treaties between sovereign states which have established common organisations, which nevertheless speaks of itself like a country in its own right. Ambiguity was built into it from the start not because of a conspiracy but because of the caution of its early members about the practicality of their ultimate goal. 'Ever-closer union', the key phrase in the Treaty of Rome, can mean as little or as much as you want. If it meant the dissolving of European languages and their replacement by English, for instance, it would be resisted by the very nations most regularly accused of pursuing a federalist agenda. We are now at the stage in the EU's development where less ambiguity and much more openness about that eventual destination, and who wants to be part of it, are needed.

It seems dishonest, however, not to expose and listen to the full force of the federalist argument. To do that, I chose a French journalist who knows Britain well, and a French MEP who originally campaigned against the Maastricht Treaty on democratic grounds, but who has now become an ardent federalist. 'Les Deux Magots' is a Parisian cliché – just off the Boulevard de Cliché in fact. It is the fine, roomy, expensive café where Jean-Paul Sartre and Simone de Beauvoir sat and decided life was meaningless – and then carried on living it nevertheless, with gusto and style. Nowadays American tourists sit there, hoping some philosophy will rub off from the cane seats, plus a handful of foreign students, trying to look intense, smoking their first Gitanes and failing to quite understand *Figaro*. But early in the morning, with the sky turning pale, it is still the haunt of proper Parisians, meeting for their croissants and *grand crèmes*.

Philippe Chatanay, the executive editor of the current affairs weekly *L'Evenement* could be mistaken in the first minutes of talking to him for an American. He is anything but. Chatanay argues that the EU is for France, first and foremost, a way of keeping globalisation – which in France mostly means the USA – at bay. He is eloquent and forceful. We live by our local particularities, our different ways of doing, eating, living. France has a glorious regional cuisine to protect, a fine heritage. Why should it allow the steady degradation and uniformity that globalisation involves? The protection of the European film industry by law, for instance against 'a world culture which is submerging us' was felt by many French to be not nationalistic, but internationalist in spirit 'because we are defending what we consider to be a very interesting and important lifestyle model which goes from food to cinema and that if we were to surrender to this world tide of homogenisation we would not be accomplishing our destiny.' There is rising irritation and incomprehension about the British inability to choose between the US and Europe.

Whose side are we on? An English-speaking Trojan horse, perhaps, less Little Englanders than Little Americans: 'Which is larger, the Atlantic or the Channel?' This is the common reaction to British Euro-scepticism but what interested me was that Chataney's protests against a world uniformity sounded uncannily like what many British anti-Europeans feel about another kind of uniformity from Brussels. Philippe talks about the furious French protests over GM food and the campaign against McDonald's, which dominates this week's issue of his magazine. What could be more important and intimate than the food we eat, he asks. I ended by asking him what the continental reaction would be if Britain actually left the EU. He paused before admitting that many people would breathe a sigh of relief. At last the 'trouble-makers' would have 'left the club'. But then, he said, there would be a second reaction, one of disquiet and self-doubt. European Union has been for so long seen as a force of history, an inevitable progress. 'There's a waiting list as long as my arm, everyone wants to be in the European Union, and I think that if one of the early members were to leave, that would bring all of us to ask questions about what exactly is this Europe that we're building ... what do we want to do with this Europe of ours?' Which, whatever its effects on the British, might be no bad thing on the continent.

South of Paris, in the suburb of Villejuif, lives the economist and Green MEP Alain Lipietz, about as opposite a politician to the UKIP's Nigel Farage as it is possible to find. A former socialist, Lipietz lives in what he calls the last bastion of Stalinism in France: Villejuif was a stronghold of the French Communists throughout the post-war period. Its roads have names like Stalingrad, Kremlin and Karl-Marx; even the local swimming-pool is the Piscine Yuri Gagarin, after the first Soviet astronaut. Lipietz finds it all very amusing. He had a classic French elite education, rising through the Polytechnique in Paris and the School of Roads and Bridges – both of them institutions which mould the real rulers of modern France. But Lipietz is a genuine radical, who broke with the socialists, campaigned against the Maastricht Treaty and now looks forward to a future which the French elite will find almost as difficult as the British. He lives in a modest home, furnished very like that of the other Green I had recently visited, George Monbiot in Oxford – all rugs, shelves of books and the occasional piece of African art. He believes that what matters in politics is the global, the great forces of finance, trade and business round the world, and the local – the community or region.

He wants a United States of Europe for much the same reasons as Philippe – a strong counterweight to American power. Brussels, he says, 'must be the bodyguard of the European identities'. He wants it to be protectionist, demanding that half the films shown are not from Hollywood, keeping American hormone-treated beef out of the European market, refusing genetically modified food. He cites an economic study of where the labour time of all the goods and services an ordinary person consumed actually came from – clothes, domestic work, education, everything – 80 per cent came from a 20-mile radius of the individual and only 20 per cent from the wider nation, EU or world markets.

> Our globalised life, even our European life, or
> even our inter-regional life, is a very small part of
> our lives, but this part of our life, 20 per cent, is
> very important because if you lose your job
> because of unregulated competition on this
> 20 per cent, you will lose your job, then your
> family, then your home – you will lose the 80 per
> cent. So what is lacking is organised protection, at
> the European level, against the tempests of the
> world markets.

This is clearly profoundly different from mainstream British political thinking; New Labour is utterly committed to world markets and against protectionism. But it represents a strong strand in continental thinking, and one which is rising at home too, in the politics of environmentalists and rural producers. The collapse of the first round of new world trade talks, in December 1999 at Seattle, shows that the protectionist agenda is still very much alive.

What, then, of the nation-state? If the local matters and so does the global, what space is left for the traditional nations, which come in between? Lipietz thought it would be easy for small and marginalised nations, like the Bretons and Welsh, the Slovaks and Scots, but much harder for the big ex-imperial countries, like France and England. England's problem, he said, was that it had had an empire for so long, its original dominance left it with little specific identity of its own when the empire disappeared. More surprisingly, he suggested the same applied to France, or at least that central swathe of France that was left when the Bretons and Burgundians, the Provençal and the Basques, were doing their own thing. Some of the French regions were doing very well now: 'the region of Toulouse are now negotiating directly with the Brussels state, that is the European state. There's a new direct connection between French regions and the European Union.' The Corsicans were looking for direct connections with Barcelona and Genoa, not merely Paris. At least England has a name, he pointed out: middle France did not even have that. No, it was the old oppressive and imperial countries that would have the trouble. He compared their plight to that of post-imperial Austria which, shorn of its dependencies, suffered a crisis of identity and eventually welcomed in the Nazis. Or, he said, perhaps it was like the crisis of modern men, who had dominated women for centuries and now found, with the rise of feminism, they did not have anything else to fall back on. Lipietz may represent the more extreme end of French federalist thinking, and he acknowledged himself that French right-wingers and even the foreign ministry at the Quai d'Orsay were worried about the future of the French state. But he represents a radical new idea of identity, simultaneously local and regional, which is spread quite widely beyond conventional party politics.

These conversations in Britain and France crystallise one of the oddest problems about the European debate. There is no great difference between different EU nations, regions and even cities in their desire to keep local and traditional differences, to protect custom and variety against the flattening impact of global business. Sometimes the issues are so different they do not echo at all in other parts of Europe; the passionate enthusiasm of small-time shopkeepers and farmers in south-west France for protecting *la chasse* – their sacred right to go out looking like paramilitary Serb units and blast small birds and animals with guns – sounds as odd in London as the rituals of English fox-hunting probably sound in Paris. Sometimes one part of the EU has an ancient tradition that other parts would like to emulate. There are plenty of lager-drinkers across Europe who admire and envy the strict German rules on beer dating back to the Middle Ages. Sometimes there are strong similarities: the battle by French cheese-makers to preserve their old ways against the white-coated hygiene inspectors are not so different from the struggles of cheese-makers in the English West Country. But, in all this, there is a massive difference between the UK and most other EU countries. We see the main threat to the nooks and crannies of daily life as being Brussels. There, they tend to see the threat as the USA, and the European Union as their natural protector. Thus, as my French journalist colleague and the Green MEP from Villejuif both insisted, it was the USA that was trying to impose bad food and hormone-pumped beef on unwilling European consumers; without a strong Europe, it would be impossible to say 'no'.

In Britain, though, campaigners against GM crops are making common cause across the EU; in most cases it is 'Europe' which is blamed for offensive innovation. The weights and measures campaign is a good example. For many of us, the question of whether we should get our sugar and timber in metric or imperial measures is not of huge moment – we can adapt and have before. But traditional measurements, related to a human pace, or the bones of a human hand, are also reassuring, familiar and not to be set aside lightly. Many people, not all of them elderly, think automatically in feet and inches and know what a pound of something feels like, who will never think the same way about metres or kilos. To take that away from them is to shake their world just a little and should not be done without careful consideration. It is disrespectful of politicians and officials to rub away the markers and grooves of ordinary life without good reason.

Generally, such things have happened at moments of national crisis, as when the French revolutionary government from 1789 rewrote the months and seasons in pursuit of Reason. Changes to food laws, ways of measuring and describing, undermine, just a bit, people's sense of security. The change to decimal coinage in Britain in February 1971 may have been a necessary act of modernisation – certainly the old system seems outlandishly complicated to children now. But it was widely disliked and fused, in many minds, with the rampant inflation, the terrorism and the industrial strife that made the 1970s so unhappy. The basic motivation of the French peasant rebel, fighting to save inefficient but time-hallowed methods of cultivation, and the group of men in a London club, fighting to save the traditional British system of weights and measures, is identical. They are both reactionaries, in the proper sense of the word. So why is one constantly turned against the USA, seeing Brussels as the ally, while the other is against Brussels, and far likelier to look to the American as the natural ally?

One simple answer is history and language – that we are indeed not Little Englanders, but Little Americans. We share far more than English. We are, more and more of us, the 'Atlanticians' described earlier. We share entertainment, popular reference-points, even political fashions. Our economies move more closely together than the British economy does

with any continental one. There are clear signs in the growing debate over the euro of a coherent alternative to British
involvement in the EU beginning to emerge on the right of
politics. Newspaper commentators and conservative economists are suggesting that instead we might join NAFTA, that
brings together the US, Canada and Mexico. Some even
argue that we should join the US as an offshore state or
group of states. Better known politicians are beginning to
talk up the American connection as an alternative to Euro-
peanness. At the Tory conference in Blackpool in October
1999, Margaret Thatcher summoned up Churchill's phrase
about British–American co-operation, when she told a late-
night gathering: 'In my lifetime, all our problems have come
from mainland Europe and all the solutions have come from
English-speaking nations who have kept law-abiding liberty
alive for the future.' Her pro-USA and anti-Europe sentiments were echoed the following day by Francis Maude, the
Shadow Chancellor, who told the conference:

> We can look towards America: a high-tech, low
> tax, lightly regulated economy which has created
> a million jobs a year for the last 25 years …
> Where success is not a dirty word. A true
> enterprise culture. Or we can look to the
> continent: higher taxes, more regulation,
> governments that don't know when to get out of
> the way – and unemployment at twice Britain's
> level … The simple fact is that our economy is
> aligned with North America, not with the
> Continent.

So are we more European or more American? The question is even asked, *sotto voce*, inside New Labour, which has its
share of Atlanticists too. Tony Blair and Gordon Brown owe

a considerable political and personal debt to Washington politicians and thinkers, more than they owe to socialist and social democrat politicians in continental Europe. They feel more at home with President Clinton and his advisers than with French or German colleagues – something that contrasts sharply with the instinctive pro-Europeanism of Labour modernisers in the Kinnock period. Prime ministers of any stamp tend to deny that there is a choice – we must be America's gateway in Europe, and also the eloquent European nation in America, and that is our destiny.

Yet there is a struggle between the European style of capitalism, with higher welfare spending, less social division but also less economic dynamisms, and the US style; and it is very difficult to take both sides. When the euro-referendum hots up this will become a real cultural, economic and emotional choice whose outcome is hard to predict. Against the Atlanticists, a new generation of historians has recently emphasised the artificial nature of original Britishness and, more radically, the complex interconnections between Britain and the continent which make our destiny seem quite obviously there. Norman Davies uses the French names that famous English monarchs would have called themselves – Eduoard I, King Etienne de Blois rather than King Stephen and various Henris – thus undercutting the familiar stories of English medieval history. He writes strongly about the 300-year Norman and Plantagenet empire in France, mostly ignored in traditional 'Our Island Story'-style history, and describes the British Isles through most of their history as an integral part of the European story. Of the reformation, classically seen as a great period of English and Scottish self-assertion, Davies writes that it

> cut off the Isles from much of the Continent and
> from that main body of Christendom which had

been its spiritual home for the previous millennium. This spiritual isolation was arguably more profound than anything that has resulted from all the political invasions and geographical changes since the Ice Age. All the great shifts of previous times, whether the establishment of the Celts, the rule of the Romans, the arrival of the Anglo-Saxons or the conquests of Normans and Angevins, had usually fostered a rapprochement between the experience of the islanders and that of the Continentals. But the Reformation set them apart. It drove a wedge down that Channel that was higher than any cliffs. It erected a barrier that was as durable as it was forbidding ... It put England into a position of unprecedented isolation surrounded on all sides by sullen Irish subjects, by reluctant Scottish allies, and by powerful Catholic powers in France and in the Spanish Netherlands.

You do not have to work very hard to discern Davies's sympathies. But they are shared by quite a number of British politicians, business people and ordinary citizens too. For the pro-Americans the problem will be to convince us that Britain can really leave the EU, the project at the heart of continental Europe's hopes for the future and our greatest market, without very damaging economic and political penalties – and, perhaps, convincing us that we have more in common with US corporate and mass culture than with Europe. Certainly, a subservient relationship with an America looking ever more to the Pacific, and wanting to deal with the whole EU, would not be easy or comfortable.

For the pro-Europeans, the problem is to persuade people that there can be a living democracy among so many languages, and that the EU can be reformed or rolled back so that it is not oppressive. Then there is the harder question still of what we have to defend against global culture, alongside the French, Germans and Italians. French life is, for all its morose intellectual self-questioning, particular and confident. The French have their language, their cuisine, their landscape and *savoir vivre* to protect. The little civilities of French life, the polite handshakes between men as they pass, the *bonjour* and air-kissing, the care over clothing and the elaborate language of compliment which fails, quite, to hide moments of astonishing rudeness – all that is at the heart of the French lived life. They perceive this as being undermined by the Anglo–Saxon economic force which we call the liberal market system.

What do we have that is as deeply rooted – what are the things we would fight to the death for? Queues? Pub signs? Double-decker buses? London is far more internationalist and less English, than Paris is French. Nor do we have a distinct agricultural tradition or great cuisine to defend against outsiders. Our fights tend to be about power and democracy. Britain, being an outward-turned, post-imperial country which is an internal coalition of nations, and now of many smaller communities, has loaded a lot of its public identity onto political traditions and institutions, its separate laws and currency – the very things that Brussels threatens, in trying to build an order which will protect entirely different parts of continental life. The Paris elite defends food and countryside; the British elite is more worried about common law, Parliament and the pound.

That is, we are choosing to identify ourselves as a nation on the basis of precisely the institutions and habits that continental Europeans are less concerned with. Partly, it is simply a question of who joined the club and when, and therefore who it was designed for. No European system designed by

British politicians would ever have devoted such a huge proportion of its budget to farming subsidies – and the
Common Agricultural Policy still swallows half of all the EU
taxes. No EU strongly influenced by Britain would be pursuing the withholding tax proposal which could do such
serious damage to the City of London. But farm subsidies
and anti-tax avoidance measures like that make perfect sense
to France and Germany. Decades of British suspicion and
arrogance about European politics have had their inevitable,
bitter reward – an EU designed by, and for, others. The Spanish businessman or the Bavarian farmer might have moments
of hostility to the waste, bureaucracy or petty-mindedness of
aspects of the EU. But neither doubts, deep down, that it is
there to make the future better for them.

All this throws up some uncomfortable questions. People
across the Western world are less interested in, and impressed
by, the self-importance of the state. They are more interested
in the environment, the food they eat, the conditions they
work in, local culture. In the longer term, is a politics which
is dedicated to preserving the nation-state going to be more
popular than the politics of all that – of food, environment
and lifestyle? And there is another dilemma. The more closely
you look at the detailed complaints of many businesses and
individuals in Britain about European legislation, the more
often you discover that much of their problem is with British
officialdom and the British interpretation of European law.
Take the campaigners for pounds and ounces. It was no
Brussels body that failed to warn the British people about
compulsory metrification; it was British cabinet ministers,
both Tory and Labour, who sneaked it through. It was not
scheming Commissioners who refused a longer UK opt-out
from all this; it was the utter failure of the Department of
Trade and Industry in London to seek one. And it was not
the European Parliament which nodded through the relevant

legislation with a few jokes in 20 minutes when no one was watching; it was the House of Commons.

There was a huge amount of anger in Britain about the French and German bans on British beef and the long delays on lifting them when the nation's cattle herds were finally declared BSE free. It was, no doubt, partly about getting a commercial advantage for their own cattle and keeping out cheaper British meat. But what was at the heart of the problem? BSE itself: one of the most catastrophic malfunctions of the post-war British state, a catalogue of blunders, Whitehall departmental incompetency, state secrecy and ministerial failure that led to the bankruptcy of thousands of farmers, some of whom killed themselves, to the destruction of the British beef herd, to the closure of abattoirs and to the terrifying brain disease deaths of dozens of innocent people. This was a British political failure long before it had anything to do with continental agriculture ministers in Brussels.

Critics of the European Union find themselves, more often than they care to admit, defending the constitutional independence of a British state which, whatever its theoretical glories and proud history, is the main culprit and author of their woes. The people who tell us, with great sincerity, that they are fighting for freedom and democracy are doing so to defend the autonomy of a state which is highly centralised, secretive by instinct and practice, often contemptuous of Parliament, and which has been horribly incompetent. Its ministers are weak and its parties cannot maintain reasonable numbers of members. If the Westminster Parliament is the bastion of freedom, why do so many of its citizens, in Scotland, Wales and Northern Ireland, wish to leave it? If 'Euroland' is an undemocratic, oppressive fix, why is it so many well-off British people are buying houses there and even choosing to emigrate? Very often, it is the over-zealous, aggressive and mean-spirited application of general European

law by British officialdom that puts the shopkeeper out of
work, or closes the light industrial unit. Many of the regulations and form-filling that oppress people are hatched and
administered from London. Yet it has become the fashion to
blame everything bad or inconvenient in public life on
'Brussels bureaucrats'.

Actually, it is odder than that. The people who complain
about the EU most are rarely keen political reformers when
it comes to the British state. There, they are conservatives.
The case for freedom of information legislation, a more
effective parliamentary scrutiny of ministers, or greater freedom for local councils tends to come from a separate group
of campaigners – who are, by and large, pro-Europe. But do
these liberals attack similar failings in the EU? Again, rarely.
It is as if both groups are shouting at the same volume, about
related grievances, but in different directions, and never to
one another. There is, however, one great difference between
British government failure and European failure. We in
Britain can eject our governments occasionally; we cannot
kick out the European Commission.

There is an invasive and sometimes aggressive EU agenda
on many aspects of daily life that seems far removed from
what Brussels needs to do. Parts of that agenda are designed
to satisfy continental interest groups who have little in
common with British island interests. Beyond that, the EU is
seeking to create a political union from which it would be
difficult to secede and which would, inevitably, be controlled
by a pan-European elite of appointees and national ministers
operating far above the heads of citizens of the member
states. That presents huge problems not just for Britain but
for any other part of the Union whose citizens have a lively
democratic culture – which is, chauvinism aside, most of it.
If the democratic gap is not bridged, then it is not Britain
that will collapse, but the European project. A system built to

prevent war between states will eventually produce another kind of random, mundane violence, against itself.

Today, Britain faces three different possible European futures. There is the Europe of the sceptics, in which we turn our backs on their continental project and accept our cultural and business destiny, to be Americans in all but name – but off-shore Yankees, rewind button colonists who have crossed the Atlantic one more time, this time mentally, from west to east, and taken up position on a European island. Or there is the Europe of the Europeans, in which the British, or the English, seize their European identity back again, share the currency, and drive fully into the project, so that we start to see our children and grandchildren's destiny as working in Bordeaux or Milan, multilingual offshore Euros. Finally, there is the fudged identity, in which the Europe of the Six or Eight forges ahead with a single currency and deeper political union, leaving a skirt of second-division European associates, tied to it with trade agreements but retaining more political independence and, if they wished it, their individual currencies.

This may be the likeliest outcome of all, since it would allow some hesitant nations, above all Britain, to enjoy some benefits without the most difficult costs. It is advocated by senior figures in Brussels and by Conservative politicians in Britain. And it would be no disaster. The problem with it, however, is that accepts what no previous London govern-ment has accepted, which is that there is a grand, world-scale political union taking place on the continent which neither can nor should be influenced by the British. If at some stage, this Union wished to keep out our products, or people, or caused us problems in other ways, there would be nothing, short of some appeal to international bodies, that we could do. And it would make England more isolated if the Scots, Irish and even Welsh wanted to be part of it – which on cur-rent trends they would. Third, changing world demography and power, plus the emergence of the EU, would push the British out of those top-division organisations we are currently in. Perhaps that would not matter. But this second-division option is not, all in all, a glittering vision of a happier future. It looks like what it is, an unhappy and reactive compromise.

Why are we reactive? It is because of the failure of the British state to evolve into a popular modern democratic society. The unpopularity of British political culture and our institutions, which seem so often the property of the 'top ten thousand' of politicians, hacks, fixers and officials, means that there is a core weakness which the EU can easily exploit. Britain, which had a democracy which was hugely popular, has not renewed that democracy sufficiently to keep it popular. There is not the automatic mass instinct to preserve British constitutional freedoms that there would have been in the 1920s or the 1950s. On a range of issues, from clean beaches to food safety, the EU has been able to offer consumers information and scrutiny which, by rights, Westminster ought to have offered first. People have no affection for the Commission or the Council of Ministers, if they even understand what these are; but they have no affection for the parliamentarians of London, or much faith in Whitehall, either. If some continental observers see Britain as an exhausted post-imperial remnant, full of self-doubt, rather than a vibrant and proud democracy – well, they are half-right, anyway. Vultures do not hang over healthy cattle. In the end, there is no solution to Britain's European problem that does not begin at home, with Britain's British problem.

7

Is There an Answer?

Is there a question? Political writing is littered with journalistic warnings of imminent apocalypses which never quite
occur. It is possible that nothing much will happen here,
either – if the Scots do not want further separation from the
British state, if Northern Ireland settles into a devolved structure that the two communities like, if for some reason, perhaps a crisis in London or financial disaster on the continent,
the referendum on the euro never happens. There are, however, many assumptions in that – a chain of 'ifs'. The likelier
thing is that the future of the British state will be a matter for
all of us within a few years. In common with many of the
people quoted in this book, from all over the political spectrum, I expect that there will eventually be a euro-referendum and that that will be a moment of national truth, an
intense argument about who we are, our place in the world
and our real interests.

People on both sides of this coming argument say similar
things about its significance. Nigel Farage, from the UKIP,
believes that Britain will vote to keep the pound but 'that still
won't solve it, because even if we say no to the euro, it's just
an impossible position to be in the EU and not in the euro.'

So there would be a further stage; many Tories, he says, share his view about leaving the European Union 'but think it's easier just to talk about the euro for now and then to try and deal with the other part of the business later.' From the other end of the spectrum, Billy Bragg, the left-wing singer, sees it as a wonderful opportunity for another kind of break:

> It gives the English a chance to vote. We can't vote ourselves out of Britain but we can say we are looking forward to the future and embracing a European future rather than looking back to a little English imperial past. That's part of our history and part of our legacy; but there are people in this country who want to live there and I'm afraid that when I see those guys with the little golden pound sign on their lapel, I want to remind them that it stands for a Lire, which is an Italian word given to us by some Romans who turned up here from Europe a long time ago.

That argument between Farage and Bragg, and the millions standing with each of them, cannot forever be delayed.

What of the other questions discussed in these pages? It is unlikely that corporate power will be reined in again by individual nation-states. We live, in the words of the political philosopher David Marquand, in a world of 'restive, masterless, productivity-enhancing but community-destroying new capitalism'.[1] The state will never again own and run great industrial enterprises, or limit its citizens to a certain amount of money they can take with them abroad, or successfully censor what they see and read. Britain's establishment will never again rally the people around a constitution of parliamentary absolutism, a significant monarchy and a popular, Established Church, never mind the politically abolished hereditary peerage.

Britain will never again be a white nation, with only tiny fringe groups of a different colour or faiths; the mingling of people and the growth of New British communities has gone too far for that. It will never have an empire again. We will not return to boiled cabbage, thick coats and hats in winter-time, or the rationing of television. The new towns and suburbs, covering land which was forested or planted for centuries, will not be removed. If the fox-hunters are banned, they will be banned forever. In the age of the Internet, we will never again have to take what we are told by politicians or company bosses as gospel, but can find out for ourselves. It is hard to imagine us ever again fighting a conventional war, with years of sacrifice, slaughter and privation. Future wars, if they come, will be shorter and perhaps more catastrophic. We will not stop visiting the continent in an almost routine way, whatever happens about the EU, or half-thinking in American English.

The Old Britain into which I was born is dead. When was the day it died? Was it Indian independence? Suez? The Treaty of Rome? Or of Maastricht? Was it when Margaret Thatcher agreed to the Single European Act? Or was it those other great events of her premiership, when the end of exchange controls, then privatisation, and then, in the Major years, the World Wide Web and the signing of the Uruguay Round of the GATT Treaty, created today's global economy? Or is that too economistic – should we look inside the state? Was it the day when Scotland voted 'yes' to its own Parliament? Was it 1994, when the last volume car producer in Britain went into German ownership? It was, surely, all of those dates and none of them. A certain kind of nation-state, with its rituals and hierarchies, its place in the world and its self-assumptions, has certainly slipped away and quietly died when no one was watching. But 'Britain' is still here, that splatter of rock and earth, crammed with 238 people for every square kilometre – and a lot more if Scotland is excluded.

Britain today is far from being the England that Shakespeare's John of Gaunt lauded. It does not think of itself as a 'Throne of Kings' or the 'seate of Mars' nor as an Eden, nor, in the age of jet travel and nuclear weapons, as a 'Fortresse built by Nature for her selfe /Against infection, and the hand of warre'. The 'Moate defensive', as Shakespeare called the Channel, has been, quite literally, undermined. We would not call today's Britain, however much we admire it, a precious stone set in a silver sea; there are rather too many motorways, peripheral estates and out of town shopping centres for a precious stone. Nor are today's Royal Family famed throughout the world 'for Christian service'.

Britain is, however 'a little world' in ways Shakespeare never imagined and remains a place many of us prefer to anywhere else on earth. It is often forgotten that John of Gaunt's speech is not a simple hymn to England, but a bitter looking-back, which ends protesting that 'this deere, deere Land /Deere for her reputation through the world/ Is now Leas'd out (I dye pronouncing it)/ Like to a Tenement or pelting Farme.' That England, he continues, 'is now bound in with shame, /With Inky blottes, and rotten parchment bonds. /That England, that was wont to conquer others, /Hath made a shamefull conquest of it selfe.' John of Gaunt sounds like a contemporary Euro-sceptic, writing in aged mortification to the *Daily Telegraph* letters page. His England, and later Shakespeare's own England, was in fact not in decline at all, but on the verge of an extraordinary forward leap in power, riches and self-confidence. And so, very possibly, it is again. Out of the husk of the Old Britain, who knows what bright-winged creatures may be crawling?

So if the question is, do we want to preserve Britain, my answer is no, I do not want to 'preserve' Britain. There is nothing terrible looming if Britain dissolves into its earlier constituent nations, because the dominant one, England, is more liberal and open than its critics presently understand. For many people in Britain, the loss of the British state would be a minor thing. That might seem a shocking statement but if, in due course, we lived in different federal regions of the European Union, or in separate states called England, Scotland, Wales and Ireland, the majority of people would carry on doing more or less exactly what they did before. They would eat the same food, do the same jobs for the same companies, support the same football teams, read the same papers and magazines, listen to the same music. From their windows, the view would be unchanged and the big things in life – love, children, deaths and little inexplicable eruptions of happiness while walking through the autumn leaves – would feel identical. There would be moments when we found ourselves fumbling with 'British … I mean …' and the disappearance of some familiar objects like the Union Jack would produce, in many of us, a sentimental pang. But assuming that a violent nationalism did not arise and that there was no idiotic new economic policy which erected new borders, and that whatever political dispensation we lived under was cautious and clever about not interfering too much in daily life, then the middle classes would be fine. Life would be a little shaken, certainly. But not deeply stirred.

The same is not true, however, for many of what we could call the lost people of Britain, those stuck in a cycle of joblessness and poverty on estates across the country, many white poor, from Essex to Liverpool, Falkirk to Plymouth, many Bangladeshis and African-Caribbean people, many Irish and travellers and refugees. These people would be vulnerable because they are so heavily reliant on the state and have so little to start with; major constitutional arguments are rarely settled by reference to the interests of the powerless. This is going to be an argument conducted in newspapers and metropolitan newsrooms, among well-paid and secure people on both sides, not in the peripheral estates. There are nearly 4 million people living on income support and 4.6 million on housing benefit. Child poverty is acknowledged to be among Britain's most damaging social problems. The people at the bottom, generally defined as about a fifth of the total, are the ones who suffer most directly from the withdrawal of politics from public life. Only the state, with the vast resources of compulsory taxation, has any chance of providing the huge amount of educational and financial support that can lift them, or at least their children, back into the economy and society where the rest of us live. A strong, functioning national community is essential for them, or has been so far, because national identity and belonging are the basis on which richer people have agreed to see their money flow through the state to help their fellow nationals. Taxation is a form of coercion, because it is ultimately backed up by the force of the state. But we accept that because we live among, or near, people who clearly need help – who need education, better opportunities, more spent on their housing – and who are, after all, our 'fellow citizens'. In part, the motivation is human solidarity, in part it is fear of crime and disorder.

This is a subject that liberals shy away from, but the brutal truth is that people are readier to see their money go to help others from their own community than the poor of other nations. Compare, for instance, the amount spent on combating poverty in the UK with the paltry sums that are sent by the British government as official overseas aid. This has not come about by the wickedness of politicians, but through political choices assented to and even insisted on by voters, in ballots, opinion polls and focus groups. Charity still begins at home. The people most at risk in any major constitutional resettlement will be the poor, because they depend most on the state as it is. In the long run, they might be better off – if, for instance, a Scottish government decided to spend more generously on state education and housing than the previous British government had done, notwithstanding the much smaller tax base it had to work from.

But it is a fair working assumption that, overall, the bottom fifth of the population would not find such a change liberating. A state like Britain depends on huge cross-regional subsidies, on money flowing from richer areas to poorer ones. In any unitary state, the scale of these transfers is hidden. Legislation for a London mayor and assembly has produced calls from would-be mayors for the capital to 'get its money back' from Scotland. The Scots are vulnerable to this because they have a separate system of administration, and the gap between Scottish tax-take and public expenditure in Scotland is (relatively) easy to work out. The old figure of Scottish spending being 20 per cent above that of England in per capita terms is hefty, though it is now falling. But the transfer of funds from, say, the south-east of England as a whole, to the north-east would be equally striking. Because the British economy has become so tilted towards the south, including London, East Anglia and the M4 corridor, the effects of the breakup of the UK on the funding for other parts of the country would be serious – serious, that is, for the people at the bottom of the pile. (The rest of the UK offers the south-east of England plenty of other 'goods' including a reserve labour force, military bases, water, recreational space and so on, but these are hard to price.) So that is a reason to think twice.

There are others. For all its faults and weakness, Britain has provided a non-ethnic, invented, loose and relatively comfortable home for a huge number of different kinds of people and communities. One of the reasons I do not support the idea of creating a republican model of Britishness, on the American revolutionary model, or the French 1789 model, is that it implies a citizenry who are all essentially committed to the same ideas, the same culture.

It is exclusive, not inclusive, and that does not match the Britain of the 2000s. The very fact that Britain was developed for purposes which are now almost ludicrously inapt is a kind of strength. We could be a mosaic country, a 'community of communities' as it has been termed. Those communities include many that cross the internal borders. Nearly a fifth of the population of Wales is English-born, and 8 per cent of the population of Scotland. In the 1991 Census, 743,000 Scottish-born residents of England were registered; that would not include, of course, the very many who think of themselves as Scottish, or partly Scottish, who were born south of the border, such as the bagpipe-playing Alastair Campbell, press secretary to the Prime Minister. There are also, with the same caveats, at least 545,000 Welsh-born people in England. A further decade of economic pull from the south-east suggests that these numbers are higher now. Then there are the 'visible minority populations', as the Census called them, who were counted at 2.72 million then, the vast majority by number and proportion living in England. The same Census found 3.99 million people living in the UK who had been born outside the country and one experienced observer concludes that 'it is reasonable to guess that the census figure of 7.27 per cent of population foreign-born is a serious underestimate of our total foreign-descended population.'[2] We do not know the full picture, partly because of a mix of political correctness which inhibited the earlier counting and partly because the next Census is due in 2001. The fact that some 70,000 people sought asylum in Britain during 1999 plus the youth of some of the New British groups suggests that the proportions of 'minority' British are set to rise quite fast. Britain has benefited hugely from the influx of different groups, from German Jews to Ugandan Asians to Americans, and there is a case, made eloquently earlier in this book by Yasmin Alibhai-Brown, for keeping the 'loose overcoat' definition of belonging and allowing the island to remain plural and complex.

Overall, though my friends tell me Scotland is going and will not be stopped, and are perhaps right, and though nothing terrible is likely to happen if Britain returns to its constituent nations, I would prefer some kind of British political identity to be kept. But that cannot happen simply by staying, frozen, at this moment of constitutional change. It implies making choices about what kind of Britain would work in the future, and what kind we want. Everyone takes different, private messages out of the history of their own country, community and family. We all absorb some bits and forget others. You could look at the history of Britain as the story of a singular, successful, military and imperial people who have had some blows, but are still essentially the same people, who must pull up the drawbridge of John of Gaunt's 'Moate defensive' and wait for better times. Many people think that way. Let 'Europe' simply go away, or collapse, or something. Ignore the Scots and the Irish.

Or you could take the Atlantic view, favoured by the proprietors of some of our newspapers, and conclude that we are, essentially, an old and distinguished branch of the same family as the North Americans who ought to shamble back to kith and kin, rather like a frail grandparent being offered a small room upstairs in the spacious home of the loud, robust and self-obsessed family. You could reflect on how recently immigration and Europe have changed Britain, wallow in stories about Ted Heath's deceit, and join some fascist group or other. You could, with equal logic to any of those, conclude that British greatness coincided with the time when

Britain was a staunchly Protestant country, keeping Catholics out of public life, and decide that 'Papists' were the most obvious termites undermining Britishness. Barmy, but there's enough history there to back you up if you want it. You could go with Norman Davies and read our history as that of an essentially European people who became distracted during their imperial adventures, and should now come home again.

So where do I go? With what seems to me the truth of the matter, that Britain is plural and mixed, a land where Muslims and Catholics, Scots and English, conservatives and radical socialists, can all feel at home. Britain should be even more engaged in the world economy, not less engaged, but able to offer its citizens the good government that can compensate for the insecurity and unpredictability of global trade. It will not be a Britain with internal barriers but it will be a Britain whose peoples have different identities. Billy Bragg elegantly explained the difference between Englishness and Britishness:

> British is a bit like 'our street'; it's us and our neighbours. It's not our house, but it's our street and we know our neighbours' houses and we come and go from one another's houses. I would include the Irish Republic in that as well. I know they don't feel themselves to be part of that, but I would include them as neighbours in that we come and go and we have so many things in common.

Well, I like that street. I live there too. And that is another reason for asking: can Britain be reformed, secured, put back together again for another 300 years? Does it have to part? Or could it evolve into some kind of happier, less post-imperial, union of the island peoples?

Cruder, faster attempts at 'rebranding' Britain have been made already. There was a vogue for 'Cool Britannia' shortly after New Labour took power which was overhyped, and then much ridiculed. It seemed to be mere metropolitan swagger, the conceit of the Islington ruling classes – an early attempt to stamp the country as a progressive one, shedding its monarchical pageantry and history in one quick, slick, ad-man's makeover. People protested, not unnaturally, that Britain was its past, that you cannot simply deny yourself and your roots, though some metropolitans try. The 'forces of conservatism', as Tony Blair put it in his famous 1999 conference speech, saw Cool Britannia as light and trite and an easy target for mockery. Perhaps they were right, but the anxiety about Britain's image was not misplaced. The notion of rebranding Britain, which came from the impossibly trendy Demos think-tank, was championed by the Design Council and supported by many hard-nosed exporters. It is not so hard to see why: Italy, France and other countries sell themselves on the supposedly rich and humane texture of their everyday lives, Germany on its technical efficiency, and so on. If Britain is seen as essentially a 'past' country, reliant on pageantry, tourism and 'heritage', it makes life for its exporters significantly harder.

In the global country, nations as well as companies have brands. In Britain's case, the pageantry model has been out of kilter with the real country, with its successful creative industries, global services and openness to change. The attempt to re-imagine Britain in brand terms was not all silly and it was not all vanity. There were down-to-earth, sensible proposals for better and more welcoming ports and airports, better co-ordination of how Britain projected itself, and so on. The youth of the people who proposed it was not a good reason for mocking them.

Yet, in the end, Cool Britannia proved as evanescent as the

I'm Backing Britain campaigns of the 1970s, a passing mood. It had no more success than the ethnic art tailfins adopted by British Airways in recognition of its role as a global airline, mocked by Margaret Thatcher and then partly phased out again in favour of the familiar Union Jack. Recent surveys show no noticeable impression so far on overseas audiences, who persist in associating Britain with Big Ben and London fog. So why did rebranding not work? The answer was given by Stephen Bayley, the designer who was briefly and unhappily involved in the Millennium Dome project:

> The vexatious matter of national identity is a delicate and precarious mixture of shared symbols, happy accidents, evolutionary chaos, historical inheritance, genetic roulette, political interference, history of artistic whim, palaeo-anthropology, economics, the weather, geology, sunspots, Iron Age migration patterns, religion, bus routes, taste, sex, the Gulf Stream, football results and investment decisions made in Lower Saxony and Detroit.

British identity was too complex and contradictory to be subject to branding, which was only a posh word for good-will, with a logo attached, 'a logo being a trademark that went to art school and lives in Soho or Covent Garden.'

Thus, concluded Bayley, while it would be nice to get away from some of the Olde Worlde images of Britain that had dominated us since the 1950s, 'the coruscating alternative – of national destiny being in the hands of spoon-faced trainee brand managers who think 1688 is a French lager – is not welcome either.'[3] The trouble with the Bayley counterattack is that it leaves you with – what? A wry smile, a hopeless shrug, and little else. The fact is that we are in deep trouble in terms of our national identity and wry smiles are not a sufficient response. They leave the people who will be damaged by the decay of Britishness with nowhere to turn. Many of us who had become sick of the starchy, nostalgic and hectoring British tone of the past few decades found the idea of a more stylish and relaxed British cool rather attractive. It might have been excessively metropolitan, too much of Manchester and London and insulting to some of the rest of the country. But it reflected the feeling of those cities better than anything that had gone before. And it gave a new generation a hope of making a good living in a country they felt they recognised. The trouble was, it was all words.

In truth, what Britain needed was not rebranding, a quick makeover, but re-imagining, and then restoring. The deeper causes of national malaise, which have been the subject of this book, involve the constitution and democracy, power and values, and could not be addressed by branding. Among mainstream politicians, Gordon Brown seemed to understand this fully, and worked in a series of pamphlets and speeches at the idea of what he called 'the Great British Society' in which a prudently run economy and a new deal for unemployed people would stitch back together the popular democratic state that had emerged from the ruins of 1945.

In *New Scotland, New Britain* Brown and another Scottish MP, Douglas Alexander, argued that Scotland and England shared not just a common island and language, but also 'a commitment to openness and internationalism, to public service and to justice, to creativity and inventiveness, to democracy and tolerance.' The British expression of these went far beyond a defence system and an integrated economy:

The National Health Service was not a
specifically Scottish creation. Indeed, it was

created by a Welshman, but it serves the whole of
Britain. Of course, we can have a separate NHS in
Scotland – indeed, it is already administratively
devolved – but the ideal that inspires and
motivates the staff and the patients of the NHS is
that any citizen of Britain has an equal right to
treatment irrespective of wealth or race and,
indeed, can secure treatment free of charge in any
part of Britain. So when we talk of the National
Health Service, national means Britain.

They argued that it was more modern to embrace a multi-
layered identity; that instead of asking how the Scots could
create a nation-state, the more important question was 'How
as a people do we advance the well-being of all?' And they
concluded by posing the choice facing Scotland as 'the battle
between social justice and separatism'. Their essay, published
by the Smith Institute, a Scottish think-tank set up in
memory of the former Labour leader, was targeted at mainly
Scottish audiences. Brown and Alexander reminded their
readers of the number of Scottish jobs dependent on exports
to the rest of the UK – the figure was said to be 367,000 –
that more than half of Scotland's top 50 private sector companies were registered in England; and that identifiable
public spending per head during 1996-7 was almost £5,000
in Scotland, against about £4,000 in England. These are serious questions for the Scots to consider. But they do not
address the question of 'New Britain' in a resonant way for an
English audience; and they do not deal at all with any democratic deficit south of the border.

Brown's New Britishness takes its emotional energy from
the patriotic enthusiasm generated by the 'new Jerusalem'
socialism of his youth and attempts to apply it to modern
conditions. His model of Bank of England monetary

independence and his caution in public spending helped to create the foundations for this; the jury is still out on whether the New Deal has worked properly, but many more people have been offered training and a fresh start at work. This 'Great British Society' should not be dismissed. To put it crudely, there was a fundamental problem with the Thatcherite idea, when the state appeared to be saying that it was too weak to offer help to the people at the bottom, that there was less and less it could effectively do – and yet at the same time it demanded more respect and authority. Brown's economic and social programmes at least acknowledge that the modern state has to work to earn its respect. But what of the constitutional agenda, outside Brown's remit (and about the only thing that was)?

Before and after the 1997 election there were a series of detailed and intelligent attempts to rethink what the constitution of a revived Britain might look like. At the Constitution Unit, a committee including academics, former senior civil servants and others met under the direction of Robert Hazell, a one-time Home Office official, from 1995 on, to draw out a set of principles and a route-map for the major set of changes New Labour was already committed to. But New Labour was not conspicuously grateful. It made it clear that it would keep to its original agenda; and so lost the chance to follow what had been a clearer and more coherent path than the one it took. Hazell, who subsequently became a professor of government at University College London, has kept a close watch on constitutional change since and, a moderate in these matters, has pointed out the major gaps in government thinking, on Parliament, the courts – which are asked to take on new powers – the English question, and Whitehall. 'To come to terms with the new political culture the centre will have to relax and be willing to let go ... Constitutions alone cannot bind nations together: but constitutions embody

values, and to work they need politicians who accept those
values and can give force and expression to them.'[4]

A similar conclusion, expressed more saltily, came from
the most dogged and radical of the reformers, the writer
Anthony Barnett, who had been a founder member of Char-
ter 88 and whose book on constitutional reform proposed a
written constitution, a much greater role for elections and
the wholesale demolition of the hereditary principle at the
centre of formal public life. Barnett's achievement was to
push notions of citizenship and a written constitution to the
centre of the argument during the Conservative years, so that
when John Smith was Labour leader he felt obliged to
respond with a ground-breaking speech and set of proposals
which was, in turn, inherited by New Labour.

Since then, as with the Constitution Unit, there has been
something of a falling-out. Tony Blair's attitude to the whole
thing had seemed ambivalent from the start. He wanted to be
a disciplinarian devolver, a liberal controller. His speeches
mentioned political reform, but the subject tended to come
in the dead zone of his oratory, three-quarters of the way
through a long list of issues, and before the resonant sum-
ming-up. It was carefully embedded in other bread-and-
butter questions, almost as if the Prime Minister would
rather it was skipped over by an inattentive listener or fast
reader. A classic example of the technique came in his speech
in January 1999 to the Institute for Public Policy Research
(IPPR), a centre-left think-tank:

> Make no mistake, this government has embarked
> on a radical shift in the balance of power in
> Britain. We are, in the words of our constitution,
> shifting 'power, wealth and opportunity' into the
> hands of the many not the few. Power for the
> citizen against the state, the consumer against

> vested interests, and the people of Scotland, Wales
> and London to decide on their own future.
> Wealth spread more widely, private pensions
> extended, more child benefit for all mothers.

He slips very quickly from 'power' to pensions, from the constitution to child benefits. This was certainly influenced by the advice that constitutional reform, or even political reform, was a turn-off for voters. But the IPPR is hardly Basildon high street; and from the start, New Labour risked simply failing to get its case over for the very serious changes it was committed to, never mind the ones it was still thinking about. The Blair government pursued devolution and incorporation of the European Convention on Human Rights into British law, but flinched at voting reform for the Commons or on moving briskly towards an elected second chamber. Its Freedom of Information Bill bitterly disappointed campaigners and, in certain ways, made the state less open, not more so. Blair had moved ahead on many of the things constitutional reformers had talked about at local level, legislating for the return of London government and directly elected mayors; suggesting local referendums, voting in supermarkets and at the weekend to boost the very low turnouts (at the bottom of the European league table) in local elections; and accepting the idea of 'citizens' panels' and other new forms of democratic involvement. Yet, at the same time, New Labour's early commitment to inner-party democracy, with one person, one vote replacing the trade union-brokered deals, was ditched pretty quickly when 'the wrong person' seemed likely to be chosen to lead the new Welsh Assembly or to become Labour's candidate in the London mayoral elections. As with Freedom of Information, the impulse to reform and the instinct to control were in sharp and embarrassing conflict.

Reflecting on all this, Anthony Barnett, having hailed the new government with a book ecstatically titled *This Time: Our Constitutional Revolution*, went public with his sense of hurt and disappointment. In an open letter to the Prime Minister, Barnett recalled that in his book:

> I argued then that the country was ready for a new democratic constitutional settlement. But I had an inkling of the alternative direction you might take. 'What 1997 has made possible,' I wrote, 'is not inevitable. As well as constitutional democracy, there are adverse forms of modernisation. Centralised, populist rule from above is one, which rests on the awe-inducing glamour of media and electoral manipulation, rather than the glint of bayonets or coronets. This, I fear, is the course you have taken ... you have started to lose the initiative. If you are to start winning again, you must inspire the independent action of others. Once, you turned three good words into your mantra: education, education, education. Now, you need another three words, not as an alternative to economic and social reform, but as their companion. They are democracy, democracy, democracy.[5]

Barnett's many qualities as a lobbyist do not include a talent for ingratiation.

There are some signs that New Labour remains interested in the coherence and future of its own reshaping of the British system of government. Another book, by the *Guardian* journalist Jonathan Freedland, called *Bring Home the Revolution* attempted to restore the reputation of American democracy on the left, proposing a republican Britain, with no monarchy and a vast increase in the number of public elections for office-holders.[6] It attracted the interest of ministers, and was a bold effort to change the terms of debate. In it, Freedland set out a Barnett-like agenda for a written constitution, a culture of rights, strong and entrenched local powers and a reformed democracy, but cleverly set it in the context of the vibrancy and success of the United States constitutional story, itself borrowed from the writings of Britons like Locke, Paine and Mill. As with Robert Chesshyre, a decade earlier, Freedland had been a Washington correspondent and had come back enthusiastic about American democratic freedoms. This has the effects of making radical reform seem less threatening, since it would be mimicking another nation's success; of flattering the reforming tendency, since it implied Britain could be like the far more powerful US; and of reminding the British left that it too had a liberal tradition.

In his concluding peroration, Freedland said:

> Britain's progressives have let their inheritance be stolen. But it was our entire nation which lost its birthright – to America ... Britain *did* have a revolution. The trouble is, we had it in America. The Founding Fathers were English radicals, who took a revolution intended for us and shipped it across the Atlantic. With it, they exported our rightful destiny. It is time to bring it back home.

This is calculated to appeal to the strong pro-American instincts at the heart of New Labour, a party which has fed and watered itself intellectually with US Democrat policymakers and in the Library of Congress.

Every push which reminds New Labour of the importance of democratic reform is to be greatly welcomed. There are, nevertheless, some caveats to be made. It ignores the

English question almost entirely; yet that is what now stands right in the middle of the debate, still barely articulate, embarrassing, immense, but clearly there. Further, the Freedland proposal plunges us straight into the argument about whether we want the British future, if there is one, to be more like the European or the American models. He has written of his surprise and delight that some conservatives have engaged with his argument, and that the *Sun* was particularly enthusiastic. But of course it would be: its staff saw a rare opportunity to forge an alliance with a centre-left thinker for its, and its proprietor's, project of making Britain more American. The anti-British republicanism of Rupert Murdoch is resourceful, relentless and highly opportunistic.

One of the most influential writers in this field, a historian whose book *Britons* has had a huge impact, is Linda Colley. Her retort, as someone who lived in the United States for 16 years 'and loved it' is that the cultural and political differences put Britain more with continental Europe than with our cospeakers:

> Are we like the Americans in terms of our
> attitude to death sentences? No, we are not. They
> execute people, we don't. Are we like them in
> terms of gun law? Emphatically not. We are not
> like them in terms of the sports we play. And are
> our politics and our attitudes about the relations
> between money and politics the same as theirs?
> Emphatically not. In many ways we are like the
> Americans. Increasingly, as the American empire
> deepens its grip, we are all going to be like
> Americans. To say that and to say that we should
> like the Americans, which I do, is not the same
> surely as saying that we want to be the 55th state.

It was an illusion, she said, that Britain could take advantage of America's world-wide position 'as if we can be the mouse on the lion's head and it's rushing through the jungle and people are running away from it … That is not how Washington sees the world. The United States is a melting pot of an enormous number of ethnicities. The Anglos are a tiny minority and an ever less influential minority in the way that the United States looks at itself. I wish some Brits realised that.' Given that Freedland had bravely admitted his enthusiasm for direct democracy implied a return to the death penalty in Britain, it is clear that, once again, there is a fundamental conflict of values at stake.

Even if Britain is held together, and does not die off – a big if – then the tone and atmosphere of the restored Britain that would have to be created is unresolved, fluid, open. But it cannot be left open forever. For myself, and with hesitations, I am more European than American. Neither model is entirely happy, for instance, when it comes to relations between different communities and religions. Europe boasts resurgent fascists in Austria and Switzerland, but does not have the hideous apartheid of American cities. In the end, Europe is made up of crowded, historic nations living cheek by jowl and sharing more common history than they do with the USA.

I changed my mind on a number of things while working on this book. One of them is a written constitutional settlement – the new start, critics like Barnett and Freedland have argued for. After 15 years of reporting Westminster, I thought that, although we needed a reformed politics (no one who has actually sat and watched our system in operation can sanely deny that) it was best done piecemeal and crabwise. Scotland's long march to self-rule was unstoppable, certainly after Margaret Thatcher came to power; we needed a Freedom of Information Act because too much had been hidden, even basic things about the safety of food and hospitals; the House of Lords had to be reformed and the Commons had to claw back its own self-respect from the internal party police called 'whips'; the erosion of local government had to be reversed, using a return of powers removed during the Conservative years and the election of more powerful, directly elected mayors. But these were individual changes which could be best be dealt with one by one, by a new government which understood the importance of restoring British democracy to the British people. The argument was that one reform provokes the next – the image was of a dry-stone wall, where you move one stone and others start slipping.

How far has this been vindicated? This is my third book on British politics. The first, *The Battle for Scotland*, predicted that there would be a Scottish Parliament but argued that 'questions about sovereignty, devolution, Home Rule and federalism are being asked by many more people than the Scots' and suggested that a big question for the future was the mood of English nationalism when it eventually awoke.[7] The second, *Ruling Britannia*, attempted to analyse Britain's centralised and malfunctioning political system during the Conservative years, and proposed a plan of reforms familiar since New Labour came to power two years later.[8] It was a programme of evolutionary change and some people criticised it for not being radical enough and going for a full written constitution. In the second edition, I replied: 'Why could I not be braver and go the whole hog? Because, in brief, the whole hog won't go. It is a phantom hog, a hog with wings, flying across a rose-tinted sky.' It would require a radical breakdown of Britain's political economy

> for there to be the kind of political revolution the architects of political reform await. In its absence,

> there is no mechanism for the upending of our
> institutions and culture. The Commons would
> have to suspend its activity and start again. But
> Britain is a place where we live, not a blank sheet
> of paper … Reformers must work with the
> parties, politicians and social forces that exist now
> and urge them forward.

That is quoted because it is, in general, better to be frank about shifting your opinion. The critics were right. The Scottish Parliament did come and the stones are slithering, and we must work with the parties and politicians of today. But Britain now needs the wholesale rethinking I argued against in the mid-1990s not just to improve things, but for its own survival. The radical breakdown has arrived, not only after Home Rule but also because of the democratic and political challenges posed by European Union, which have smashed two administrations, the Thatcher and Major ones, into splinters, and can certainly break another. If Britain is not re-imagined and restored, Britain will die as a state and as a constitutional tradition. It has been a large part of this book's purpose to explain why. Where I disagree with Freedland and others is not, any longer, in rejecting a constitutional revolution but only in its content.

Scotland will probably go at some time; or if it does not, is unlikely to be strongly affected by reform programmes in London. In Northern Ireland, the beginnings of a new politics can be seen for the first time in generations, as nationalists and pro-agreement Unionists slowly build ties of mutual respect, if not yet of trust, and try to work together. The longer-term future of Northern Ireland may be inside the UK, but the demographic forces and the greater prosperity of the Republic are among the pressures that will bear down on Unionists for a generation to come. Republicans point out in private that the Republic today is very far from the Catholic, reactionary, priest-dominated society feared by Orange Protestants. They believe that the logic of cross-border economics, one-island transport systems and health services and the rest of it will, in time, erode Ireland's internal border to the point where it becomes meaningless. Just as Unionists think that a period of peace in Northern Ireland would increase the proportion of Catholics who want to stay inside the UK, preferring to be a loosely ruled and democratically safe part of a larger association, so the Republicans think Protestants would begin to reassert their Irishness and accept the logic of a single state. But if the UK loses Northern Ireland, and if Scotland leaves the British Union, then that takes us straight back to the English question. Ireland and Scotland as well as the profound question of monetary union in Europe are multiple detonators bringing us to the point where we do indeed require 'the upending of our institutions'.

Englishness exists. England's senses of itself go back more than a thousand years, albeit in different forms, and unless England is recognised and given a new sense of its own security, then all the hopes for a liberal, open, democratic and tolerant future are in danger. England cannot be ignored, tied down, balkanised or dissolved. Yet England has been pushed into a corner where it is expected to passively await its future. That, in itself, is dangerous. One of the most striking things in recent years is that while conservative writers have been slowly burnishing and practising the language of Englishness, creating a word-picture of an ancient, sovereign nation oppressed by the Celts in cabinet and the European federal plotters, the centre and left of politics have shied away from the very question of whether English consciousness exists.

This is mad. For any party to feel, or to seem to feel,

queasy about the national identity of 85 per cent of the people and votes it depends upon would be an act of political suicide. It would also be unhistorical. So the first thing that needs to be done is journalistic, or novelistic, rather than legislative. It is the re-imagining of a progressive, open England. There are so many English histories available, a great treasure-chest of achievements, stories and individuals, that it is easy to reveal the democratic, open, radical side of England, and to celebrate that and to build a programme around it.

I go back to John Bull and Hogarth and his side of beef, and discover that, though John Bull was originally a caricature of the English, a fictitious cloth-merchant created by a Scottish writer in the early 1700s (in the context of a trade war with France, interestingly, though it was cloth that was at issue then, not beef) the English readily adopted him for their own democratic purposes. In his early guises John Bull was drawn as a shaggy headed bull-man, a kind of homely English minotaur. As the historian Derek Jarrett put it, when the caricaturists wanted an aggressive image they chose the royal lion of England to symbolise the nation,

> but when they wanted to comment on the
> nation's domestic troubles, the taxes it had to pay
> or the corrupt politicians it had to endure, they
> showed it as a bull. And bulls need to be led by a
> particular sort of man: someone with firmness not
> humour, someone not afraid to get his clothes
> dirty, someone used to the honest toil of country
> life. The moral of it all was that the ordinary
> freeborn Englishman would take almost anything
> from those who respected him and understood
> him but would paw the ground ominously in the
> presence of canting moralizers or villainous
> courtiers.[9]

There is meat in John Bull for any democrat today. Indeed, hostility to cant and court is at the heart of the radical England which needs to be rediscovered in this new century.

It is there in the great William Cobbett, the farm-labourer's son from Farnham, soldier, patriotic Tory, radical journalist, parliamentary reformer, defender of the rural poor. Or Tom Paine, whose *Rights of Man*, in helping to create the intellectual climate for two revolutions, the American one and the French one, must make it the single most influential political book ever produced by an English writer. Or William Hazlitt, the greatest of all journalists, who described political hacks in his essay 'Illustrations of *The Times* newspaper' by noting that 'Man is a toad-eating animal … He sneaks to court; and the bland accents of power close his ears to the voice of freedom ever after; its velvet touch makes his heart marble to a people's sufferings. He is the intellectual pimp of power … For one tyrant, there are a thousand ready slaves.' It is there in the great struggles for parliamentary reform, and the abolition of slavery, for the emancipation of Catholics and votes for women. It is there in George Orwell, England's second most influential political writer after Paine. It is there in the determination to build a working welfare state for everyone after the Second World War, and in the long tradition of radical anti-colonialists who fought successfully to get Britain out of its empire without the all-out wars the French fought. It is there in the dignity of Stephen Lawrence's family. It is there in the country's inability to take 'Cool Britannia' quite seriously. It is there in Alan Bennett. There are many Englands. The reactionary England exists but it is not the only England and it will not be the England of the next hundred years.

Finding the other, better stories has become a political project as important as improving Britain's hospitals or building new bridges. The core of the Englishness worth preserving is democracy, fair play and that suspicion of cant. Politicians who recoil from these are seen, rightly, as unpatriotic. Anthony Barnett has proposed a series of qualities of 'democratic Englishness' which include a return to the very high levels of literacy that marked England in the sixteenth and seventeenth centuries; pluralism; force, vulgarity and money-making; gender and urbanity. Certainly, a successful re-imagining of England will have to be popular and robust, not a dry political affair. It must begin with the Englishing of its main political parties, and a project to put England back at the centre of its own political life.

One school of thinking in New Labour argues for a system of strong regional assemblies throughout England to match the Edinburgh Parliament and the Cardiff Assembly. That was what New Labour promised to do in its 1997 election manifesto for every region that demonstrated through a referendum that it wanted an assembly. In power, the party has been a little quieter, but regional government remains the passion of John Prescott in particular, as he reminded the 1999 party conference in Bournemouth. Behind the scenes, he and his officials have been wading through the thicket of tangled, difficult issues that need to be resolved first. How would these referendums be triggered, and where? What would happen to those parts of England that did not want to be a region? What of the historic counties and the equally historic internal regional rivalries between cities?

The trouble is, English regional government has been, very much, a politicians' answer to politician-made problems. In the north-east of England, where regionalism is strongest, a sense of worry and anger about being outplayed by the neighbouring Scots is one motive. Though there have been various campaigns for regional identity, such the Northern Assembly and Yorkshire Democracy campaigns, there has not so far been the kind of mass, bottom-up demand for regional democracy that the Scots experienced. All sorts of people who might benefit from assemblies – local politicians, newspapers, public sector officials – have been more prominent than ordinary voters. And the great motive is of course the European Union, whose funding for less well-off areas is based on a system of regional assistance which England, without regions, finds hard to exploit with the same skill as the German Länder, the French or Spanish. But the EU grant-distributing system is not a good mechanism for dealing with English identities, in a country whose counties and towns retain more loyalty than regions. In any case, this is the same regionalism that English nationalists regard with such horror and alarm since it retains the nations of Wales and Scotland as single entities while carving England up, part of a grand plan to dismember the EU's 15 member states into 111 regions that will deal directly with Brussels.

English regionalism would help get grants. It would also correct one of the great democratic failures of the modern British state, the rule by quango and unelected government officials of provincial England. And yet, in a heavily governed nation, we have to be suspicious of yet another tier of administration, yet more tax-funded offices, councils and bureaucrats to serve them. There is a strong suspicion on the right of British politics that it is all a Labour plot to stop any moves towards an English Parliament which – so the thinking goes – Conservatives would be much likelier to dominate. This is a thick brew – envy of the Scots, hunger for European grants, local democratic failures, and rancorous party-political suspicion. Is it possible to solve the 'English question' with a dose from that pot?

I doubt it. Better by far to take John Bull by the horns and give England its own Parliament under an entirely new British settlement. This is a conclusion I have been driven to, almost against my will, by the impeccable arguments in its favour. When this was first hinted at by William Hague, I reacted with visceral hostility, pointing out that he was heading in an English nationalist direction, leaving New Labour as the nation's last true unionist party. But if it is good enough for Scotland and Wales, there is no legitimate reason to deny a Parliament to England, at least as natural and historic a nation as they.

How might we get there? The mood of English national feeling has not risen to a high pressure, but feels to me uncannily like what was happening in Scotland in the mid to late 1980s. The time is right for the options to be openly discussed. This could happen in the conventional way, through a Royal Commission on the government of England. Or, other kinds of leaders, from politicians outside government, to trade unionists, religious leaders and others could mimic the Scots and form an English Constitutional Convention, without formal authority, to hear evidence and make recommendations. It is hard to believe that such a body would not attract great public interest.

Meanwhile, what of New Labour? Tony Blair seems to be divided on these matters. The press of daily business and his impatience for bread-and-butter reforms to education, health and welfare, drive him, as all prime ministers, to want more control and more effective delivery from the centre. Constitutional change was never one of his burning issues, and we may doubt that he would have moved as fast on Scottish Home Rule had it not been for the legacy of John Smith. Yet Blair is also a courageous and strategic politician, a man who keeps his gaze on the middle distance (infuriatingly so for some colleagues) and who is famously in love with modernity. He is much mocked for his hammering emphasis on newness, and his sweeping remarks about 'the forces of conservatism' all around him. Marquand put his finger on the tone:

Even before the election, Blair and his associates
insisted that the 'Old' Labour Party of the past was
now subsumed in – had indeed been replaced by
– a radically different 'New' Labour Party,
uniquely suited to a 'Young Country'. After
victory, the rhetoric of youth and novelty became
louder and more intense. 'New, new, new', Tony
Blair told a meeting of European socialist leaders
in a characteristic outburst, shortly after entering
office, 'everything is new'. This is the myth in a
nutshell. The world is new, the past has no echoes,
modernity is unproblematic.[10]

But Blair's optimistic energy and intensity is exactly what
voters first responded to. It seems hard to believe that his
mind is closed to the English question, however uncomfortable it seems just now.

Dealing with it, however, would mean a radical recasting
of the whole system of British power as it is now. That, too,
is needed for and in itself. The same *Economist* poll quoted at
the start of this book had a striking question which was
mostly lost in the excitement about the decay of British
national feeling. The pollsters had also asked, 'How much say
do you think people in England/Scotland/Wales have over
the way they are governed?' The numbers answering 'too
much' were 2 per cent for Britain and England, and less for
the rest. Those who said 'too little' were 67 per cent for
Britain, 66 per cent for England, 78 per cent for Scotland and
77 per cent for Wales. We are not people who have too much
democracy, and we know it. As the EU extends its legislative
grip over Westminster and more law is made by judges, a new
settlement for democracy is now needed. So suppose, as a
thought experiment, that a government agreed that England
could not be refused a Parliament with the same rights and

limitations as the Scottish Parliament. Depending on the Northern Ireland peace process, we would then have a system of three or four national parliaments in the UK. Unless we were talking about the formal dissolution of the Union, there would then have to be a federal, overarching Parliament, to oversee disputes and to carry on with the very substantial business not dealt with by the national chambers.

Would this be really necessary in today's world, with the EU taking over so many other powers? I believe it would be hugely useful. The intermingling of the people of Britain, their companies and their property; the imbalance between the huge wealth of one part of England and the rest of England, never mind the other countries; the need to boost the north to relieve pressure on the congested south; and the existence of effective British armed forces with their own distinct British identity, are all obvious reasons for persevering with a unitary chamber, albeit it one exercising fewer powers over daily life. There is also the very large question of who guarantees and oversees a new constitutional settlement, based on rights and clear principles, which I will come to shortly. The British federal Parliament need not be large or more than a single chamber, but would deal with foreign relations, including European Union legislation, defence, human rights, and some other all-UK issues, such as welfare payments, company and income taxation. It would, or could, act as the final arbiter in disputes between the national assemblies and, for some classes of legislation, would act as their revising chamber, with suitably limited powers.

So we can picture it in the mind's eye, imagine this as a British Commons of some 150 members sitting in what is now the chamber used by the House of Lords – which would be finally abolished. This is certainly no more cumbersome or costly than the system of regional assemblies suggested by the current government. It has two huge advantages. First, it treats England properly as a nation, and by doing so, suggests a way the nations of Britain could continue to work linked together, in a looser Union. Second, by instituting a federal system in Britain, it would make us a more natural member of the EU than we can ever be with our current system of theoretical, but not real, parliamentary absolutism.

The clearest definition of the current creed is still that of England's great jurist, Sir William Blackstone, who declared in 1765 that 'what the parliament doth, no authority upon earth can undo ... the power of parliament is absolute and without control.' The irrelevance of Blackstone's formulation in the year 2000 is, or ought to be, a spur for change: no healthy state rests for long on a self-evident absurdity. Critics of change like to say that our system remains the best because 'we can kick the rascals out'. Well, so can the French, the Germans and every other democratic nation. The Italians are manic rascal-kickers, though that may be because they have so many political rascals. But these other nations manage to do the kicking without a parliamentary absolutism that stops them sharing power easily with others. They have constitutional guarantees which their citizens find more useful than theory about total parliamentary control – something that seems to belong to Cromwell's short-lived republic rather than to today. In short, we either have to change our constitution to allow federalism to work; or leave a federal Europe. The current situation is not indefinitely sustainable.

What about the argument that this is all very un-British, the tearing up of a constitution that has served us well for centuries? It depends which version of history you choose to highlight. A state which has changed from aristocratic management board to democracy, which declared itself an empire, then lost it again, which withdrew hurriedly from most of Ireland, created state bureaucracies in Scotland and

Wales only in recent times, which extended the franchise to women as late as 1929, which removed the key powers of the Lords in 1911 and kicked out most of the hereditary peers in 1999, which introduced departmental select committees as long ago as 1979, where any attempt by a monarch to exercise her theoretical political powers would cause uproar, which undermined and neutered local democracy, joined the EEC and signed the Maastricht Treaty, which introduced jury-less 'Diplock' courts in Northern Ireland, became a nuclear power by stealth, has celebrated and then quietly sidelined cabinet government, which handed control over monetary policy to a committee of the Bank of England, which included a former American government servant; how can this state be thought a model of continuity?

Our constitutional story has been one of constant change and turbulence, dominated by the endless wheezes and dodges of a small number of ministers to exercise the maximum amount of power. The facts that we have not decapitated a monarch recently, been invaded or suspended the rule of law, are all true, but ought not to hide our history as a country that has changed the rules of the power game (which is what the constitution is) time and again.

Furthermore, federalism is not as alien to British ways as we sometimes assume. A version of the scheme outlined above was being promoted in 1604, when William Shakespeare was in his prime and writing *Othello*, by one John Doddridge, a lawyer and MP for Horsham. King James VI and I was sitting on the English throne as well as the Scottish one, trying unsuccessfully to persuade the English Parliament to consider political union, and working on what would become the Union Jack. Doddridge argued that

> there cann bee no perfect unyon of twoe
> kingdomes except there bee established a meeting

of bothe states and, as it were, a common
parliament for bothe kingdomes for the generall
causes which shall equallie concerne bothe
people. Suche a parliament or assemblie have all
the cantons or confederat states of the Helvetions
and Swisors for their generall causes, althoughe
every estate perticulerlie have nevertheless his
proper and peculiar parliament.[11]

The case for a looser, federal system was argued passionately
a century later in the run-up to the Act of Union. Again, the
Swiss comparison was used by the Scots, as well as the examples of the Netherlands and ancient Greece. But, in the
words of one recent historian of British federal thinking,

The brute reality was that the English had no
interest in sharing political power. If the Scots
wanted to keep their cultural forms intact, that
was acceptable, if not entirely agreeable, because
the English recognized that key decisions
involving key economic and political issues would
be made in the seemingly 'British' but still
patently English-dominated parliament.[12]

Federalism was nevertheless adopted by the rebel American states, and exported as a practical idea inside the British
Empire, for Canada and Australia, then other territories. In
the middle of the struggle over Irish Home Rule, Liberal
ministers took up and vigorously promoted what Asquith
called, shortly before the First World War, a policy of 'Home
Rule All Round'. At around the same time, there was a
strong campaign for the white colonies of the British Empire
to be joined in one grand federal imperial Parliament, ideally
directly elected, led by the 'Round Table' movement. World

federal government was advocated by British constitutional writers between the world wars and, after 1945, West Germany's new federal republican constitution was designed not by Germans but by British officials. The British history has been one of parliamentary absolutism; but federalism has been a larger part of the national conversation than conservatives today are inclined to admit. It is there in the grab-bag of history if we choose to reach in and pull it back out.

If we did, however, we could do more than restore English democracy. No federal system could work without a written and agreed set of rules about the relationship between the British chamber and the national parliaments or assemblies. That means, of course, a constitution, of a singular kind, sitting above 'the Queen in Parliament' – a document that we have not had before. But this, surely, is a great opportunity, not a threat. If it was founded on a Bill declaring the fundamental rights, freedoms and responsibilities of all British citizens, from free speech to freedom from religious persecution, it could be the basis for that diverse, open and tolerant Britain that we glimpsed earlier, a constitutional assertion of the kind of country we were determined to be. It would require a British Parliament to do something never before done; to tie the hands of its successors, since constitutions must be hard to change. The process would mean ending the polite fiction that we are subjects of the Queen, not citizens, and asserting the sovereignty of the peoples of Britain. This would not necessarily stop us keeping the monarch as head of state, though I would like to see that question put to a referendum following a new constitutional settlement; and I would vote for a republic. This constitution could give guaranteed rights to the diminished local councils, the shires and towns, who have suffered under successive central governments. It could establish the ultimate duties and loyalties of civil servants. It could do so much to turn round our jaded, cynical attitude to our democracy. It would then, of course, be put to a referendum vote itself. For the rules of power are not primarily for the political parties, but for the rest of us.

How, you may ask, does this fit with the great question of the European Union? Just consider, first, the democratic effect of turning back to restore the foundations of democracy in the British nations. For as long as I can remember, we have been reacting to the pace of change on the continent of Europe, hobbling and wheezing behind the grand project as we try to catch up with its logic. Could there be a more satisfying, significant assertion of popular sovereignty than to start afresh at home instead? The idea, which you hear on the continent, that the British are simply too exhausted, too knackered to act for themselves, would be exploded. Any fears that Britain, or England, was being subsumed into an undemocratic superstate, on a hidden timetable, by unelected commissars, would be brought immediately into the open, since here would be a bold remaking, a home-made democratic initiative.

If Britain had a healthy political culture, liked and trusted by its citizens, freshly minted, giving full rein to local initiative, then it would be simply impossible to take a continental bureaucratic plan of government and stick it on top. For once, the rest of the EU could only stand and watch. Whether Scotland leaves the UK or not, this seems an appropriate and necessary act of national assertion. In terms of domestic politics, it would instantly return words like democracy and freedom from the anti-European right to the mainstream of moderate opinion. And until England feels happy and secure in its democracy, how can there be a successful and settled relationship with the rest of Europe?

For, though I emphatically do not mean this as a way of 'getting back' at the EU or getting out of it, a new constitu-

tional settlement in Britain would be a useful pointer to the
necessary but skeletal progamme for democratic reform in
Europe as a whole. The more one looks at the problems of
modern Britain and the problems of the European Union,
the more the one seems to be a kind of warped mirror of the
other. Britain is an asymmetric and over-centralised Union
in which historic nations and groups are weighed down by
the centre. That goes for the EU. Britain has an increasingly
insecure sense of itself. So does 'Europe'.

Britain has found its role and position in the world
shrinking. But actually – though no one says it – is this not
true of Europe as a whole? Europe's population is fast-falling
as a proportion of the world's. For nation-states like Portugal,
Belgium, Austria and Spain, which once ruled large overseas
territories, federal union is a refuge, a way of replacing lost
singular importance with part of a common importance –
like struggling companies which merge and merge again as
they try to survive. In Brussels, it often seems that the permanent bureaucracy is in command of elected politicians;
that lobbyists and special interest groups are benefiting constantly at the expense of ordinary voters. There is an in-group
of chummy business people and public officials, networks of
mutual obligation and friendship that are always potentially
corrupt and sometimes actually so. Exactly the same applies
to London and has done throughout my working life. Anti-
EU politicians in Britain complain that Brussels is incompetent, interfering and arrogant, and are surprised that more
British people do not complain. The reason they do not is
that they are used to it. British politics has been inept, interfering and arrogant too. The EU had incompetent and (in
some cases) corrupt Commissioners and senior officials;
Britain has had 'sleaze', ministerial resignations, fat cat privatisation bosses and charmed circles of politicians and media
barons, cronies and influence-pedlars.

Reforming Britain using principles of clear divisions of power and responsibility, human rights and a plural vision of citizenship would be a great act in itself, and the only thing which might hold the British Union together for the next century or two. But it would also offer a model for some of the major reforms needed for the EU, including an open and democratically accountable Council of Ministers to act as its ruling body, a slimming-down of what the centre is expected to do, the return of 'nation-states' rights' to the constituent members of the EU and an acknowledgement that the people of that Union too, are sovereign as national citizens first and foremost.

There can be no successful Europe without a people who regard themselves as active democratic citizens on several levels, just as there can be no successful Britain for the future unless we learn to be Scottish and British, English and Cornish and British, Londoners and Black-British, and so on. Multiple identity is the key to a looser Britishness and it is the key to a better European future. As with London, the trend has been for Brussels simply to amass more and more authority for reasons of 'efficiency'. Again, the only long-term way of halting and reversing this trend, which occurs in every power system, is for there to be a European constitution, based on agreed political principles, which lays down the rights and powers of different parts of the Union. In current circumstances, such a constitution, no doubt hammered out over months in some 'Congress of Europe', would be a decentralising measure, since the nations and regions would regard it as their final explicit settlement and would not vote for self-destruction. Again, we have nothing to lose by clarity and frankness, which is what a constitution offers. That is what subsidiarity and true federal democracy means. I am not scared of the European superstate because, particularly as it expands, it is simply impossible to run an oppressive system across so many peoples who have been schooled in democracy. The EU is many times likelier to collapse in chaos than it is to take away our freedoms.

As we have seen, there are various possible Europes on offer, including a two-speed one, with a smaller and more integrated core, and a trading 'skirt' of secondary members, including Britain, or England. But like many millions of others, I would prefer to see a Europe-wide movement for democratic change, and to see a revitalised British democracy leading it. When the referendum comes on a single European currency I will vote unhesitatingly for the euro, but not with the expectation of becoming a passive, if prosperous Euro-serf: I want us 'in Europe' to cause trouble and shake it up until it is a proper federal system, whose political rulers are elected and know themselves to be the servants of its people. I want to be part of an assertive, self-confident democracy, British or English, which is as keen to change the world around it, as these islands ever were in the sixteenth or nineteenth centuries.

Is this hopelessly ambitious? It is the job of political journalists to be ambitious. We lead easy enough lives. We have no constituency, no need to listen to Sir Humphrey, no need to check our radio-pagers. If we are not ambitious, then who will be? Second, I have a profound belief in the likelihood of the British Union dissolving within a decade. The day Britain dies is not today, nor yesterday, but it is coming unless bold action is taken. I was there when the Scottish Home Rule movement got started and I can smell what is coming down south.

But whether Scotland goes, or England revolts, the latter country still needs to consider its future. If this country, which has done so much and taken so many risks, journeyed through such tumultuous changes in decade after decade, really finds the notion of a new 1688, the restoring of its political energy, too frightening or tiring to contemplate, then perhaps it really is bust. That is a matter for the individual, for everyone. It is for your imagination, your decision. Whatever happens, political change is beginning not ending. We either embark on an ambitious and risky plan of further democratic reform – an English Parliament, federal Britain, a written constitution – or we will end up, one day, in a chilly churchyard of the mind, throwing handfuls of clay on the Union Flag. Which is it to be?

Notes

1 Roll-back

1 Rowan Moore in the *Evening Standard*, 11 October 1999
2 Oliver James, *Britain on the Couch*, Arrow, 1998, p. 308
3 James, *Britain on the Couch*, p. 314
4 Raphael Samuel, 'Unravelling Britain' from *Island Stories*, Verso, 1998
5 Norman Davies, *The Isles: A History*, Macmillan, 1999, pp. 1032–3

2 Are There any British Left?

1 Boris Johnson in the *Spectator*, 9 October 1999
2 Lawrence James, *The Rise and Fall of the British Empire*, Abacus, pp. 169–70
3 Andrew Jack, *The French Exception*, Profile Books, 1999, p. 47
4 Memorandum for the Imperial Conference, 2 June, 1926, reproduced in full in Ian Jarvie, *Hollywood's Overseas Campaign: the North Atlantic Movie Trade, 1920–1950*, Cambridge University Press, 1992
5 Jarvie, op cit.
6 Jarvie, op cit.

7 'The Anglo-American Media Connection,' by Jeremy Tunstall and David Machin, Oxford, 1999, page 17

8 Raphael Samuel, *Island Stories / Theatres of Memory*, vol. 2, Verso 1998, p. 185

9 See Dominic Hobson, *The National Wealth*, HarperCollins, 1999

10 Anthony Sampson, *The Essential Anatomy of Britain*, Hodder & Stoughton, 1992, p. 58

11 Ben Pimlott, *The Queen: A Biography of Elizabeth II*, HarperCollins, 1996, p. 558

12 Pimlott, *The Queen*, pp. 560–1.

13 Simon Schama in the *New Yorker*, October 1997

14 Hobson, *The National Wealth*, p. 135

15 Christopher Lee, *This Sceptred Isle*, BBC/Penguin, 1999, p. 5

3 The Natives are Revolting

1 See Maire and Conor Cruise O'Brien, *Ireland – A Concise History*, Thames & Hudson, 1972

2 Andrew Marr, *The Battle for Scotland*, Penguin, 1994

3 MORI poll for the *Mail on Sunday*, March 1988

4 See John Davies, *A History of Wales*, Allen Lane, 1993, p. 548

5 Leighton Andrews, *Renewal* magazine, vol. 7 no. 3

6 See Brendan O'Brien, *The Long War*, O'Brien Press, Dublin, 1993

4 The English: a Secret People

1 P.H. Ditchfield and Fred Roe, *Vanishing England*, Studio Editions Ltd, 1910, 1993

2 From *The Ingerland Factor*, edited by Mark Perryman, Mainstream, 1999

3 Mike Marqusee, *Anyone But England: Cricket, Race and Class,* Two Heads Publishing, 1998, pp. 43–4

4 Robert McCrum, William Cran and Robert MacNeil, *The Story of English*, Faber & Faber/BBC Books, 1986, p. 19

5 From Gerrard Winstanley, *The Law of Freedom and Other Writings*, edited by Christopher Hill, Pelican, 1973

6 Samuel Bamford, *Early Days*, 1849, quoted in Victor E. Newburg, *Popular Literature*, Pelican, 1977

7 See Jenny Uglow, *Hogarth: A Life and World*, Faber & Faber, 1997

8 Simon Heffer, *Nor Shall My Sword: The Reinvention of England*, Weidenfeld and Nicolson, 1999

9 Fiona MacCarthy, *William Morris*, Faber & Faber, 1994, pp. 311–12

10 David Mellor, Gill Saunders and Patrick Wright, *Recording Britain*, David & Charles for the Victoria & Albert Museum, 1990. I am indebted to Alan Berman for telling me this story.

11 Simon Jenkins in the *Sunday Times*, 24 October 1999

12 From the opening of Graham Harvey, *The Killing of the Countryside*, Jonathan Cape, 1997

13 Raphael Samuel, *Island Stories / Theatres of Memory*, vol. 2, Verso, 1998, p. 61

14 Robert Chesshyre, *The Return of a Native Reporter*, Penguin, 1988, ch. 2

15 Neil Ascherson, 'The English Riot' in *Games with Shadows*, Radius, 1988

5 The New British and the World

1 *Pocket World in Figures 1999*, The Economist/Profile

Books, 1999
2   Dominic Hobson, *The National Wealth*, HarperCollins, 1999, p. 1063
3   Stephen Bayley, *Labour Camp*, B.T. Batsford, 1998
4   Hobson, *The National Wealth*, p. 592
5   Louisa Buck, *Moving Targets*, Tate Gallery publishing, 1997
6   Cabinet Papers, December 1953, CAB 124/1191, quoted in evidence by Anne Owers for the Commission on the Future of Multi-Ethnic Britain, 'Race, Asylum and Immigration', 1999
7   These paragraphs rely heavily on papers by Roger Ballard for the Commission on the Future of Multi-Ethnic Britain, to be published in 2000 by Profile Books
8   Bhikhu Parekh, 'South Asians in Britain', in *History Today*, September 1997
9   Dominique Moisi in the *Financial Times*, 23 August 1999

6 Intimate Enemies: Britain in Europe

1   Margaret Thatcher, *The Downing Street Years*, HarperCollins, 1993, p. 792
2   See Hugo Young, *This Blessed Plot*, Macmillan, 1998, pp. 10–16
3   See John Pinder's essay in *Eminent Europeans*, edited by M. Bond, J. Smith and W. Wallace, Greycoat Press, 1996
4   Young, *This Blessed Plot*, p. 93
5   Young, *This Blessed Plot*, p. 64

7 Is There an Answer?

1 David Marquand, *The Progressive Dilemma*, 2nd edn,
   Phoenix, 1999, p. 228
2 Ann Dummett in *Constitutional Futures*, edited by
   Robert Hazell, Oxford University Press, 1999
3 From Stephen Bayley, *Labour Camp*, B.T. Batsford, 1998
4 Robert Hazell, 'The New Constitutional Settlement', in
   Constitutional Futures, Oxford University Press, 1999
5 Anthony Barnett in the *New Statesman*, 28 June 1999
6 Jonathan Freedland, *Bring Home the Revolution*, Fourth
   Estate, 1998
7 Andrew Marr, *The Battle for Scotland*, Penguin, 1992
8 Andrew Marr, *Ruling Britannia*, Penguin, 1995
9 Derek Jarrett, *England in the Age of Hogarth*, Hart-Davis,
   MacGibbon, 1974
10 Marquand, *The Progressive Dilemma*, p. 226
11 Quoted in John Kendle, *Federal Britain: A History*,
   Routledge, 1997
12 Kendle, *Federal Britain*, p. 11